Philippe, Duke of Orléans

MEN IN OFFICE

General Editor:
Professor Ragnhild Hatton

J. H. SHENNAN

Philippe, Duke of Orléans

Regent of France 1715–1723

with 34 illustrations

THAMES AND HUDSON

For Andrew

*Printed in Great Britain by
Latimer Trend & Company Ltd, Plymouth*

Contents

Contents

Preface

No political biography of Philippe d'Orléans has been published in English during the present century. That is a serious omission since the eight years of the regency were of profound significance in the history of the *ancien régime*. Following the long reign of Louis XIV the period of his great-grandson's minority saw the fundamental questioning of conventional values in the country's political, socio-economic and cultural life. The regent's posthumous reputation has been so tarnished by his notorious life-style that a balanced judgment of his period of office is not easily made. Yet, he inherited a defeated country surrounded by a hostile Europe and rescued her from isolation; and he succeeded where most of his regent predecessors had failed, in preserving France from the even greater dangers of civil disorder. From inauspicious beginnings Philippe guided his young charge, Louis XV, to his majority without compromising royal authority, at the same time offering new initiatives for France at home, in Europe and overseas, and through his patronage stimulating her artistic and intellectual life. The ideas and achievements of that formidable triumvirate consisting of Orléans himself, the abbé Dubois, his life-long counsellor, and the Scottish financier, John Law, offer the key to an understanding of the approaching crisis of the *ancien régime*.

My interest in the regency spans a number of years and I have accumulated many debts to academic colleagues and library staff on both sides of the Channel. I am also grateful to the Leverhulme Trust for a generous research award and to the University of Lancaster for its enlightened attitude to sabbatical leave which has allowed me the opportunity to write. Among individuals I am particularly happy to acknowledge my debt to Ragnhild Hatton, the General Editor of this series, who has given me much wise advice and encouragement. The perceptive criticisms of style and content levelled against the original draft by my wife and eldest son triumphed eventually over an outraged *amour-propre* and now allow me to accept sole responsibility for what follows with a little more confidence.

Brookhouse, Lancaster, 1978

Prologue

No one with an *entrée* to the royal palace of Versailles in 1715 could have been surprised at the news of Louis XIV's death for the king had been ailing for more than a year as he approached his seventy-seventh birthday. Yet when word finally came on 1 September, just five days before that anniversary, the sense of shock was still profound. Louis had worn the crown for nearly three-quarters of a century: most of his contemporaries and their children were long since dead, and to their grandchildren it must have seemed almost part of the natural order that Louis XIV should be king of France. It was to be expected, therefore, that after his departure from the political scene a crisis of government would ensue, especially since Louis had been no mere figurehead, no prisoner of his office, but the prime mover in every area of administrative activity.

The disastrous events of Louis' last years added to the uncertainty. The War of the Spanish Succession brought humiliation to French arms and made fiscal demands on a peasantry, already undermined by famine and epidemic, which it simply could not meet. In the French church the Jansenist controversy raged on, despite the king's authoritarian efforts at suppression and his belated recourse to the pope for assistance. The traditional gallicanism of the parlement of Paris began to stiffen the opposition of religious zealots and to drive the magistrates towards their first head-on clash with the king since 1673.[1] Louis was becoming embattled and at court a sense of apprehension and gloom replaced the old spirit of self-confidence and *élan*. The final and supreme tragedy of the king's old age touched his own family: in the space of little more than three years between 1711 and 1714 Louis suffered the deaths of three eldest sons in the direct line, his own son the dauphin, his grandson the duke de Bourgogne, and his great-grandson the duke de Bretagne, besides a younger grandson the duke de Berry, and his favourite granddaughter-in-law, Marie Adélaïde of Savoy, duchess de Bourgogne. These personal disasters contributed to the gathering sense of doom. By 1715 only a five-year-old child, the second of Louis' great-grandsons, who had himself narrowly missed death in 1712 from what was thought to be smallpox, survived to carry on the legitimate Bourbon succession, since his one remaining grandson, Philip V, the king of Spain, had been forced in the interests of European peace to renounce his claim to the French throne. Even if the child Louis lived he would not reach his majority until 1723, a date which, for all the robustness of the king's constitution, seemed now to be beyond his reach. At best, therefore, a regency appeared certain; at worst the direct line would come to an end. In either event, assuming the validity of Philip V's renunciation,[2] the best claim to the office of regent and even to the crown itself, should the young Louis die before producing an heir, would lie with the king's nephew, the highly controversial figure of Philippe, duke d' Orléans, whose once deserted apartments at Versailles began to fill up with visitors during the month of August 1715, as the mortal nature of the king's illness became apparent.

I

The Regent Elect and the Problems of the Regency

Philippe II d'Orléans, the future regent, was born at the royal palace of St-Cloud on 4 August 1674. His father, Philippe I, was the younger brother of king Louis XIV and his mother was Elisabeth Charlotte, the daughter of Karl Ludwig, the elector palatine. At the time of Philippe II's birth only the dauphin and his own father stood closer to the throne. He himself was a great-grandson of Henri IV whom in later life he claimed to resemble, though according to the peevish duke de Saint-Simon he did so as much in his vices as in his virtues.[1] Philippe was, therefore, a member of that exclusive inner royal circle, a *petit-fils de France*, recognized on his father's death in 1701 by Louis XIV as the premier prince of the blood, who could look with legitimate expectations towards the throne itself. Yet, because he was of the collateral line, it was not surprising that from time to time he should be viewed as a rival by the king's immediate family. Orléans' ambivalent position, so close to the throne yet on a lower step than Louis' son, grandsons and great-grandsons, is a factor of crucial importance for an understanding of his career and life-style.

This sense of ambivalence, stemming from birth, was heightened by the complexities of his personality and personal relationships. One can only guess at the effect of his parents on the young duke de Chartres – Philippe's title while his father was alive – but theirs was so outlandish a union, even in an age of ill-matched marriages, that it can scarcely have been negligible. Besides, in the goldfish bowl of Versailles, such a marriage was bound to be the object of intense public scrutiny, and it does seem probable that as a child the future regent felt himself obscurely disadvantaged. His father – Monsieur – was an effeminate dandy, ill-equipped to play a leading role and treated by Louis with mingled affection and scorn. His mother was a German lady of sturdy and un-compromising character and entirely devoid of feminine charm: according to one contemporary pleasantry, Orléans owed his very existence to his mother's masculine appearance.[2] The *ménage* at St-Cloud was certainly bizarre yet it was also ideal for Louis XIV's purposes. Under no circumstances could his younger brother be allowed to outshine *le roi soleil*; Monsieur had been raised for the shadows. So much the better, therefore, if he seemed quite unsuited to hold the highest office. In fact, his environment had shaped him: looking back over his career one discovers with a sense of surprise his spirited command of the victorious French troops at the battle of Cassel in 1677. He bequeathed courage to his son as well as good taste. It was his misfortune, and his son's, that they were in no position to excel, at least not in those skills which went traditionally with the *métier du roi*. Monsieur never again distinguished himself in battle after 1677 and his son's military career was reduced to a series of brilliant episodes. The sense of irritation engendered by perpetually having to take second place would grow in proportion to the talents frustrated, and Orléans was an exceptionally talented man. Moreover his royal cousins were no match for him. On every count save one he held the advantage over them; however, that single accidental exception was decisive: proximity to the throne.

His military record amply demonstrates the point. While the dauphin's martial exploits were, in the words of Louis XIV's most recent biographer, 'largely confined to long horseback rides',[3] and both the illegitimate duke du Maine, Orléans' life-long rival, and the duke de Bourgogne, Louis' eldest grandson, disappointed the king with their less than enthusiastic approach to campaigning, Philippe showed early signs of real talent. His first campaign, under marshal Luxembourg, was undertaken in 1691 at the age of seventeen, and in the following two years he distinguished himself at Steenkerk and Neerwinden with displays of courage and *bravura* which endeared him to his men rather more than to the king who remembered the Fronde and the Great Condé's reputation. Thereafter he was not allowed to add to his laurels until the War of the Spanish Succession was entering its fifth year and Philippe his thirty-third. The king's armies had suffered two crushing defeats at Blenheim and Ramillies, the latter virtually predicted by Orléans to his sovereign when he learned of marshal Villeroy's choice of ground for the battle, and Louis found himself in need of the kind of charismatic leadership which his nephew had already demonstrated in Flanders more than a decade before.[4] In June 1706 he was appointed to titular command of the French army in Italy. Though the subsequent battle before Turin, which his troops were besieging, marked a major disaster for the French, it did no damage to Orléans' military reputation. Real authority in the army lay with the shell-shocked marshal Marsin, whose refusal to be guided by Orléans' much sounder assessment of the situation, in favour of an aggressive sortie against prince Eugène's relieving force, brought about an ignominious defeat. Orléans' judgment was vindicated and his courageous conduct on the battlefield contributed further to his reputation. He was warmly received by the king on his return to Versailles even though *en route* he had characteristically dallied at Grenoble for a few days in order to entertain his latest mistress, Madame d'Argenton.[5]

Having proved himself worthy of genuine high command, he obtained his reward in the following year when he was appointed commander-in-chief of the army in Spain. That year, 1707, was the *annus mirabilis* of his short though spectacular military career. It began with the French victory at Almanza in Valencia where his army, commanded by his deputy, the duke of Berwick, the illegitimate son of king James II of England, put to flight a mixed force of English, Dutch and Portuguese troops. Orléans' misfortune was to miss the battle and, therefore, the glory, by some twenty-four hours as he hurried south from Madrid, having cut short the tedious formalities required of him at the Spanish court. Despite the disappointment which he must have felt at that moment, Orléans accepted the fact that Berwick had had no alternative but to fight when he did. It was a generous reaction from one who admired good-natured loyalty and honest stubbornness more than he valued self-esteem, and his regard for Berwick continued to grow. The immediate question was how best to capitalize upon the victory. Saint-Simon, whose virtues and vices so complemented the vices and virtues of Orléans (thereby accounting perhaps for an otherwise incongruous friendship), hastened to proffer his advice: an immediate march across Spain to the Portuguese border which would bring the Peninsular war to a triumphant conclusion. The *duc et pair* solemnly noted Orléans' tongue-in-cheek reply, 'that the plan itself was a good and a sound one, and perfectly practical for an army of non-eaters and non-drinkers'![6]

In the event, Orléans decided to pursue the vanquished army, intent on expelling the enemy from Valencia. He quickly subdued that province and then took Saragossa in Aragon before turning his attention to Catalonia, the heartland of opposition to the French in Spain. His army laid siege to the fortress of Lérida before which the Great Condé had met his first defeat when he failed to capture it in 1647. Its capitulation on 12 October 1707 sealed his martial reputation. Orléans was back in Spain in the following year, on the Ebro, where he successfully besieged Tortosa, treating the defeated governor of the fortress with characteristic chivalry.[7] That campaign marked the end of his military career.[8]

Philippe also possessed striking qualities of intellect and taste which tended to set him apart from his Bourbon cousins. As a child he showed quickness of mind, and later a ready comprehension of a variety of subjects: history, geography and mathematics, Latin, Spanish, Italian and German. He interested himself in the work of Descartes and indulged in intellectual debates with his friend, archbishop Fénelon, on the subject of the existence of God. Another of Orléans' intellectual pursuits – a dangerous one for him as it turned out – was the study of chemistry. He was much impressed by a distinguished chemist from the Dutch East Indies, Wilhelm Homberg, who became a member of the French Académie des Sciences in France in 1691. Philippe made him his chief personal physician and lavishly equipped a laboratory specially constructed for him. There the two men worked together, the serious scientist and his enthusiastic patron, who for their pains were transformed in 1712 by malicious and hysterical court gossip into the sorcerer and his apprentice. Homberg died in September 1715 within a few days of Orléans' assumption of the office of regent.

With maturity Orléans developed an aesthete's sensibility to add to his robust intellectual curiosity. His enjoyment of poetry and *belles-lettres* demonstrated his impeccable literary taste; he patronized Jean-Baptiste Rousseau and Antoine de la Motte; and Fontenelle lodged at the Palais-Royal for eighteen years. But he reserved a special affection for the fine arts, revealing a near-professional appreciation of music and painting. He composed at least two operas and was something of a musicologist; and he painted competently under the tutelage of the court painter, Coypel *père*, whom he commissioned to decorate the Palais-Royal.[9] It is as a great collector of paintings that we may best judge both his enthusiasm and his taste. He began collecting at the age of twenty and by the time of his death owned some five hundred canvases, most of them of high quality, including twelve Raphaels, more than twenty Titians, many examples of the work of Veronese, Caravaggio, Tintoretto, and Correggio, a Bellini, six Rembrandts, three works by Gerard Dou, and two by Ribera. He possessed Bellini's *Circumcision*, Rubens's *Judgment of Paris*, Van Dyck's *Charles I and his Family*, Holbein's *Portrait of Sir Thomas More*, and among French artists paintings by Poussin, Rigaud, Claude Lorrain, Philippe de Champaigne, and his contemporary, Watteau.[10] It is not to belittle Louis XIV or the members of his family to maintain that in powers of intellect and delicacy of feeling Orléans was incomparably better endowed than any of them.

Yet that fact simply added to the frustrations of a gifted man, bored by the enforced pointlessness of his life and irked by his limited opportunities to excel. The effect was to exaggerate that fundamental trait in

Orléans, his sense of being an outsider at the royal court, and to persuade him to adopt anti-establishment attitudes which scandalized Versailles and thus encouraged his own isolation still further. As he outstripped adolescence, he found his pleasures increasingly in Paris. He owed his notorious contemporary reputation as a womanizer less to the impressive scale of his activities, in which he matched his hero and great-grandfather, Henri IV, than to the dubious reputation of many of his conquests and the publicity surrounding them. Actresses from the Opéra and the Comédie-française appealed to him more than the aristocratic mistresses available at Versailles and he made no secret of the fact. Similarly, his euphemistically styled 'suppers', which he held regularly during the regency at his home in the Palais-Royal, offended polite society, partly because of the lubricity of those occasions, but equally because of the notoriety they attracted, which Orléans made no attempt to play down, and the composition of the guest lists: ladies of easy virtue and for the most part undistinguished pedigree, and the regent's male companions, the *roués*, dissolute and convivial cronies in the business of eating, drinking and wenching, but of no great social or political consequence.

Orléans' attitude to women was equivocal. Though he sought their company from an early age he seemed capable of establishing only superficial relationships except, possibly, with Mademoiselle de Séry, countess d'Argenton.[11] He enjoyed a series of brief, physical liaisons any of which could be terminated as soon as his old enemy, boredom, put in an appearance. Collecting mistresses was one of the few occupations available to him and he applied himself to that task as enthusiastically as to his collection of paintings, though with less taste and discernment, as his mother wryly observed: 'He is not fastidious; so long as the ladies are good-humoured, eat and drink to excess; and are young, they do not have to be beautiful. I have often reproached him for choosing such ugly ones.'[12] No doubt on a deeper level of perception, his parents' unsatisfactory marriage had contributed to the shaping of Orléans' attitude to women, which was at all events in striking contrast to his habitual relationship with men; that being marked by a generosity of spirit and a degree of personal loyalty uncharacteristic of the backbiting environment in which he lived.

Orléans' hostility towards the court establishment may also be detected in his attitude to religion. In Louis XIV's later years Madame de Maintenon succeeded in creating at Versailles a spirit of near-religiosity which Philippe found uncongenial and oppressive. He was by conviction a sceptic and a deist though in this matter too there may have been an element of bravado, a desire to shock and outrage the bastions of conventional morality. Saint-Simon relates an incident occurring one Christmas in the royal chapel at Versailles when Philippe accompanied his uncle, the king, to midnight mass. Throughout the service he appeared to be engrossed in his prayer-book though it subsequently transpired that he had in fact been reading a volume of Rabelais. While accepting as genuine Orléans' lack of religious enthusiasm, Saint-Simon was convinced that this particular demonstration was fraudulent, since a perfectly adequate distraction was already to hand: not only was the music played during the service of high quality, 'far better even than at the Opera'; but it was also played for a long time, through matins, lauds and the three Christmas masses, and Orléans was a noted music lover. With his usual mixture of shrewdness, self-righteousness and *naïveté*, Saint-Simon summed up the regent's disposition towards religion:

> Like his debauched companions he longed to persuade himself that God did not exist; but he was far too intelligent to be an atheist, which is a rarer type of madness than most people imagine. . . . It would have comforted him to believe that he had no soul but, despite all his efforts, he could not quite convince himself of that.[13]

His behaviour was calculated to shock, and so well did Orléans achieve his effect that he acquired a reputation which quite travestied the real man. His sexual indulgence and his hedonistic attitude in general were not, of course, mere gestures aimed at the court and the establishment: his sensual nature threatened to undermine his public authority and perhaps ultimately deprived him of political ambition. Yet there is little in common between the debauched monster of contemporary myth and the amiable, pleasure-loving man who inspired it. Gossipmongers accused him of incest with his daughter, the duchess de Berry, of whom he was indeed extremely fond,[14] and with even more inventiveness, of seeking to acquire the throne by the simple means of poisoning those who stood in his path. Thus the dauphin, who died in 1711, his son the duke de Bourgogne who followed in 1712, and the latter's son, the duke de Bretagne, who survived his father by only a few days, were all allegedly done to death by their ambitious relative who had acquired his lethal skills in Homberg's laboratory; apparently he had also carelessly removed the duchess de Bourgogne who posed no threat to him at all while allowing the future king, Louis XV, to survive! Though the king himself repudiated these calumnies, he could not dispel the mutual hostility which increasingly alienated Orléans from the court. Other, more tangible, issues added to that sense of alienation.

His marriage was a case in point. In the course of 1691 Louis XIV decided that his nephew should marry Mademoiselle de Blois, his natural daughter by Madame de Montespan. Both the prince and his parents were hostile to the proposal for they believed that the family would be dishonoured by such an alliance. No doubt there were advantages to be gained from becoming the king's son-in-law, but the price – marriage to a royal bastard – was one which no foreign prince would have been asked to pay. However, there was no gainsaying what was virtually a royal command and in February 1692 the union was duly solemnized, the bridegroom salvaging from the occasion the king's assurance that he would inherit intact all his father's possessions, titles and prerogatives. Ironically, the moment of inheritance came when Monsieur suffered a stroke which may have been precipitated by a violent quarrel with the king on the very subject of Philippe's neglect of his wife. Certainly, Orléans' marital links with the king added to the tensions already created by his dissolute way of life.

A few months earlier, in November 1700, Louis had received the details of the last will of Charles II of Spain according to which the Spanish inheritance was to pass to his grandson, the duke d'Anjou, on condition that the crowns of France and Spain were never to be united. To forestall that possibility Charles stipulated that in the event of Anjou's death or of his accession to the French throne, the order of succession to the Spanish crown should be as follows:

> ... the Spanish succession will pass to his brother, the duke de Berry, the third son of the Dauphin, ... and should this Duke also die or succeed in his turn to the French Crown, in that case I nominate to the Spanish Succession the Archduke who is the second son of my uncle, the Emperor, similarly excluding in the interests of the peace of Europe and of my subjects the Emperor's elder son. And should the said Archduke also die, in that event I nominate for the succession the Duke of Savoy, and his children.

The renunciations of their rights to the Spanish throne by Anne of Austria, daughter of Philip III of Spain and wife of Louis XIII, and Maria Teresa, daughter of Philip IV and wife of Louis XIV, were waived, on the assumption that the threat of Spain's being joined to France, which had caused them to be made in the first place, no longer existed.[15] Louis himself had long opposed the second renunciation and the language of his acceptance of Charles's will seems to reflect a distinction between the two cases:

> We accept the testament of the late Catholic King on behalf of our grandson, the Duke d'Anjou: Our only son, the Dauphin, also accepts it; he abandons without reluctance the just rights of the late Queen his mother, and our very dear wife, which have been acknowledged as of incontestable validity, as well as those of the late Queen our most honoured Lady and mother.[16]

Louis never raised the question of his own rights through his mother, though if Anne of Austria's renunciation was rendered ineffective the cadet branch of Orléans could mount a better claim to the succession than either the Austrian Habsburgs or the house of Savoy.[17] Both Monsieur and his son were indignant at the absence from the will of any reference to their rights and Monsieur made a formal legal complaint in the parlement of Paris at the omission.[18] After his father's death, Orléans pursued the matter with the new king of Spain, Philip V, who in October 1703 signed a declaration recognizing his cousin's claim to the Spanish inheritance.[19] In a state still dominated by dynastic considerations it was inconceivable that Orléans would allow his claim to go by default, and he was far too ambitious and able not to make the most of his opportunity. If he felt slighted at what seemed one more example of the inferior station ascribed to the ruling family's collateral line, he could not on this occasion blame Louis XIV who was neither responsible for the contents of the will nor in a position to modify them. In fact, Louis was anxious that the younger branch should properly establish its claim (foreseeing the possibility of Philip V's translation to the French throne) and in 1712, following the deaths in the royal family, he proposed to the Allies as a basis for peace that Philip V should eventually inherit the French crown and be replaced in Spain by the duke de Berry or, if he refused, by Orléans.[20]

Spain was the setting for a more puzzling episode in 1709 which followed on from the matter of the Spanish succession and further estranged Orléans from the court. The details remain obscure but it appears that in August 1708, when both Orléans and general Stanhope, commander of the British forces in Spain, and a future secretary of state, were in the Peninsula, the former raised the possibility of his succeeding to the Spanish throne in the event of Philip's being forced to abandon his kingdom.[21] Before leaving Madrid in November to return to Versailles Orléans instructed his agent, Regnault, to remain in Spain in order to sound out Spanish opinion on such an eventuality. However, the scheme was uncovered by the influential princess des Ursins, *camarera mayor* to the queen of Spain. This formidable lady, an old friend of Madame de Maintenon, had become the power behind the Spanish throne, and she and Orléans had been temperamentally at odds with one another since his first campaign in Spain in 1707. Under the influence of drink, Orléans had made his dislike of the princess public, and his vulgar remarks reached her ears.[22] Given the opportunity for revenge she complained to Louis XIV of his nephew's compromising behaviour. Louis' reaction was low-key: on 29 April 1709 he replied, 'I have spoken to my nephew; he has vowed to me that never during his stay in Spain has he concerned himself with any matters of government.'[23] Nevertheless, he did agree that Orléans should not return to Spain that year. Instead, the duke despatched his private secretary, Flotte, charging him to maintain his rights to the Spanish crown in accordance with the declaration approved by Philip V himself in 1703. Flotte and Regnault were both arrested in Spain and at Versailles the word spread that Orléans was guilty of treason. His enemies at court, headed by the dauphin, disseminated rumours of an attempted *coup d'état* and so inflamed matters that at one moment Louis asked his chancellor to prepare a form of arraignment against his nephew: it seemed possible that the premier prince of the blood would stand trial, perhaps even face execution. But that remote possibility was removed by the king himself who let it be known that he considered the affair exaggerated and ordered that the malicious gossip was to stop.

Louis XIV's role is significant in interpreting the degree of Orléans' guilt in the Spanish affair. In October 1708, under the most severe pressure from the Grand Alliance, Louis had accepted in principle that his grandson would have to be removed from the throne of Spain before a peace treaty could be signed. This drastic step was a preliminary to the 1709 negotiations which only foundered on the brutal allied stipulation that Louis should, if necessary, make war on his own grandson. These negotiations were conducted at the same time as Orléans' alleged treachery was being plotted in Spain and the two episodes are closely linked.[24] Orléans explained the connection and gave his account of his own part in the imbroglio to Saint-Simon:

> ... the prince confided to me that many eminent Spaniards, grandees amongst others, had convinced him that the King of Spain would not long be able to retain his throne, and that he had been strongly urged to expedite that monarch's abdication in order to replace him. M. le Duc d'Orléans told me that he had rejected this proposal with all the contempt it deserved, but that he had at the same time agreed to the possibility of his changing his mind should King Philip fall unaided, without hope of recovery. In that case, he contended, there would be no disloyalty, but great benefit to the King and to France, because the Spanish throne would be thus kept in the family – a result no less desirable for King Louis than for the prince himself. What is

more, if all this could be achieved without King Louis' knowledge or participation, the latter would be relieved of the obligation to renounce his grandson in a treaty, and the Allies be willing to accept a king elected by the Spaniards themselves and independent of France; for the appearance of union and alliance would then be less obvious than under King Philip.[25]

Saint-Simon's account carries conviction though it may not be the whole story, for that fussy courtier was not as privy to Orléans' innermost thoughts as he imagined. Orléans was sufficiently tempted by the prospect of gaining the advantage for his house over the Bourbon line in Spain to undertake secret negotiations with Stanhope. Nevertheless, it is highly improbable that he would have entered into the kind of conspiracy which he assured Saint-Simon he had rejected and which would have properly laid him open to the accusation of treason. He could only have held Spain with the active support of the Allies and the passive approval of the Castilians, upon neither of which could he depend and he would have had to take up arms against his father-in-law and the French troops with whom he had so recently distinguished himself. Though his enemies might point to his political ambition and to his estrangement from the French court to justify their accusations, there was nothing in his record to suggest that Orléans was capable of such a dishonourable course of action, in which, incidentally, he seemed content to rely upon only two – highly inefficient – agents.

The second possibility, however, that the king of Spain might in any case have to relinquish his throne, was a very different matter. If that happened Orléans would be intimately concerned since his claim to the Spanish crown had already been recognized by Philip V. Thus the second part of his *exposé* to Saint-Simon also rings true, though in one area some doubt remains: was Louis XIV as unaware of what was taking place as he, by his actions, and Orléans quite specifically, according to Saint-Simon, maintained? The diarist himself reports Orléans' assertion that no sooner had Louis forbidden him to return to Spain than he suggested privately that Orléans should send someone to protest his loyalty so that, if Philip were forced to quit the Spanish throne, Orléans' own claims would not be placed in jeopardy. The king also tried to calm any fears in Philip V's mind about Orléans' designs on his crown.[26] On the British side there was a good deal of scepticism about the independence of Orléans' actions. The duke of Marlborough wrote to lord treasurer Godolphin in January 1709: 'I really believe the Duke of Orléans would not act this part, but that he had the king of France's permission';[27] and Stanhope himself observed, 'The judgement I am able to form by all I could gather from what has passed is, that when things went ill for France, that court has indirectly led the Duke of Orléans to believe it would be no disagreeable expedient to get a peace to let him be King of Spain.'[28] Louis' subsequent attitude to Orléans was ambiguous. It appears that the virulent court gossip momentarily convinced him of his nephew's involvement in a more serious plot than he had at first comprehended or approved, though he soon reacted strongly against this idea. At the end of his life when seeking to effect a reconciliation between Orléans and Philip V, Louis, through his distinguished foreign minister, the marquis de Torcy, implied that the accusations levelled against Flotte and Regnault, who were still in prison, were probably false.[29] However circuitous the means, it appears certain that Louis XIV had indicated his support for some kind of initiative from Orléans.

In opening discussions with the British there was no question of a *coup* in Orléans' mind; if Philip was forced to abandon his kingdom it would be as part of an overall peace settlement. Orléans' conduct may have been incautious and clumsily contrived but it fell far short of treason. However, the episode had the effect of further compromising his reputation, which was to plummet still lower in the following years with the deaths of successive heirs to the French throne and the consequent allegations of poisoning levelled against him.

This series of royal fatalities exacerbated the interconnected problem of the successions in France and Spain, making the Allies hypersensitive to the danger of one man inheriting both kingdoms. By this time neither Louis nor Philip was in a position to hold out against the Allied demand that the latter should renounce his rights to the French succession and the house of Orléans its rights to the Spanish. These renunciations were incorporated into the treaty of Utrecht. Neither Louis nor his grandson, however, considered such enforced renunciations to be binding. Speaking on Louis' behalf Torcy told the British ministers that the required renunciation was null and void according to the fundamental laws of the kingdom which stipulated that:

> ... the Prince who is closest to the Crown must inherit it. He receives his patrimony neither from the King who precedes him nor from the people, but from the law which bestows it. ... This law is regarded as the work of he who has established all monarchies and we are convinced in France that God alone can annul it.

Philip, too, contrasted the hereditary law of succession with the usurpation by William III which the British had solemnly confirmed.[30]

Consequently, when the duke de Berry died in May 1714, Philippe d'Orléans knew that only the fragile life of the future Louis XV held at bay the threat of a disputed succession. The death of his youngest grandson also persuaded the king of the need to take further steps to safeguard the Bourbon line. But at the end of a long life, in which the last years had been the saddest, Louis allowed his heart to get the better of his political judgment and he produced two enactments which flew in the face of those fundamental laws which he had stressed unavailingly to his enemies before Utrecht. In July 1714 he made his two sons by Madame de Montespan, the duke du Maine and the count de Toulouse, eligible to succeed to the French crown if all others in the direct line died without heirs, and in the following month he drew up a will naming Orléans as merely the head of a regency council which would act for his great-grandchild and giving the duke du Maine charge of the young king's education and command of the royal household troops. Together, these royal acts increased the air of misgiving already surrounding the French succession by introducing a third, extremely dubious, candidate at the expense not only of Orléans but of Philip V who continued to protest his own pre-eminent rights. In May 1715 the latter despatched the prince de Cellamare on his embassy to Louis XIV's court with instructions to uphold and to rally support for his master's pretensions.[31]

As for Louis' own expectations, he must surely have recognized how unlikely it was that his illegitimate children would ever ascend the throne of France; a royal decree was no more likely than the insistence of a victorious enemy to reverse a fundamental law of the French state. He certainly had no illusions about the effectiveness of his testament. No French king could bind his successors, and Louis had the example of his father's vain attempt to do so as a recent reminder of that fact. He made his doubts clear, indicating that it was the pressure exerted by Madame de Maintenon which had persuaded him to resort to a will. She was anxious, as was the king, to safeguard the duke du Maine's future: hence the testament's careful division of power between Maine and Orléans.[32]

Louis XIV's attitude towards Orléans towards the end of his reign was not as hostile as it had been previously. Following the Spanish *débâcle* of 1709 Orléans had offered an olive-branch to the king by ending his liaison with Madame d'Argenton and in the same year his daughter was betrothed to the duke de Berry, adding to the already bewildering set of relationships between the houses of Bourbon and Orléans. Later, when the succession of royal deaths caused wild accusations to be levelled against Philippe, Louis refused to give them any credence; while his efforts at the end of his life to bring about a reconciliation between his nephew and his grandson have already been noted. Louis was a good judge of men and he knew that Orléans had talents and a charismatic personality which neither Maine nor Philip V could match. By the time of his final meeting with his nephew, on 26 August 1715, the king seemed to have accepted that until the dauphin's majority, and notwithstanding his own testament, the future of the kingdom would lie incontrovertibly in Orléans' hands.[33]

*   *   *

The problems confronting Orléans as he contemplated the future during the last week of Louis XIV's life were formidable, and suggested that 1715 might become as ill-omened a date in French history as 1559, 1610 or 1648. At the end of the regency, in February 1723, the keeper of the seals, Fleuriau d'Armenonville, was to remark that regencies were always stormy times;[34] and undoubtedly the history of the preceding century and a half amply bore out his observation: the Wars of Religion, the troubles of Louis XIII's minority after the assassination of his father, Henri IV, and most recently the events of the Fronde.

The matter of the king's will posed an immediate difficulty, for Orléans had to choose between seeking to establish his authority by directly asserting it or making political compromises with the accompanying risk of diminishing it. Yet it was only the immediate hurdle for Orléans to negotiate: beyond it lay a host of long-term problems. He had two rivals for the office of regent in Maine and Philip V of Spain, and in the latter an arch-rival for the French succession. Shortly after the beginning of the regency the Spanish ambassador, Cellamare, reported after discussions with members of the 'old court', including Torcy and Villeroy, that the country overwhelmingly favoured the succession of Philip V if Louis XV should die childless. Nor was this merely the partial view of men hostile to Orléans: even the faithful Saint-Simon admitted in 1718 that were the situation to arise he too would be forced to opt for the king of Spain.[35] The dangerous uncertainty of the situation was compounded by the controversial character of Orléans himself, especially when seen against the background of the previous reign. His rule seemed as likely to encourage dissension and opposition, conspiracy even, as to command respect not least because it marked the dissolution of the apparently changeless perspectives of Louis XIV's world.

Not that that dissolution was universally regretted: tensions that had existed for some time behind the bland conformity of Louis' régime had now to be reckoned with. During the War of the Spanish Succession France had suffered the most shattering military setbacks since the Italian campaigns of Francis I early in the sixteenth century; but by this time the implications of defeat were global and not simply European. It is true that the treaty of Utrecht did not represent the supreme humiliation for France that seemed likely in 1709–10, due partly to the revival of French arms under marshal Villars and partly to the withdrawal of the British troops following the Tory peace party's electoral victory in 1710 – perfidious Albion running true to form, though on this occasion to France's advantage. Nevertheless, morale was low and a number of Frenchmen began to ponder whether the basic philosophy and structure of government in France were at fault. After all, its troubles might broadly be said to stem from events in England in 1688 when divine right monarchy, the very cornerstone of the French system, had been rejected in favour of an elected ruler whose inspiration had a good deal to do with subsequent French defeats. Though the swingeing attacks of the *philosophes* on the sacerdotal nature of kingship lay in the future, there were some already willing to argue that God's lieutenant had taken a wrong turning. Saint-Simon's notorious belief that all would be well if the peers received their proper due provides an extreme example of aristocratic criticism of the régime. A more plausible view was taken by Fénelon with his advocacy of a revived and noble-dominated estates-general: besides, his influence with the duke de Bourgogne offered some hope of practical results. The count de Boulainvilliers was uncompromisingly direct in his characterization of Louis' reign as 'despotic, money-minded, very long, and consequently odious'. For him feudalism, with its recognition of the importance of the nobleman's role, was 'the masterpiece of the human mind', and he had this to say of the monarchy of Louis' age:

> It is astonishing that nowadays it is thought fitting to treat it as founded on the absolute power of the prince, without hearkening to the testimony of thirteen centuries during which we see the kingdom established solely by the blood, the labour, and the expenditures of the old nobility.[36]

Not all aristocratic critics, however, looked to the past, real or illusory. Boisguillebert and Vauban criticized the uneven tax burden which allowed the privileged groups to escape the ever more onerous financial exactions borne by the third estate.[37] There was aristocratic support for the idea of universal taxation but only if as a *quid pro quo* the king would introduce reforms favouring increased noble participation in government.[38]

This ground-swell of aristocratic criticism reached a crescendo as the possibility of change could at last be discerned with the passing of the old order. Though it did offer a challenge to the status quo, there were no signs of any serious matching discontent among the unprivileged which might have produced conditions conducive to revolution. There was some rapport, however, between noble and business interests which heightened tension further in Louis' last years. The mercantilist state structure elaborated by the king and his minister, Colbert, antagonized both groups. It was inclined to deprive the nobleman of his political importance and independence since it was centralist and bureaucratic in tendency, and it threatened the merchant's profits with its policy of intervention and direction. There were, of course, long-established links between the nobility and the wealthy bourgeoisie and a steady recruitment from the latter into the former. With the cumulative financial strains imposed on France by the last two wars of Louis XIV's reign, the Nine Years War and the War of the Spanish Succession, these links were strengthened to provide a firmer bulwark against government policies.[39]

There were difficult and dangerous currents, therefore, for the new regent to negotiate, many of them swirling around the rocks of financial disaster which in 1715 threatened the country with ruin. In that year the controller-general of finance, Nicolas Desmaretz, estimated that the national debt had reached 2,000 million livres, a figure which a distinguished recent historian of Louis' reign, Pierre Goubert, describes as 'fantastic but possibly accurate'.[40] However, at the very end of the regency, when Orléans began daily instructions to the young king Louis XV on the state of the kingdom which he was shortly to inherit, he was to put the figure at Louis XIV's death in September 1715 even higher at 2,200 million livres, with the revenues due from the following years 'mangés d'avance'.[41] The cause, as he also explained to his pupil, was war. Between 1688 and 1697, when the Nine Years War was being fought, the state's expenses doubled and more than doubled between 1701 and 1714 during the War of the Spanish Succession. This period of colossal public expenditure, reaching a peak of 264 million livres in 1711, coincided with and exacerbated the serious depression which was affecting country areas in particular. The government's various financial expedients only made matters worse.[42] The War of the Spanish Succession demonstrated that the cost of participating in world-wide conflict could not be borne without imposing dire strains upon French financial resources. A more sophisticated monetary system was needed but that could only accompany changes in the country's socio-economic structure and especially in the psychology of the privileged classes. Though there were signs of willingness by some noblemen to accept a more equitable distribution of the tax burden, the price to be paid by the government was high: an end to administrative innovation. There was an important paradox in this, for to turn the clock back would be to risk making the country less rather than more capable of coping with its problems. Largely under the influence of Torcy, a training school for professional diplomats had been established, and there were many other examples from that long reign of the incipient state bureaucracy which increasingly limited the amateur's scope in government.[43] The king himself had to be a professional, *un roi d'aujourd'hui*, as Louis XIV undoubtedly had been, though that new style raised a further question about the nature of royal authority: was it no longer to be exercised in favour of the old dynastic and patrimonial interests but only of the impersonal state whose chief servant the king had become?[44] The Bourbons failed with tragic consequences to resolve that particular dichotomy. In 1715, however, the new regent faced grave economic difficulties and crucial decisions about how the country should be administered and governed which were daunting enough in themselves.

One other issue also threatened to rend the country, the recurring crisis of Jansenism. This was not merely a dispute among theologians: during the *ancien régime* such quarrels at once became matters of state since the king's authority was embedded in his subjects' spiritual conformity. The problem of Jansenism engaged the king's prestige as *le roi très chrétien*, and also revived the vexed question of his relationship with the pope. In addition, it helped to focus the dilemma of *le roi bureaucrate*, whose administrative régime was likely on occasion to clash with the dictates of established law. In this area Jansenism was responsible for recharging the political batteries of the parlement of Paris.

Jansenism had taken root in France from the mid-seventeenth century, following the appearance of bishop Jansen's *Augustinus* (1640). The position of its adherents has been pungently, though not altogether unfairly, categorized by Sainte-Beuve as that of good Catholics who disliked the Jesuits. In fact the theological argument, centering upon the relationship between divine grace and free will in the matter of personal salvation, was an ancient and complex one. Jansenism offered an ascetic way of life for it emphasized man's inadequacy in the absence of divine assistance. Its French adherents, headed by the abbé de Saint-Cyran and Antoine Arnauld, had their spiritual base at the convent of Port-Royal-des-Champs and numbered Racine and Pascal among their disciples. By 1713, however, the movement was under fierce attack from the vehemently orthodox king. Its leaders were dead, Port-Royal had been razed and Louis requested the pope, Clement XI, to deliver the *coup de grâce*. The latter responded in September 1713 with the bull Unigenitus dei filius whose acceptance throughout his realm the king had guaranteed in advance.

Such a guarantee, however, was contrary to Gallican tradition and in particular to the fourth of the Four Articles of 1682 which had been approved by the French bishops and registered in the parlement of Paris as a law of the state, with the whole-hearted support and consent of the king himself.[45] This article stipulated that the pope's judgments in matters of faith were irreformable only when they were unanimously backed by the French clergy. Unless an assembly of the French bishops provided such support Unigenitus could not become a law of the French church. The king went some way towards following the recognized procedure by summoning a council of bishops comprising fewer than half of the French episcopate, yet even from this smaller body he could not extract a unanimous acceptance. A minority of bishops led by the cardinal-archbishop of Paris, Louis Antoine de Noailles, refused to receive the bull save with the addition of written explanations.[46]

Armed with this dubious majority among the bishops, the king consulted his chief law officers in the parlement of Paris, the *procureur-général* and future chancellor, d'Aguesseau, and Joly de Fleury, the *avocat-général*. They expressed their opinion firmly and courageously: no paper pronouncement could be considered a law of the church unless it had been accepted by the French bishops and the episcopal support so far received fell short of that requirement. Nor was it possible for the parlement to register Unigenitus as a law of the state before it had become a law of the church. Finally, they opposed proposition 91 of the bull according to which the pope claimed the right to excommunicate the French king and free his subjects from their obligation of obedience, as also being contrary to the Gallican Articles.[47]

The king decided to ignore the opinions of his legal advisers and in February 1714 he sent the bull and letters-patent enforcing it as a law of the state to be registered by the parlement. This precipitated a stormy debate in the Palais de Justice and, although the attack on Unigenitus was mounted by Jansenist magistrates, there was widespread opposition to the anti-Gallican posture which both king and pope were now adopting. For the first time since the prohibition of 1673, remonstrances before registration were demanded and the first president – the court's chief judge – had to intervene to prevent this opinion gathering support. As it was, the bull was not registered 'purely and simply' as Louis wanted, but with qualifications protecting the liberties of the Gallican church, the rights of the crown and the authority of the bishops.[48]

By ignoring the traditional Gallican doctrine which he himself had defended in the articles of 1682 the king was doubly guilty in the eyes of the magistrates of the *parlement*: he was undermining one of the traditional bases of kingship in France and he was flouting a law which had been validated with his full approval. His overbearing attitude in the matter of Unigenitus, therefore, stimulated the law court's political revival, for the *parlement* had long taken pride in its role as the chief bulwark against arbitrary government. That role, of course, was based upon the preservation of existing laws and legal procedures: in changing circumstances such precepts might seem inadequate or obstructive but as yet they still offered the supreme, traditional guarantee of political stability. The *parlement's* reaction to Unigenitus certainly struck a responsive chord in the capital: Madame de Maintenon observed that 'From the moment the Bull was translated all Paris appeared to be Jansenist'.[49] The king, however, was not to be gainsaid and in July 1715 he decided to summon a national council of bishops. The indications were that Louis intended to use this council as a means of enforcing unanimous acceptance of Unigenitus and for that reason almost all the senior magistrates expressed their disquiet to the first president during August 1715.[50] However, Louis died at the beginning of September before the council could be convened.

The new regent would, therefore, face a divided church and the underlying threat of a divided kingdom. In this situation the *parlement* of Paris had a crucial part to play. It also figured prominently in another context: in the last month of his life the king handed over to this court's safekeeping the will through which he sought to regulate the affairs of the regency.

Orléans did not doubt his unpopularity at court vis-à-vis the duke du Maine nor the widespread belief that Philip V of Spain had a prior claim to the regency and to the throne. The king's will added a further complication, though in excluding the king of Spain and nominating Orléans as the titular regent it could be exploited in the latter's favour. Equally, the very fact that it had been deposited in the *parlement* suggested a method of proclaiming the regent's authority with the maximum legal endorsement. This greatest of the sovereign courts, in which peers and princes of the royal blood were still entitled to sit beside the magistrates, had played a prominent part in the nominations of the two previous regents, Marie de Medici and Anne of Austria. Both of these ladies had responded by inviting the court to proffer whatever counsels it thought appropriate to the good of the state. There were precedents here for Orléans to reflect upon. He had begun to negotiate with some leading members of the *parlement* even before Louis XIV drew up his will. They included president de Maisons who died less than a fortnight before the king, the *gens du roi*, d'Aguesseau and Joly de Fleury, the abbé Pucelle, a senior and much respected Jansenist member who had led the attack on Unigenitus in the court, and a lay-councillor, Joseph Charles de Fortia, as well as Jean-Baptiste du Gaumont, a *maître des requêtes* prominent in the legal establishment of the capital.[51]

Orléans had other allies too, notably the duke de Noailles. This nobleman's uncle, the cardinal-archbishop of Paris, had become a hero in the parlement as a result of his intransigent opposition to Unigenitus, so that a strong rapport with the Noailles family was bound to assist Orléans' relations with the sovereign court. In addition Noailles was the brother-in-law of the duke de Guiche, a colonel of the French Guards, the largest regiment in the *maison du roi* and the one best placed to influence events in Paris. Temperamentally, Noailles had much in common with Orléans. Intelligent, cynical, amusing, he had organized his own political academy to study universal history in 1707. A free-thinker, he calculated that his considerable political ambition would best be served by a close alliance with the arch-libertine.[52] The new king of England, George I, was also anxious to proffer assistance since Orléans' title to the throne derived from the British insistence at the peace of Utrecht that the king of Spain should renounce his claim to the French throne. The British ambassador at the French court, lord Stair, was ordered to assure Orléans of the king's support. Efforts were made to stiffen his resolve for there was great concern in London during August 1715 that Orléans might lack the ambition and the application necessary to capture the regency. This fear was misplaced, and Stair was reassured on 23 August by the abbé Dubois, acting as the duke's confidential emissary, about the strength of Orléans' position. Three days later, on the 26th, when it was apparent that the king's death was imminent the chancellor, Voysin, and Louis' old confidant, marshal Villeroy, revealed to Orléans the contents of the king's will though one may doubt whether the revelation came as much of a surprise.[53]

Orléans had been quietly consolidating his position at the duke du Maine's expense and when the old king died early in the morning of 1 September he acted promptly and with a sure touch. Having decided to rule with the assistance of a series of councils he had already offered the presidency of the council of finance to the duke de Noailles. Now he promised to marshal Villars the presidency of the War Council and had formal discussions with cardinal de Noailles and the duke d'Antin, destined to be presidents respectively of the council for religion and of the council for internal affairs. Then he left Versailles for Paris where he had discussions with d'Aguesseau and other leading members of the parlement.[54] The first president, de Mesmes, had been taken into Orléans' confidence shortly before the king's death and doubtless the meeting on 1 September simply served to confirm the arrangements tentatively agreed upon in the course of earlier discussions. By the time he returned to the palace at nine o'clock that evening, his plans for the meeting of the parlement on the following day were complete.

This crucial debate took place in the ancient Palais de Justice, for over four hundred years the parlement's permanent abode which stood on the western side of the Île de la cité. Early on the morning of Monday, 2 September, detachments of troops from Guiche's French Guard began to take up their positions, blocking the main approaches to the palace and controlling the river banks around the island. Orléans was thus able to forestall a similar demonstration by the Swiss Guard whose chief was the duke du Maine, though the danger of that happening was slight: the bastard Maine seemed unaware of his rival's clandestine bargaining which included an arrangement with M. de Reynoldt, Maine's own deputy in the guard. Within the palace two of Orléans' chief allies, Guiche himself and lord Stair, were installed in prominent positions in boxes overlooking the *grand'chambre* where the session was to be held.

It was a session attended not only by the magistrates but by the peers and princes of the blood, all of whom sat by right in the *grand'chambre* of the realm's chief court. Only the king himself was absent from this gathering of the high nobility. Before this distinguished company Orléans rose to claim the office of regent by right of birth and in accordance with the laws of the kingdom.[55] At one point in his address he came close to adding the parlement's approval of his title as another necessary attribute:

> I am convinced, therefore, that according to the Laws of the Kingdom and to the precedents established in similar circumstances, and likewise in accordance with the intention of the late King, the office of Regent belongs to me; but I would not be satisfied unless to the many titles which can be mustered in my favour, you add your votes and approbation which will gratify me no less than the Regency itself.

At another, he made more explicit his reliance on parlementaire support:

> But by whatever title I may aspire to the Regency, I venture to assure you, gentlemen, that I will deserve it through my zeal for the King's service and through my devotion to the public weal, being assisted chiefly by your counsel and by your wise remonstrances. I request them of you in anticipation.[56]

Orléans had already agreed to restore the right of remonstrance to the traditional form in which it had existed before 1673. In other words, the magistrates were to be given the opportunity to examine and to criticize proposed legislation prior to registration, thereby resuming the political role denied to them for the greater part of Louis XIV's reign.

In his reply the *avocat-général*, Joly de Fleury, picked out the same theme, referring to Orléans' confidence in the court's opinions and remonstrances, and making an equivocal distinction between his right to the regency by birth and 'les suffrages de cette auguste compagnie' which would bestow upon him the title of regent.[57] By general acclaim without recourse to a vote, the parlement pronounced Orléans regent.

There was still the knotty problem of Louis XIV's will to be disposed of, with its nominated regency council and its stipulation that Maine should have control of the king's education and of his household troops. The parlement resumed its session in the afternoon when the shape of Orléans' bargain with the court became clearer. The regent elaborated his intention of governing the country through a council of regency and a series of subordinate councils, on which he hoped that some members of the parlement would agree to serve. In the regency council itself he was willing to submit to the majority decision in every area but one, on condition that he was allowed to nominate the membership. The exception concerned the distribution of offices, benefices and favours in which he demanded complete freedom of action. He also insisted that the household troops should come under his direct command. The parlement accepted all these propositions, leaving the chagrined duke du Maine with no more than the empty title of superintendent of the king's education.

At Louis XIV's death Orléans' authority was by no means assured. It would have been dangerous for him to assume power arbitrarily as if the will had never existed, yet had he accepted its terms his authority would have been circumscribed. By acting as he did he gained public recognition, effective control and the support of the parlement. But he paid a price for these advantages. From a strictly legal point of view Orléans' claims to the regency by birth, and through the late king's will, had much to commend them. Yet the one depended on the validity of Philip V's renunciation and the other Orléans himself had been instrumental in destroying. Consequently, he leant heavily upon the magistrates' support. In order to win that support he had had to encourage the parlement to resume a political role which in the past had proved embarrassing to more than one regent. His decision to establish a series of councils, the *polysynodie*, was also calculated in part to appeal to magistrates long frustrated and antagonized by Louis XIV's progressively bureaucratic régime, particularly since Orléans was willing to recruit some of them as councillors. Even before the king's death he had entered into a number of engagements with the magistrates in discussions designed to procure the court's support when the time came and including, as we shall see, certain assurances relating to the matter of Unigenitus. The members of the parlement were not the only group which had to be conciliated but they were the first. In achieving this initial success, the new regent gave himself some limited room for manoeuvre in dealing with other groups and in confronting the grave problems which beset him.

1 Philippe's father, Philippe I, duke d'Orléans, Monsieur in court parlance, brother of Louis XIV. Portrait by Charles Lebrun.

2 Philippe (to the right), before he was breeched, with his sister, Elisabeth Charlotte, and their mother, Madame in court parlance, second wife of Philippe I, Elisabeth Charlotte (Liselotte von der Pfalz).

3   Philippe as a young boy, portrayed in armour, indicating the military career for which he was trained.

4 Philippe, again in armour. A portrait probably painted before he became regent.

5 Portrait of Philippe's wife, Françoise-Marie, Mademoiselle de Blois, daughter of Louis XIV by Madame de Montespan, as a young girl. They were married in 1692, when they were both in their teens.

6 Philippe, who became duke d'Orléans in 1701 on the death of his father, took an active part in the War of the Spanish Succession, both on the Italian front and in Spain itself. This martial scene commemorates his military career which won him praise from Louis XIV. His high birth made him the obvious regent named by Louis for the child-king, who succeeded as Louis XV in 1715.

7 The *lit de justice* in the Paris parlement on 2 September 1715, when Philippe was affirmed as regent. Note the child-king under the canopy on the left.

8 Louis XV accompanied by the regent, his governor and governess, enters Paris by the Porte Saint Antoine. The castle of Vincennes can be seen in the background.

Philippes d'Orleans,
Petit fils de France, déclaré Regent
du Royaume par le Parlem.t le 2.7.bre 1715.

Tu vois dans ce Heros le parfait assemblage
Des plus rares Vertus, des plus heureux talens:
Mons, Steinkerque, Nerwinde, et les fiers Catalans
N'ont que trop fait l'essay de son noble Courage,
Sur ce grand Prince, enfin, digne de notre Homage
La France se repose, et les Coeurs sont contens.

I.F.

9   Allegorical representation of Philippe as regent holding in his hands *fleur-de-lys*
emblems. The verse below celebrates his military virtues: 'France is now at peace
and hearts are content'.

10 Louis XV and the regent at the 'Restoration of Liberty', i.e. the declaration of freedom of movement to men of the church whose non-acceptance of the papal bull Unigenitus had confined them to their local districts in Louis XIV's reign.

11 The regent in his role as educator of Louis XV. Note the fine work-desk, the dog and the decorative scheme, as well as the splendid costume of the young king.

12   One of the regency councils by which France was governed during the early years of the king's minority.

FRIENDS AND HELPERS OF THE REGENT

13   Adrien Maurice, duke de Noailles (1678–1766), president of the council for finance (1715–18) and member of the regency council (1718).

14   The duke de Saint-Simon, a close friend of the regent and author of a diary which gives a vivid picture of the regency years.

LOUIS DUC DE S^t. SIMON,
Pair de France Grand D'Espagne.

15   Henri-François
d'Aguesseau, chancellor of
France (1717–50), the most
distinguished lawyer of his
generation and an influential
political figure.

Louis Antoine de Noailles, uncle of the duke de Noailles (see ill. 13), cardinal-archbishop of
ris, and leader of the Jansenist opposition to Unigenitus.

Louis-Alexandre de Bourbon, count de Toulouse, Louis XIV's son by Madame de
ontespan. His naval career is alluded to in the background. He became the effective head of the
arine (together with marshal d'Estrées) and, though subsequently demoted in rank, remained on
od terms with the regent.

18　Philip V of
Spain, who
condoned the
Cellamare conspiracy
and whose ambitions
to become king of
France, if Louis XIV
died with heirs of his
own body, worried
the regent.

19　Louis Auguste de Bourbon,
duke du Maine, son of Louis XIV by
Madame de Montespan, who was
deprived by the regent of those
responsibilities for Louis XV's
upbringing designated in the will of
Louis XIV.

20　Louise Bénédicte, duchess du Maine, grand-
daughter of the Great Condé, ambitious on her
husband's behalf and a sworn enemy of the regent.

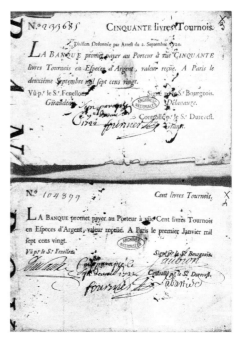

21 (*top, left*)
John Law,
controller-general
during 1720, the
financial reformer
who played such
a significant role
in the economic life
of the regency.

22 (*top, right*)
Two of the last bills
of exchange issued
by Law's bank in
January (below)
and September (top)
1720.

23   The collapse of
        Law's system.
        German satirical
print on the death of
credit.

24   View of the Palais-Royal, the regent's principal residence.

25   An engraving by Audran, one of thirty made to illustrate a French translation by Amyot, published in 1718, of Longus' *Daphnis and Chloë*. All the engravings are after original designs by the regent, and this one depicts the wedding of Daphnis and Chloë.

26   Design by G.-M. Oppenord, the regent's principal architect, for a section of Salon d'Angle, Palais-Royal.

27   Design by Oppenord for the bed-alcove of the regent in the Palais-Royal.

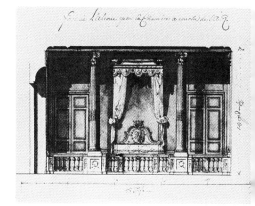

28 *Le Bal Champêtre* by Antoine Watteau, one of the many paintings purchased by Philippe.

29 A typical commode of the regency period by Charles Cressent, one of the most celebrated proponents of the form.

Marie Louise Elisabeth,
e eldest surviving daughter
Philippe, who married in
10 the duke de Berry, Louis
V's grandson. He died
ung and in her widowhood
e became a close companion
her father.

Philippe's mother in her
er years. She was devoted to
r son and her vast
rrespondence has much to
l about him.

32   Cardinal Guillaume
Dubois, the regent's chief
adviser, a skilled diplomat,
influential in French foreign
policy. The regent survived
him by only four months.

33　The Cabinet du Roi, designed by R. and J.-R. de Cotte under the direction of the regent, celebrates Louis XV reaching his majority. The regent before his death in December 1723 had succeeded in his task of keeping the power of the crown unimpaired during his period of office.

II

The Government of the Kingdom

In the early years of the regency the government of France appeared to be conciliar, following the establishment of the *polysynodie* to which Orléans had committed himself in the assembly of 2 September 1715. Yet the nature of this régime has been much misinterpreted by subsequent commentators.[1] Before examining the regent's experiment more closely, however, both the function of the king's council in the previous reign and the precise nature of the authority inherited by Orléans must be looked at.

The king's council was considered indivisible although it met under various titles and with differing personnel. Since 1661 there had been two sorts of royal council meetings, those of government at which the king himself presided and those concerned with judicial, financial and administrative matters mainly of a litigious kind. The chancellor, the crown's chief legal adviser, usually presided at these latter sessions though an empty chair always reminded those present that they were meeting as royal councillors. The government councils were the *conseil d'en haut* which dealt with all the most important affairs of state, domestic and foreign; the *conseil des dépêches* concerned with routine matters emanating from the provinces, and the *conseil royal des finances* which supervised the fiscal policies of the kingdom. The three aspects of the council at which the chancellor normally presided, known collectively as the *conseil d'état privé, finance et direction*, were the *conseil d'état privé* (or the *conseil des parties*) which was concerned with judicial disputes between individuals and corporate bodies; the *conseil d'état et des finances* (or *conseil ordinaire des finances*) which regulated judicial and administrative disputes arising from the activities of the controller-general's office, and which had ceased to function long before the end of Louis XIV's reign; and the *grande* and *petite direction*, both dealing with contentious matters in which the king had a financial interest. The presidency of the *petite direction* was held by the *chef* of the *conseil royal des finances*, whose role in both councils was largely honorary.

The membership of these bodies varied considerably in size and personnel. Only a handful of ministers of state attended the *conseil d'en haut*; indeed they became ministers as a result of their summons to that body. The chancellor was sometimes a minister and always a member of the *dépêches* and the *conseil royal des finances*. All the secretaries of state were also present at the *dépêches* and some of them were ministers of state. The controller-general of finance attended the *dépêches* as well as the *conseil royal des finances*, the *conseil des parties*, the *conseil ordinaire des finances* and the two *directions*. He too was frequently a minister of state. The thirty councillors of state* sat in the *conseil des parties* and the *conseil ordinaire des finances*; most of them attended the *directions* and two had membership of the *conseil royal des finances*. All the *maîtres des requêtes* – magistrates traditionally closely tied to the king's service – sat in the *conseil des parties*, the *conseil ordinaire des finances* and the *directions*. The intendants of finance were likewise members of the *conseil des parties*, the *conseil ordinaire des finances* and the *directions*.[2]

Since in all these councils decisions were taken in the king's name whether he was in attendance or not, it is important to have clearly in mind the precise relationship existing between crown and council. The council was always a purely consultative body and in the last resort the king, who was certainly expected to seek advice, had also to make the decisions. A distinguished eighteenth-century lawyer, Gilbert de Voisins, who was appointed by Orléans *avocat-général* in the parlement of Paris in 1718, expressed the relationship thus:

> ... the King's Council which is bound to his person and is inseparable from him, is in principle neither a jurisdiction nor a litigious tribunal. It is the King himself accompanied by those who assist him in government, for which he is responsible; and whose truly royal character demands an aura of deliberation and advice.

Louis XIV put it more succinctly to his grandson, Philip, as he went off to rule Spain in 1700: 'Ecoutez, consultez votre Conseil, mais décidez.'[3]

What, therefore, was the nature of the regent's relationship with his regency council and with the other councils established by him in September 1715? First of all it must be understood that according to the French legal and constitutional tradition his appointment as regent bestowed upon him sovereign authority, to be exercised on behalf of the minor king; authority identical with that which Louis XV would himself wield at the moment of his majority. That was the meaning of the parlement's recognition of his status as 'Régent en France pour avoir

* There had been this number since 1673.

en ladite qualité l'administration des affaires du Royaume pendant la Minorité du Roi'. Specifically, however, Orléans chose to protect and exercise his power in precisely the way his predecessor had done. After dismissing his wayward superintendent of finance, Fouquet, Louis XIV had decided that the king himself should sign and settle all the accounts which had prev ously been handled by the superintendent whose office he abolished. On 23 September 1715, a week after the institution of the *polysynodie*, a royal declaration similarly stipulated that until the king's majority the regent would be responsible for 'tous les états et ordonnances de fonds et dépenses que le feu Roy ... avoit coutume de signer et arrester luy-même', a stipulation reiterated later that year.[4]

As to whether the organization of the conciliar system diminished the regent's authority, the answer must be hardly at all. It is true that in recommending the parlement to support Orléans' claim, the *avocat-général* added the proviso, 'sauf à délibérer ensuite sur les autres propositions qui pourroient être faites par M. le duc d'Orléans'. Undoubtedly one of the proposals in Joly de Fleury's mind was that concerned with the establishment of a *polysynodie*. Indeed the court's formal recognition of Orléans' status as regent also included some details of the conciliar régime shortly to be introduced. The regent also agreed to abide by the majority verdict in the regency council. In reality, however, his position was not affected by these apparent restrictions. In the first place the distribution of offices and favours was explicitly reserved to the regent alone and, even more significantly, appointment to all the councils, including the regency council itself, was to be in his gift.[5] It was no great burden for him to submit to a majority vote when he knew that those voting depended upon his favour to remain royal councillors. Therefore, although the regent's offer to abide by the regency council's verdict seemed to clash with his obligation to exercise sovereign power on the king's behalf, the appearance was deceptive: it was part of an illusion which at the time Orléans found it necessary to create, an illusion involving the whole structure of the *polysynodie*.

In fact, the *polysynodie* failed to introduce any modifications into Louis XIV's conciliar structure. The three most technical aspects of the council dominated by legal experts, the *conseil des parties*, the *grande* and *petite direction*, continued to function as before. The government councils were all contained in the council of regency which initially met on Sundays and Wednesdays to consider matters of foreign policy when it was effectively the *conseil d'en haut*; on Tuesdays to consider war, the navy and the provinces when it was the equivalent of the *conseil des dépêches*; and on Saturdays for financial affairs when it matched the *conseil royal des finances*. At all these sessions the regent presided, but the king's empty chair signified that Orléans was merely acting as substitute for his royal master. The members of the regency council were in effect ministers of state though without the title.

There were some significant changes in personnel though in this area, too, much was unchanged. Save for the intendants of finance the membership of the *conseil des parties*, the *grande* and *petite direction* remained as it was and even the two councillors of state who had attended Louis XIV's *conseil royal des finances* were summoned to the regency council when it met to discuss financial matters. However, the former predominance of the secretaries of state and of the controller-general of finance was brought to an end. The four secretaryships were reduced to three with the suppression of the chancellor Voysin's office of secretary for war in January 1716 and only one of them, La Vrillière, was retained *ex officio* in the regency council, where he took the minutes but had no deliberative voice. That was in notable contrast to the practice observed under the previous régime when the secretaries had tended to dominate the *conseil d'en haut*. Similarly, the controller-general, Desmaretz, was dismissed and no replacement was named. Under Louis XIV, as we have seen, this official was accustomed to attending every branch of the king's council including the *conseil d'en haut*. Finally, the offices of the seven intendants of finance were suppressed.

The business of all these officials was taken over by the seven specialized councils of the *polysynodie* – established by royal declarations on 15 September and 14 December 1715 – concerned with foreign affairs, war, the marine, including the administration of the colonies, finance, the interior, religion (the *conseil de conscience*) and commerce. Each had a president who communicated his council's proposals to the regency council at the relevant sessions and was granted an entrée to that council for those sessions only. None of these bodies formed part of the royal council proper. Neither the regent nor the chancellor attended their sessions and no vacant armchair symbolized the king's presence. They did not have the authority to issue decrees or judgments; they simply assumed the responsibility of preparing material for the regency council. The business of advising the sovereign's representative and his council was thus given over to committees.[6]

Orléans, therefore, introduced a governmental system which, though in most respects identifiable with that of Louis XIV, was in comparison more elaborate and less professional. To do that a shrewd politician like Orléans must have had his reasons; and indeed he had. He was well aware of the weakness of his position on the morrow of Louis' death, and of the vulnerability of all regencies, as he indicated in a letter to the French ambassador to the Vatican, cardinal de la Trémouïlle, in September 1715.[7] Consequently, he felt it necessary to establish his authority by taking measures which he judged would be seen as appropriate to the moment. The late king's administrative arrangements had emphasized the role of individuals, the controller-general and the secretaries of state, whose powers appeared to reflect, however palely, the increasingly authoritarian stance of the sovereign himself. Orléans sensed that it would be timely to restructure government administration on a broader base and reduce the influence of particular officers. He remarked to La Trémouïlle that people were tired of seeing whole sections of government in the charge of one man, and that a new form of administration was needed to restore confidence. Indeed, the idea of a multiplicity of councils to govern the country had been debated in the circle surrounding the late duke de Bourgogne, and in 1713 Orléans himself had commissioned two members of his household to contribute to a study of conciliar government in French history.[8] The word *polysynodie* was coined by the abbé de Saint-Pierre in 1718 in a book destined to get him into difficulties with the regent.[9] Orléans knew, of course, that the parlement welcomed the concept of a *polysynodie* as a means of again influencing government, and that the magistrates' support for his authority as regent depended in part upon the execution of his promise speedily to communicate his proposals to them. In the important letter to the ambassador in Rome already cited, Orléans explained that the people would also have lost their initial confidence in him if he had delayed making his arrangements public. In this context he was thinking in particular of the Jansenist cardinal de Noailles whom he designated president of the *conseil de conscience*, an appointment underlining another advantage which Orléans drew from the *polysynodie*: the ability to balance all opinions in order to prevent a flight to extremes.

The conciliar system possessed one final attraction for the regent; it enabled him to reward his supporters and accommodate his enemies by offering them, at least on the face of it, a significant voice in government. A scrutiny of the *polysynodie*'s personnel reinforces this point. The regency council included royal princes who, despite the recent prominence of non-royal ministers and secretaries of state, might still appear the natural advisers of a minor king. The duke de Bourbon – 'Monsieur le Duc' – a great-grandson of the Great Condé, was a young man without any talent for government, as he was to demonstrate during his brief period of office as first minister following Orléans' death, but the regent was aware of his ambition for political power. The two illegitimate sons of

Louis XIV and Madame de Montespan, Maine and Toulouse, offered a potential nucleus around which the regent's enemies could gather, particularly since the late king had elevated them both in 1714 to the rank of princes of the blood. Besides these three princes, Orléans invited a number of members of the 'old court' to join him in the regency council: chancellor Voysin, and marshals Harcourt and Villeroy. A third marshal, Bezons, was added to counterbalance the uncertain loyalties of his two *confrères* though, since all three were political light-weights as well as undistinguished military men, the balancing exercise was largely academic. Saint-Simon too was a member and, though a staunch ally of the regent, he was to a remarkable degree deficient in political virtues. According to his own account he amply demonstrated that deficiency by recommending that the former bishop of Troyes, who had resigned his see in favour of his nephew in 1697, should be invited to join the regency council. His subsequent vitriolic comments on that elderly cleric were allegedly inspired by the bishop's unseemly conduct on his return to society but were probably the result of his firm support for Unigenitus which the duke neither anticipated nor wel-comed. Finally, Colbert's nephew and Louis XIV's most outstanding diplomat, the marquis de Torcy, was also appointed to the council and, in this instance, Saint-Simon accurately reflected the general sense of astonishment which followed the announcement.[10] Two of Louis XIV's former secretaries of state, Pontchartrain and La Vrillière, both represen-tatives of the great *robe* family of Phélypeaux, sat initially in the regency council. However, after some six weeks, in November 1715, Pont-chartrain was ordered to resign his secretaryship in favour of his son, the count de Maurepas, who was only fifteen years old, and to leave the regency council. La Vrillière remained, acting as the council's secretary though initially without the right to opine. Such, then, was the composition of the original council of regency though there were to be changes and additions in the course of the ensuing years. Other princes of the royal family were admitted as they came of age; in 1717 the prince de Conti, in 1718 the duke de Chartres, in 1720 the count de Charolais. The significance of the remaining additions can best be measured in the changing perspective of the later years of the regency.

Each of the satellite councils was headed by a great nobleman, not by a member of the administrative *noblesse* as would have been the case in the previous reign. It has already been noted that cardinal de Noailles was president of the *conseil de conscience*. His nephew, the duke de Noailles, presided over finance, marshal d'Huxelles over foreign affairs, marshal Villars over war, marshal Villeroy over commerce, marshal d'Estrées over the marine (though the count de Toulouse was its effective head), the duke d'Antin over the interior. The personnel of these advisory bodies included other *grands seigneurs* and magistrates whose presence reflected the various obligations inherited by the regent. Guiche and Reynoldt found themselves at the council for war, Gaumont at finance, d'Aguesseau, Joly de Fleury and the abbé Pucelle at the *conseil de conscience* and another Jansenist abbé from the parlement, Menguy, at the council for the interior. In addition, there were a number of noblemen whose collective lack of political nous may be precisely measured by their total failure to influence affairs of state: the marquis de Biron, the chevalier d'Asfeld, the marquis de Brancas, the marquis de Coëtlogon.[11]

All in all, neither the personnel of the regency council itself nor that of its various subordinate agencies inspired confidence. It is unlikely that Orléans himself viewed the system as an efficient method of conducting government business. He appears to have seen it as a useful façade behind which to shelter while his position remained vulnerable but never as a realistic means of running the country; that task he approached in a subtly different fashion.

In erecting this façade Orléans was quick to capitalize upon the example of the admired duke de Bourgogne, the new king's father, whose putative reforms had included the elaboration of a conciliar theory of government. The preamble to the royal edict establishing the councils included the following passage:

> ... this form of government appeared especially suitable to our very dear uncle, the duke d' Orléans, since he knows that its design had already been sketched by our most honoured father whose views at least we will have the satisfaction of following even though Heaven has deprived us of the advantage of being moulded by his noble example; he was convinced that when the totality of authority in a department was wielded by a single individual the burden often became too heavy for the person concerned and this could be dangerous for a prince who was not endowed with the superior intelligence of our great-grandfather; that since the prince always experienced difficulty in procuring the truth it was necessary to have several persons available to bring it before him and if provision were not made in government for a certain number of men who were as loyal as they were judicious, it would be almost impossible always to find subjects sufficiently mature and well-informed to make up for the loss of men accomplished in the science of government, and in a position to replace them.[12]

Such sentiments sounded convincing even in the context of a legal preamble, and the regent acted at first as though he believed them. Hence the dismissal of the controller-general of finance, Desmaretz, whose office was left vacant; the enforced resignation of the secretary of state, Pontchartrain; and Voysin's resignation of his office of secretary of state for war, which was suppressed altogether in 1716. Three weeks after Louis XIV's death Torcy too resigned his secretary's office which was bought by Fleuriau d'Armenonville. Only La Vrillière retained his secretaryship and for a time, as we have seen, he had to accept a subordinate rank in the regency council.

Yet the roles of La Vrillière and Torcy were to suggest a different interpretation from that embodied in Orléans' legal preamble. The former acquired the full rights of membership of the regency council in January 1716, while the latter's treatment by the regent seemed extraordinarily generous to contemporaries who saw him as a member of the 'old court' and of one of the administrative dynasties of Louis XIV's reign. Saint-Simon relates the favours accorded to Torcy by the regent: besides the 650,000 livres paid to him for his office of secretary of state, he received another 150,000 in cash when he handed in his resignation; he was allowed to retain his minister's pension of 20,000 livres besides acquiring the influential office of *surintendant des postes* in January 1716 which replaced his former office of post master. Torcy was too expert and informed an administrator to be sacrificed to any doctrinaire scheme. Saint-Simon records Orléans' explanation which was no doubt given with less embarrassment than the complacent peer imagined: 'he confessed with a good deal of confusion that he considered Torcy necessary, because, having been minister of foreign affairs for so many years, he knew all the secrets.'[13] Significantly, both Torcy and La Vrillière were left with a good deal of independent authority within the *polysynodie* structure. Orléans ordered that the most important correspondence from French agents abroad should be addressed to Torcy who was authorized to reply without giving details to the council for foreign affairs. He was also one of those key advisers with whom the regent had regular conferences at the Palais-Royal. His great experience in diplomacy and personal knowledge of the statesmen of Europe, together with the invaluable files built up as a result of his control of the postal service, made him an indispensable adviser in the field of foreign affairs even after the abbé Dubois had become foreign secretary.[14] Dubois himself acknowledged Torcy's assistance in procuring his appointment, and indicated that Orléans had agreed that Torcy should be invited to take part in future deliberations on foreign affairs.[15] In fact, Dubois found the marquis too independent an ally and at last, in October 1721, the regent agreed to add the *surintendance des postes* to the titles of the secretary of state, and Torcy withdrew in disgrace to his estate at Sablé. He was back in favour, however, two years later when Orléans approved a captain's commission for his son in the Royal Body Guard.[16] La Vrillière likewise remained a confidential adviser of the regent, and was certainly among those who successfully encouraged Orléans to reorganize the councils and restore the offices of secretary of state to their earlier pre-eminence in the autumn of 1718.[17]

A close examination of the *polysynodie* in action reveals further inequalities among its members in terms of their political significance. Administrators of no great public reputation were elevated to positions of importance, men like Jean-Baptiste de Gaumont, a member of the council for finance who went on to become an intendant of finance when that office was restored in 1722; Amelot de Gournay, the president of the council of commerce whose advice Orléans sought on a variety of problems, including those relating to the outbreak of plague in Marseilles in 1720 and the fate of the bull Unigenitus; Claude le Blanc of the council for war, already a confidential adviser to Orléans in the first winter of the regency, who became a secretary of state after the restructuring of the government in 1718; Fleuriau d'Armenonville, a future keeper of the seals, whose confidence in the survival of the old administrative order, despite the apparently drastic changes ushered in by the regent, extended to the purchase of Torcy's office of secretary of state for 400,000 livres, a very substantial investment in 1716 for an office supposedly outmoded.[18] The repeated protests made by the council for war during 1716 and 1717 at the way in which both d'Armenonville and La Vrillière were making military appointments without recourse to the council indicated the growing suspicion of some members towards the unwelcome influence of such powerful figures.[19] The truth was that few members of the advisory councils had any consultative role at all. Orléans discussed affairs regularly with the presidents and matters were arranged so that recommendations from the particular councils to the regency council were in conformity with the regent's known opinions on the various issues considered; as a result there was very little debate when the proposals came before the regency council.[20]

That body steadily declined in importance throughout the whole period of Louis XV's minority. Although in the first year of the regency the council met four times a week, twelve months later one of its sessions for foreign affairs was abolished and from March 1718 finance and foreign affairs were dealt with on a single day. The number of council sessions declined from 165 between October 1715 and September 1716 to 98 between October 1717 and September 1718. Thereafter its meetings and significance were even further restricted until finally the taking of minutes ceased. The last registers covering provincial, financial and foreign affairs conclude in September 1717, September 1719 and July 1720 respectively.[21] As its importance declined so its membership increased, Orléans having less need to balance the competing factions or to fear the influence of individual voices. By August 1718 the number had reached 24, including Le Peletier de Souzy, the dukes de Guiche, de Noailles, d'Antin, Villars, Tallard and de la Force, marshals d'Huxelles and d'Estrées, the marquises d'Effiat and d'Argenson. More names were added later and by 1722 the regency council had 35 members.[22]

A reading of the very first register of the regency council suggests something of the body's future ineffectiveness. Covering the first two months of the regency, when the council might have been expected to be at its most active in regulating political matters, the impression conveyed is of the recording of routine, often trivial, business besides dealing with the crucial issues facing the state. Though foreign affairs and finance dominated the proceedings, reflecting the situation at large, there is no hint of the grievous religious split centering on Unigenitus which threatened to divide the country. The French ambassador in England was instructed to remain neutral during the Jacobite rebellion while his colleague in Constantinople was encouraged to rally the Turks to arm against the Emperor; the intendant of St Dominique was ordered not to allow Protestants to enter his colony, and the commissioner for the marine at Dieppe not to allow foreigners without passports to remain in the port; a safe conduct through Flanders for a royal secretary and his wife and amnesty for deserters from the army were considered; the establishment of an office to issue state notes in exchange for a variety of paper money and the extreme difficulty of persuading the king of Spain to pay out the money owed to French troops were noted, the latter more than once. These minutes do contain one clue to the emasculation of the council's role. In drawing up instructions for the king's commissioners to the Breton estates, it was decided that a small committee consisting of Orléans, Toulouse, Villeroy, the duke de Noailles, the provincial intendant, the syndic-general and the estates' treasurer should meet to iron out certain financial difficulties.[23] In fact, the committee system, later formalized during Louis XV's majority, was already being employed under the regency. For example, in order to deal with the contentious affair of Unigenitus Orléans nominated an *ad hoc* body of advisers to assist him including d'Aguesseau, d'Huxelles, the bishop of Troyes, Joly de Fleury, Amelot de Gournay, the cardinals de Rohan and de Bissy and the marquis d'Effiat: 'Voila les acteurs qui décident de la religion', in the words of marshal Villeroy.[24] Most significant of all the regent's private discussions, were those with the Scottish financier, John Law, whose economic ideas were to become official policy, and the abbé Dubois, Orléans' life-long tutor and friend, whose influence in foreign affairs overshadowed that of all others. Neither of these intimate counsellors figured in the *polysynodie* though few doubted their powerful influence at the heart of government.

The conciliar system set up in 1715 never represented, therefore, the reality of government under Orléans. The pragmatic regent was willing to tolerate it as long as it served a purpose. After three years, however, the regent's authority was greatly strengthened and that fact, combined with the *polysynodie*'s collective inefficiency and the incapacity of most of its distinguished members, persuaded him that it was time to match the structure of government to the realities of the political situation. As will become apparent, policies coming to fruition at home and abroad during 1718, inextricably bound up with the personalities of the regent's associates, friends and enemies, produced the first of the regency's two climactic periods in the summer and autumn of that year. Both Dubois and Law were in favour of abrogating the *polysynodie* from the spring of 1718 and thereafter there was much talk of it in the capital.[25] The feeling that such a move was imminent was reinforced by the disgrace of the duke du Maine, the regent's arch-rival in the regency council. In the interminable – and to a later age almost incomprehensible – disputes over precedence which were carried over to the regency from the later years of Louis XIV's reign, Maine and Toulouse had already suffered set-backs, being deprived in July 1717 of their recently acquired right of succession to the throne. On 26 August 1718, at a famous meeting of the regency council held immediately before an equally dramatic *lit de justice*, the two princes lost their royal privileges and became simply peers of the realm. Maine fared far worse than Toulouse, losing his title of superintendent of the king's education, whereas Toulouse, whose relations with Orléans were good and whose work at the council for the marine provided a rare example of *polysynodie* achievement, was permitted, as a gesture of clemency, to retain the honours which had previously been his by right.[26]

The timing of this *coup* was connected with the Quadruple Alliance signed on 2 August and with the dangerous relations suspected to exist between Maine and the Spanish court. Maine, like those other stalwarts of the 'old court', Villeroy and d'Huxelles, had opposed the unfavourable implications for Louis XIV's grandson, Philip V, of this new alliance. In addition, it had come to Dubois' notice that the duchess du Maine was deeply enmeshed in a plot involving the Spanish ambassador to France, the prince de Cellamare. The Cellamare conspiracy would not become public knowledge until the end of the year but Orléans no doubt had it in mind at the meeting of the regency council on 26 August when he remarked that he preferred an open to a hidden enemy.[27] In reality the conspiracy was more a piece of play-acting than a serious challenge to the regent and, though the duke du Maine and his wife were arrested and imprisoned in December, Orléans saw no need for dramatic measures; with customary good nature he sanctioned their early release.[28] But Maine's impending disgrace had removed the one remaining obstacle to an overhaul of the conciliar system which now followed in September 1718.

On 24 September the *conseil de conscience*, the councils for foreign and internal affairs, and for war, were suppressed, Le Blanc becoming secretary of state for war and Dubois secretary for foreign affairs. There were now five secretaries of state, Dubois and Le Blanc joining La Vrillière, Maurepas and Fleuriau d'Armenonville, the last taking overall responsibility for naval affairs although the council for the marine was not disbanded and Toulouse remained influential there.[29] Provincial responsibilities appropriate to their particular area of concern were divided among all five secretaries, La Vrillière being largely responsible for the *pays d'état* and Maurepas for the *maison du roi* and the *île de France*.[30] Two other councils survived besides the marine, those for commerce and finance, though none of them offered residual support for the *polysynodie* idea. The council of commerce was converted into a bureau in June 1722 and the marine disappeared on the morrow of the royal majority in March 1723. The schemes of John Law, which also formed a strand in the decisive events of 1718, had long threatened to diminish the significance of the council for finance and that body, like the regency council itself, played little part in his rise to power. In January 1718 the duke de Noailles was replaced as head of the finance council by the marquis d'Argenson, a change made with Law's blessing. Under d'Argenson a team of professional administrators, representative of those members of the *polysynodie* upon whom the regent relied, ran the financial machine: men like Rouillé du Coudray, Le Peletier des Forts, Le Pelletier de la Houssaye, Dodun, Fagon, Ormesson, Gilbert de Voisins, Baudry, and Gaumont. All were powerless, however, to influence or challenge the arrangements reached in private conversations between Orléans and Law. The latter's true position was acknowledged in January 1720 when he was appointed controller-general of finance, an office vacant since the disgrace of Desmaretz in 1715. After Law's fall at the end of 1720 the finance council did assume an important position but only as the equivalent of the old *conseil royal des finances*. Towards the close of the regency, in March 1722, the régime of Louis XIV was further recalled by the re-establishment of five intendants of finance. Thus the old order which in reality had never been eclipsed was seen to be restored. The dominant influence upon Orléans after Law's disgrace was the abbé Dubois whose authority, especially after his appointment as first minister, harked back beyond Louis XIV to the days of the Great Cardinals.[31]

The government reforms of September 1718 were in line with Dubois' earlier proposals, which had also been backed by John Law, and there is no doubt that their implementation was left in the abbé's hands. Subsequently another of his suggestions was adopted by Orléans; the re-establishment of the *conseil des dépêches* – though not with that name – in which the regent, the keeper of the seals, and the five secretaries met regularly in order to co-ordinate the latters' various areas of activity.[32] Yet any suggestion that Dubois was effectively running the country through Orléans should be dismissed. Philippe was fully in control, surer of his position than at any time since Louis XIV's death, and disinclined to fall in willy-nilly with the opinions of any of his advisers. Indeed Dubois himself was unsure of Orléans' intentions as late as August 1718. The worried abbé, learning nothing from the regent's remark that he would use the holidays to decide on whether to reform the system of government, asked his British friends, Stanhope and Stair, to do what they could on his behalf.[33] In a letter to d'Huxelles at the time of the abolition of the *polysynodie* Orléans himself gave an indication of his determination to maintain his own hold on government. 'I will consult people of experience in important matters', he observed, 'according to my judgment.' He also remarked that he would require the various people given government responsibilities to report directly to him.[34] The point of this observation was that he had not established a consistent hierarchy of authority. For example, under the overall control of Le Blanc as secretary of state for war a number of special commissions were established; Reynoldt to have responsibility for the Swiss Guard, Biron for the infantry, d'Asfeld for fortifications, Evreux for the cavalry, Coigny for the dragoons. Similar special attributions were granted in other areas of overall secretarial jurisdiction and all these officials, as well as the secretaries of state themselves, were instructed to report directly to the regent. It is possible to interpret that fact, as one distinguished historian of the regency has done, as indicative of Orléans' weakness in failing to make a clean sweep of his government reforms.[35] But the concept of a strictly hierarchical bureaucracy was not present in France and an alternative interpretation seems more supportable: that whatever administrative machinery he established the regent intended to hold on to his personal authority. That was certainly the contemporary opinion. Cellamare wrote in a letter to cardinal Alberoni in December 1718 of the absolute power exercised by the regent and almost two years later, in September 1720, the duke d'Antin thought that Orléans wielded a more despotic authority than Louis XIV.[36] However, the year 1720 witnessed the second of the two decisive periods in the regency, marked by the bitter struggle with the parlement of Paris which ended with the magistrates' exile to Pontoise and the collapse of John Law's System and his ignominious flight from France. Thereafter, in the closing years of the regency, Orléans did allow Dubois to shoulder more of the burden of responsibility.

Again one must beware of exaggerating the significance of Orléans' withdrawal from the centre of the stage. In all crucial respects his remained the controlling voice, notably in the sphere of financial administration following the collapse of Law's System.[37] Indeed Dubois' acquisition of the office of first minister may be seen as the rationalization of government along lines already laid down by cardinal Richelieu. Though there was no thought yet of a hierarchical bureaucracy, there was in Richelieu's rule a precedent for channelling authority through one minister. This procedure could enhance rather than reduce the crown's authority since the cardinal's relationship with the king was based on total loyalty and dependence. The minister acted as a filter collecting advice and information and passing it on to his royal master. Such a device had been anathema to Louis XIV who had insisted on hearing all the opinions and then making up his own mind. The circumstances of a regency were, of course, inherently less stable than those obtaining under a strong major king, nor were they precisely comparable: the trusted minister was responsible to the regent and not to the king, so that instead of a single unifying authority under the sovereign there might seem to be two. Nevertheless, since French constitutional theory required the regent to exercise the king's plenary authority, Orléans was effectively taking the place of Louis XIII and Dubois that of Richelieu. But the question must be asked why, at such a late stage, a mere six months before the king's majority, Orléans should opt for such an arrangement.

In the first place Orléans was paying the penalty for his self-indulgent life. The suppers and especially the wine, invariably champagne, had begun to dull his quick mind and undermine his physique. His complexion became ominously puce and his manner was at times uncharacteristically laboured. He retained his capacity to separate business from pleasure but his secretaries of state maintained that there were times in the day when the regent would have signed whatever was placed before him, however prejudicial to his interests.[38] Though Orléans had no intention of relinquishing his overriding authority he was intelligent enough to appreciate that the day-to-day routine of government would be more effectively conducted by Dubois. The latter's loyalty and efficiency would in turn guarantee Orléans' position after the king's majority.[39] The regent's ambition had been sapped by debauchery and by his own sense of loyalty to the young man whose survival continued to debar him from the throne; yet he remained the heir apparent and there was no question of his abdicating the responsibility of sovereignty. He was, however, anxious to give more time to the important task of preparing the king for his majority as Louis approached his thirteenth birthday. These briefing sessions began on 26 August 1722, within days of Dubois' promotion.[40]

The pressure came in the first place from Dubois himself, who saw his own future security as well as that of Orléans in his appointment as first minister. A memorandum in the hand of the cardinal's chief secretary, Pecquet, dated 15 August 1722, elaborated the arguments in favour of his elevation: his services to the state, notably in matters of foreign policy but also in other areas, including that of religion; the need to eliminate faction and thereby increase the government's authority; and to provide a focal point for dealing with the multifarious matters emanating from the various councils.[41] All these arguments had some substance, not least the indication of the gathering complexity of central government activity. A further memorandum dated 23 August 1722, describing the new first minister's functions, testified to that complexity.[42] Dubois remained secretary of state for foreign affairs, and in that capacity he reported only to the king and the regent; the other secretaries and the keeper of the seals reported to the cardinal. He also had daily discussions with the controller-general of finance on important matters affecting revenue and expenditure, and kept a register of all the funds leaving the royal treasury. Each day he notified ministers of the petitions received by the king, the regent or himself, as they related to particular departments, and they in turn had to provide a daily account of requests received by them from Paris and the provinces. Dubois then transmitted the information to the regent who passed it on to the king. In matters requiring urgency or secrecy Dubois wrote directly to those whom the king considered to be appropriate agents. All petitions were processed through the first minister's office and six secretaries saw to it that replies were sent out no later than the day after receipt. A register was kept of each day's decisions. Thus, in this vital area of royal patronage, the new system provided consultation and information, removed the possibility of contradictory decisions and yet worked with dispatch. All ministerial reports to the regent were to be made in the cardinal's presence or after his prior approval had been obtained. Even orders directly addressed by Orléans to his ministers had to be reported by them to Dubois before execution so that he was entirely *au fait* with what was happening. In terms of the institutions of central government the first minister worked through the *conseil des dépêches*, now openly so styled, and the *conseil des finances*, both transformed by the king's presence into true royal councils as Louis XIV had understood them. Membership of the former had grown to include the princes of the blood and the controller-general of finance, Dodun, while, besides the princes of the blood and the first minister, the *conseil des finances* was composed of the keeper of the seals, Fleuriau d'Armenonville, the controller-general of finance and two councillors of state. There was also a *conseil de conscience* that must not be confused with the *polysynodie* council of the same name, which had been abolished in September 1718. Its successor, established in August 1720, was to become a fully fledged council of government after Louis XV's majority. Before then it met at the Palais-Royal under Orléans' chairmanship. Except for Orléans and La Vrillière its membership was entirely limited to clerics, including cardinals de Rohan, Bissy and de Gesvres, and the future cardinal de Fleury, later to be Louis XV's long surviving chief minister. The *conseil de santé*, established in 1721, had a more circumscribed brief and only lasted for a short time. A co-ordinated government response was needed to combat the terrible plague which struck Marseilles in June 1720 and which quickly spread over the whole of Provence, threatening to become a country-wide disaster. The first minister attended this council's sessions and when necessary its complement also included the secretaries of state and the controller-general. Its purpose had been served by the time of the king's majority when it ceased to meet. At that date the council for the marine, the last vestige of the *polysynodie*, disappeared too; until then, however, Dubois continued to work through this body for naval affairs, in close co-operation with the count de Toulouse. He attended finally the by now desultory meetings of the regency council which had even less of a *raison d'être* since the *conseils des finances* and *des dépêches* had become royal councils in their own right.[43]

Thus, in the last months of the regency Orléans ran the country through a series of councils hardly distinguishable from those of Louis XIV and with the assistance of professionals headed by the first minister himself who presided, Richelieu-like, over the state machine. In this area at least Orléans bridged the dangerous gulf which had opened up on the old king's death between the incipient bureaucratic ideal or government service and the far older concept of personal counsel to the sovereign. The regent had put the clock neither back nor forward; but he had kept the choice open for his successor.[44]

If the status quo was gradually restored in the capital it had not been altered in any way in the provinces. There the intendants continued to carry out the orders emanating from the royal will via the Palais-Royal. Letters passed constantly between Paris and the various centres of the *généralités* where the intendants had their headquarters: there were daily deliveries to Amiens, Orléans, Soissons, Tours, Rouen and Caen, and only Montauban, Limoges and Auch had fewer than three a week. Orléans or Dubois could expect an answer from Châlons in two days, from La Rochelle in five, from Perpignan in ten.[45] France was far from being a regimented bureaucracy in 1723, but this frail network, which sufficed to bear the weight of the royal will in the provinces and to convey back to the centre the problems of the periphery, 'assured the most efficient and honest government then available'.[46] Orléans was not disposed to disrupt, nor was there any pressure on him to change, the system or the personnel: d'Angervilliers moved in 1715 from Grenoble to Strasbourg and Foullé de Martargis from Bourges to Alençon in the same year; but others in the years after his death remained in the posts assigned to them by Louis XIV: Bernage at Amiens, Bignon de Blanzy in Paris, d'Orsay at Limoges, Chauvelin de Beauséjour at Tours, Doujat at Maubeuge, Ferrand de Villemilan at Rennes, Jubert de Bouville at Orléans, Arnaud de la Briffe at Dijon, Lamoignon de Basville at Montpellier, Lamoignon de Coursan at Bordeaux, Le Blanc at Dunkirk, Cardin le Bret at Aix-en-Provence, Le Gendre de Saint-Aubin at Auch, Le Guerchois at Besançon, de l'Escalopier at Châlons, Méliand at Lyons and Turgot de Saint-Clair at Moulins.[47] These men gave continuity and substance to royal authority and enough *dirigisme* to government policy to enable the central power to keep a moderately firm hold on provincial events, in matters grave and trivial relating to the law, the army, the general administration of the kingdom and most of all taxation and the economy. At one end of the scale of their activity might be placed their struggle with the recalcitrant Breton estates or their role in implementing the regent's plan of 1722 for more effective auditing of government money held in the provinces; at the other, countless routine orders requiring intendants to check up, for example, on alleged non-payment of taxes by individuals, or on a tax collector's excessive zeal and greed in the pursuit of his work or, contrariwise, on an official's failure to produce adequate statements of receipts and expenses.[48] In reading the instructions sent out to these government agents one's attention is once more drawn to the still evolving nature of French administration. Here was a network of officials who, with their manifold jurisdiction, kept the wheels of government turning in their locality, but were still essentially pragmatists having to deal with people not yet aware of the need for absolute conformity with government regulations: like the tax payers of Poitiers who moved from one parish to another in order to profit from a lower *taille* assessment; like the officials at Grenoble who failed to provide electoral rolls to facilitate collection of the *taille*; like the *élus* of Dauphiné, who debited the cost of their official tours of inspection to the unfortunate inhabitants; or like the aristocratic debtors in Pau whose arrears in payment of the *dixième* and *capitation* of 1705 and 1710 led the intendant to require two of the chief offenders from each *élection* to pay up by a stipulated date or face a summons before the royal council.[49]

The administrative reforms of Louis XIV survived under the regent; but that did not mean that bureaucratic government was at hand.

III

The Regent's Foreign Policy

The two most important factors to be borne in mind in any discussion of the regent's foreign policy are Dubois' long history of service to the Orléans family, and the imperceptible change that was taking place in the balance between the interests of the ruling dynasties and those of the state over which they presided. The first point may be pursued at once, the second requires a prior examination of what was achieved before its significance can be fully discerned.

Philippe, then duke de Chartres, was nine years old in 1683 when the young abbé Dubois was introduced into the Orléans household to act as his tutor. The accord established between them at that time lasted until Dubois' death in 1723.[1] The abbé was a stimulating and discerning teacher, the young Philippe a highly intelligent and responsive pupil. On this foundation the relationship prospered and, long before the regency began, Philippe d'Orléans was providing the means to material wealth and social status after which this clerical parvenu hankered. He enjoyed an odious reputation in later life, and his character was magnificently demolished in a typically uncompromising fashion by Saint-Simon who could never be accused of taking a balanced view when the opportunity for personal vituperation presented itself:

There are many examples of great fortunes being made, some of them by men of little account, but never by one so entirely devoid of the requisite talents as was Cardinal Dubois, if one discounts his gift for low and secret intrigues. His mind was mediocre in the extreme, his learning unremarkable, his capabilities non-existent. In appearance he was much like a ferret, but also looked ill-bred. . . . His morals were too bad for concealment; his transports not to be excused as madness; his head was incapable of holding more than one subject at a time, and he of conceiving or following any line of action save for his personal advantage. Nothing to him was sacred; he had no respectable attachments, but was outspoken in his contempt for loyalty, promises, honour, truth, and integrity. . . . he was sweet-spoken, a toady, a trimmer, admiring, fawning . . . but still never managing to charm . . .[2]

and so on for several pages. Dubois was by no means worthy of his religious vocation though equally no man could have mastered all the vices attributed to him. Not the least of his sins in the eyes of the *duc et pair*, of course, was his modest origin as the son of a provincial apothecary. In return for the Orléans' patronage, Dubois devoted his talents, which (whatever Saint-Simon's view) were considerable, to the family's interests, particularly in the field of diplomacy.

His diplomatic career began in 1698 when he accompanied marshal Tallard to London on the latter's appointment as ambassador to negotiate the Partition treaty of that year. His true role in that negotiation remains obscure, though it is tempting to infer that he was keeping a watchful eye on an issue which was of the greatest significance to the house of Orléans, as witnessed by Monsieur's solemn protestation in 1700 of his rights to the Spanish crown. The evidence, however, is lacking and it may be that Dubois, who was well thought of by Louis himself, was simply acting as a well-informed though quite unofficial adviser. In any case he made the acquaintance on this visit of a number of English political figures, one of whom, lord Stanhope, was to feature prominently in the lives of the abbé and his erstwhile pupil. Dubois next made his mark on international diplomacy when he travelled to Spain in an official capacity. Following the death of Monsieur in 1701, the new duke d'Orléans sent the abbé to persuade Philip V to recognize the hereditary rights of his house to the Spanish succession; and the royal declaration approved by the council of Castile in October 1703 brought Dubois' mission to a successful conclusion. For these services Dubois acquired an apartment in the Palais-Royal and the abbey of Nogent-sous-Coucy.

In 1707, when Orléans was sent to command the French armies in Spain, Louis forbade Dubois to accompany him. His reasons can only be guessed at though they almost certainly included a suspicious awareness at the court in Madrid of the abbé's political skill and his strong influence over the new commander-in-chief. It would be foolish to link too closely the early part of 1708 with the events of 1708–09 when Orléans contacted Dubois' English acquaintance, Stanhope, and talk of an Orléans succession to the Spanish throne was in the air. Certainly Dubois was involved in those machinations, albeit from a distance, but it is not necessary to infer the existence of any prior conspiracy. It is enough to note that Philip V was well aware of Orléans' rights in the matter of the Spanish succession and of the Allies' unwillingness to allow the thrones of Spain and France to be united under a single sovereign. Since only the dauphin and his son, the duke de Bourgogne, stood between Philip and the French crown, it was not difficult to envisage the time when

Orléans' claim to the Spanish crown would become a matter of the utmost significance. Besides, Philip V's position in Spain was very insecure at that time. As yet he had no heir (his eldest son Luis was not born until August 1707) and his military prospects were in the balance. Not until the battle of Almanza in April 1707 would the Bourbon fortunes take a turn for the better. Orléans' very presence in Spain made Madrid uneasy. His magnanimous attitude towards the people of Valencia after the crucial battle – issuing a decree on his own authority as commander-in-chief which pardoned the Valencians for their opposition to Philip V, and opposing the latter's decision to revoke the *fueros*, the traditional liberties of Valencia and Aragon – persuaded the Spanish court that the duke was seeking to establish a party favourable to his own pretensions.[3]

Following Orléans' return to France under a cloud Dubois retired for some time to his abbey in Poitou, while the future regent occupied himself in acquiring as great a notoriety for his debauchery at home as for his controversial activities abroad. With the approaching death of Louis XIV, however, both Orléans and Dubois were drawn back on to the diplomatic scene. George I, the new king of Great Britain, made the initial move. He dispatched lord Stair as ambassador to France with instructions to assure Orléans of British backing in support of his right to the French crown, established by Philip V's renunciation at Utrecht.[4] His desire for the regent's support, if indeed Orléans were to become regent, was apparent: the Pretender was nearby in Lorraine and might, with the support of French armies and an incalculable number of British Jacobites, still threaten the Hanoverian succession. For his part Orléans needed all the support he could find against the king of Spain, who, though formally reconciled with Orléans in the last months of the old king's life, remained as determined as ever to retain his rights to the French throne. Philippe knew that since May the Spanish ambassador, Cellamare, had been working clandestinely to this end on behalf of the king of Spain as Stair had on behalf of Orléans, that Maine, the 'old court' and, for that matter, most of the political world in France rejected the Utrecht renunciations as invalid. Yet it should not be forgotten that the house of Orléans had also renounced its rights to the Spanish throne at Utrecht in favour of Savoy: if Philip came as king to France then Orléans had as much right to go as king to Madrid. Indeed the latter eventuality seemed to offer far more chance of success than any attempt to succeed to the French crown with only the support of France's recent Protestant enemies, the British and the Dutch, and in opposition to Spain and the overwhelming majority of Frenchmen. So although Orléans was beckoned towards one possible haven by George I's ambassador, he was unlikely to be easily persuaded to turn his back on Spain or indeed on the Pretender. A Stuart restoration was by no means a remote possibility at this time. Though the débâcle of the 1715 rebellion would shortly demonstrate the lack of British support for the Pretender the Hanoverians seemed no more likely to provide a stable régime.[5] Besides, the house of Stuart, which had enjoyed French support and hospitality since the Glorious Revolution, would need French backing after a restoration and would thus be unlikely to pursue policies inimical to France. Orléans even nursed hopes of marrying one of his daughters to the Pretender.[6]

During the first year of the regency, therefore, Orléans avoided being pinned down either by the Whigs or by the Jacobites and also being pushed into the anti-Spanish camp. His aim was to maintain the peace, for he knew that France was in no state to be caught up in a renewed European conflict. The fact that his own personal position would have become even more insecure in the event of war – which certainly would have been the case – does not invalidate his correct assessment of the country's best interests.

Even before Louis XIV's death Orléans had resolutely refused to become implicated in spying on the Jacobites in France or in monitoring Louis' relations with them.[7] Shortly after his assumption of power, the regency council resisted Stair's pressure to have the two ex-Jacobite ministers, Bolingbroke and Ormonde, expelled from Paris and as far as the Pretender himself was concerned it merely insisted that France would abide by the obligations of the treaty of Utrecht. Later in the same month (October) the French ambassador in London, d'Iberville, was ordered to maintain a neutral stance vis-à-vis the Jacobite insurrection.[8] About the same time Orléans rebuffed approaches from lord Stair who was proposing a Franco-British treaty guaranteeing the French and British successions as established at Utrecht, maintaining that the regent of France recognized only the interests of the king and the state.[9] Instead, he broached the idea of a purely defensive treaty which would contribute to the maintenance of the peace, between France, Great Britain and the Netherlands. However, when the British sought to follow up this initiative they received no further encouragement from Orléans.

French policy towards the United Provinces, on the other hand, was less ambivalent and more subtle. At The Hague enthusiasm for the long-standing alliance with the British and the Emperor had considerably diminished, following the former's unilateral withdrawal from hostilities in 1712 and the latter's failure to agree over the terms of the Barrier which was to guard the Dutch border with the Southern Netherlands (in the hands of the Emperor following the Utrecht settlement). Anglo-

Imperial relations had also been soured by the Tories' peace-making, especially by the recognition of Philip V as king of Spain to whom the Emperor continued to refer as duke of Anjou. There were clear opportunities here for French diplomacy to exploit, thereby further weakening and dividing the Grand Alliance powers. At the same time the British ministry was aware of the need to heal the rift before the French dealt the alliance a serious blow, and Stanhope succeeded in persuading the Emperor and the Dutch to sign a new Barrier treaty in November 1715 which was ratified in January of the following year. This did not extinguish French hopes of reaching a separate agreement with the Dutch. Orléans was well served by the French ambassador at The Hague, the marquis de Châteauneuf, at whose suggestion the regent proposed a Franco-Dutch treaty guaranteeing the permanent neutrality of the Austrian Netherlands.[10] This was an interesting proposal which should not be interpreted simply as an attempt to detach the Dutch from their allies or as a means of playing for time until the uncertainties in the international situation were resolved, though both motives were present in the regent's mind. Yet, Orléans was also actively interested in limiting the areas of possible conflict. His proposal for a defensive treaty in October 1715 was to some degree the time-wasting exercise that it was assumed to be by the British cabinet but it was more besides: it represented a tentative move towards a mutual security pact which would lessen the danger of renewed war.

The proposal of perpetual neutrality for the Austrian Netherlands fitted into a pattern first discernible in the making of the Partition treaties of 1698 and 1700, and later to be clearly delineated in the Triple and Quadruple Alliances of 1717 and 1718. The reaction in Britain was predictably indignant. The secretary of state, lord Townshend, wrote to Horace Walpole in December:

> Indeed the project seems so chimerical, and is so full of delusion, that it was hardly fit to be seriously offered by one, or received by the other. And none but France, who is used to contriving such amusing schemes, could pretend to propose to stipulate with a third power, a neutrality for the dominions belonging to another, who may not consent to it. For what could such a convention between the Dutch and the French signify if the Emperor, who is master of the country, should not think it for his interest to mind it? Methinks we are giving opportunities to France to play over the same game they did after the Peace of Ryswick, when the terrible apprehensions of a new war, made us and the Dutch run into the measures of the Partition Treaty, which was believed might be a wonderful preservative against a war, but in effect, proved the source, and chief occasion of it.[11]

Townshend's comparison with the Partition treaties was apt for both they and the proposal for the neutrality of the Southern Netherlands flouted the head-to-head diplomacy to which European statesmen were accustomed. Instead of the conventional type of settlement, of which Utrecht was a characteristic example, these were attempts to establish a broader collective security. Louis XIV and William III arbitrarily divided the spoils of the great Spanish empire in their Partition treaties, although William had no rights to the inheritance and the Bourbon claim was disputed by the Emperor who played no part in the negotiations. The principle underlying their intervention was that of *force majeur*: to prevent a world-wide conflict the two strongest powers in Europe sought to impose a settlement on the rest.[12] Though Orléans' proposal was more modest it was of a similar kind: France and the Dutch Republic were the two strong powers bordering the Austrian Netherlands and those best situated to guarantee its neutrality. The Emperor, based at Vienna and on the point of war with the Turks, looked a much less convincing guarantor than Orléans did in Paris. That was how it seemed in The Hague and the Dutch took up the regent's proposal with some enthusiasm.

Despite strong representations by the British ministers, the Dutch would not adhere to a Triple Alliance with their former allies while the possibility remained of an arrangement which would include the French. Eventually in June 1716 the British government was forced to sign the defensive treaty of Westminster with the Emperor but without the participation of the Dutch: Châteauneuf's diplomacy had been brilliantly successful. Yet Orléans could not be content with a destructive policy alone for France; the regent still had few friends in Europe and the threat of renewed war was real enough. Only with the utmost reluctance was Orléans eventually forced to accept that he could look for no help from Spain. He had made every effort after Louis XIV's death to bring about a genuine *rapprochement* with Philip V. The president of the newly established council for foreign affairs, marshal d'Huxelles, was ordered to neglect no avenue which could lead to the establishment of a close friendship between the two crowns. In November 1715, following a disaster to the Spanish fleet off the Bahamas, the regent offered several vessels to help in salvage operations and shortly afterwards promulgated a regulation very much to the advantage of Spanish merchants vis-à-vis their French rivals in the Mediterranean. Philip's response was to sign a commercial treaty with Britain which gave British merchants more privileges in the American colonies than French merchants had ever possessed: concessions likely to lead to the ruin of French trade, according to Ripperda, the Dutch ambassador in Madrid.[13]

Stanhope and the British government clearly misjudged Orléans' attitude to Philip V at this time, perhaps because Stanhope remembered the 1708 discussions with Orléans in Spain when the latter had been interested in the possibility of replacing Philip V on the Spanish throne. The British minister's estimate of Orléans' personal ambition led him to overlook the difficulties which the regent would have faced if Louis XV had died and Orléans had supported the renunciations of Utrecht. Therefore, when Orléans refused in October 1715 to conclude a treaty of mutual guarantee with Britain to which the Dutch would have been at once invited to accede – thereby underlining the British and Dutch support for his claim to the French crown – it was assumed in London that he was waiting to see how the Jacobites fared. So indeed he was, but, as his attitude towards Philip of Spain indicated, that was not his only consideration. Stanhope's comment to lord Stair, that such an arrangement based on mutual guarantees would be entirely in the interests of France and the regent, implies a possible division of interests which Orléans himself would have been loath to recognize.[14]

Despite the rebuffs from Madrid and that court's evident determination to eschew a Bourbon compact, Orléans decided, after receiving news of the treaty of Westminster, to make one more attempt to secure a *rapprochement* with Philip V. This time he chose to send an unofficial envoy, the marquis de Louville, an old friend and adviser of the king of Spain during the early years of his kingship. The embassy was opposed by the council for foreign affairs on the grounds of the unsuitability of the envoy and the inopportuneness of the initiative. However, backed by the influential duke de Noailles, Orléans ignored its censures and approved the mission. Louville arrived in Madrid on 24 July 1716.

He was instructed to discover whether Philip still wished to return to France, the attitude towards that idea of his wife, Elisabeth Farnese, and of Alberoni, his most influential adviser, and whether a genuine reconciliation between the regent and the king was possible. He was to counter Cellamare's clandestine work in France by engineering his recall. Louville was also ordered to initiate a conspiracy aimed at dislodging the powerful figure of Alberoni and substituting a Spaniard as chief adviser to the Spanish crown. This last objective was in keeping with the regent's desire to prevent any renewal of international conflict which could involve France. Neither Philip V nor the Emperor Charles VI had recognized the Utrecht settlement, and Italy was a likely arena for future hostilities. However, Alberoni moved too quickly for Louville and, by persuading the king to decline any request for an audience, blocked Orléans' initiative; the latter was forced to recall his envoy from Spain, thus vindicating his critics in the council for foreign affairs.[15] At the same time France's negotiations with Britain were reaching a crucial point as the abbé Dubois, albeit surreptitiously, took the reins of French diplomacy into his expert hands.

The disastrous failure of the 1715 rebellion reduced both the degree of uncertainty surrounding the Hanoverian succession and the options open to the regent. In December 1715 lord Stair renewed his efforts to persuade Orléans to make an arrangement with George I. He proposed a treaty, mutually guaranteeing the successions to the British and French thrones as established at Utrecht, positing only the precondition that the Pretender should be sent into more distant exile in Italy though also acknowledging that the existence of the fortified port of Mardyk presented a problem still to be resolved. However, matters were complicated by the regent's unwillingness to act against the Pretender until an Anglo-French treaty had been signed and by his stipulation that the Dutch should also be signatories to the proposed treaty. By April 1716, when the hopelessness of the Jacobite challenge was universally acknowledged, the British government was insisting on three preliminary points before serious negotiations could begin: (1) James Edward, the old Pretender, should be dispatched into Italy, (2) his supporters should likewise be expelled from France, and (3) the port of Mardyk, established by Louis XIV to circumvent the stipulation at Utrecht that Dunkirk should be destroyed, was to be similarly dismantled. Although the 'three points' were an obstacle to an agreement, by the middle of that year Orléans had decided, under Dubois' influence, to pursue the British alliance which according to the abbé would determine the European system for a long time to come, an opinion with which the regent concurred.[16] The moment had arrived for serious negotiations to commence and Orléans dispatched Dubois to The Hague where George I and Stanhope were due to stop on their journey to Hanover. The abbé's visit to the Republic was in the best tradition of 'cloak and dagger' diplomacy. Dubois travelled incognito, posing as a collector of books and paintings, adding realism to that role by purchasing Poussin's *Seven Sacraments* shortly after his arrival. Though he carried Orléans' full authority to negotiate he preferred his meeting with Stanhope to appear fortuitous. In that way he could indicate the French position and sound out the British government's attitude in discussions with his old friend without resorting to formal negotiations which might prove sterile.

The conversations between Dubois and Stanhope were mutually satisfactory. Dubois insisted on the need to link the Pretender's expulsion from France with a reiteration of the Utrecht renunciations, though he

vigorously rejected Stanhope's offer of British support for Orléans'
personal ambitions:

> It is not necessary to put into the mind of the duke d' Orléans considerations
> with which he does not concern himself. Has he not attested that he had no
> other interest than that of the King and the State? Has he not made it clear
> to you that he would not sign any treaty which took into account only his
> personal rights?

The conversations included a light-hearted exchange illustrative of the
growing difficulty in defining the separate interests of the crown and
the state. Dubois maintained that the French king was richer than his
British counterpart since legally he was the owner of his kingdom, to
which Stanhope responded: where did you learn your public law, Tur-
key?[17] For the rest, Stanhope discovered that the French were unlikely
to make difficulties over the demolition of Mardyk and Dubois that the
British would be flexible on the matter of the Pretender's expulsion.
Nor was Dubois left in any doubt about British resentment at Châteauneuf's negotiations with the Dutch and he promised to recommend their
suspension. On 24 July Stanhope resumed his journey to Hanover and
Dubois set out for Paris. There the regent and the abbé brushed aside
the opposition of d'Huxelles and the 'old court' and Dubois was sent on
his travels again, this time to Hanover with instructions to conclude a
formal agreement.

Despite Dubois' earlier strictures, Stanhope remained under the impression that Orléans' interest in a treaty was related exclusively to his
personal stake in the Utrecht settlement wherein his own rights to the
French crown were guaranteed. Therefore he proposed an article indicating king George's support for the regent's cause and was surprised
to find the abbé resolutely opposed. The latter wanted a comprehensive
guarantee of the treaty of Utrecht, partly, it is true, because Orléans had
no desire to highlight the undoubted advantage which he personally
would draw from such a guarantee; but partly too because he sought as
comprehensive a settlement as possible in the interests of France as well
as of the house of Orléans. For three days Dubois held out and the success of the negotiations seemed in the balance. 'We have reached a
critical point', Dubois wrote to the regent;[18] however, the danger passed
and the discussions continued. The abbé was eventually persuaded that a
direct reference to the guarantee would be perfectly acceptable in the
context of the overall prospects for peace embodied in any Anglo-French
agreement; and he was convinced that the treaty which he and Stanhope
envisaged would make a momentous impact on the whole of Europe.

At this point the ambivalence of the king of Great Britain's position became an important factor in the negotiations. As elector of Hanover, George I had become thoroughly alarmed at the growing threat to the adjoining state of Mecklenburg from Peter the Great's Russian army. Since France was traditionally an ally of Sweden and appeared also to enjoy good relations with Muscovy, the elector suddenly decided that a French alliance would offer the best means of securing his German base.[19] Consequently the tempo of the negotiations quickened and on 9 October Stanhope and Dubois agreed a convention embodying the results of their lengthy discussions. The formal treaty was to be signed later at The Hague and the Dutch were to be invited to join. Their interests had been taken into account in the discussions, though they had little choice but to accede to the Anglo-French agreement.[20]

The Triple Alliance was signed on 4 January 1717.[21] It sought to establish a pacific relationship between the three powers following certain specific agreements: that the Pretender should leave France as soon as the treaty had been signed and before ratification, and should not be allowed to return; nor should he receive any assistance in the future from the king of France; that no rebel subjects from any of the three contracting states should be allowed asylum in either of the other two; that the fortifications of Dunkirk and Mardyk should be destroyed; that all those articles of the treaty of Utrecht which concerned the three powers, including those relating to the successions to the crowns of Great Britain and France, should retain their full force and vigour, all the signatories offering reciprocal guarantees of the others' rights and promising military, naval or financial support.

There can be no doubt that this settlement greatly benefited Orléans' personal position, and French historians have been inclined to depict the treaty entirely in that light.[22] There is much contemporary support for such an interpretation. Though a hostile witness like Cellamare might be expected to accuse the regent of inventing specious precepts about the public good and universal peace in order to mask his self-interest, Stanhope, a much more sympathetic and highly informed observer, did not take an essentially different view. Indeed, Dubois' own observations indicated how prominently the interests of the house of Orléans figured in his calculations, and the regent himself was well aware of the advantages won for him by his old tutor.[23] At Utrecht the overriding requirements of international security had dictated the order of succession in Great Britain, France and Spain in flagrant contravention of the laws of dynastic kingship, an indication of the diminishing force of the idea that the interests of the ruler and of the state were necessarily identical. Of course, as Utrecht's nominee for the French throne, Orléans was particularly conscious of his own interests, especially while he was regent and not king. Indeed, the clandestine diplomacy embarked upon by Orléans and Dubois could be interpreted as presaging the later eighteenth-century cleavage between the king's secret diplomacy and the official government conduct of foreign policy.[24] Yet if the implications of Utrecht (and of the abortive Partition treaties of 1698 and 1700) were to be built upon then what France and indeed the rest of Europe most needed was some system of collective security to protect and guarantee the hard-won and still fragile peace. Orléans and Dubois adopted that stance, a posture in which political realism at least vied with self-interest. Motives are rarely unmixed, though a distinction should be made between those of the regent and of the abbé. The latter was largely preoccupied with serving Orléans' interests and thereby his own. In a famous letter written immediately after the signing of the Triple Alliance Dubois indicated to the regent, with a minimum of subtlety, the direction of his own ambitions: 'I consider myself very fortunate to have been honoured with your orders in a matter so essential to your welfare, and I am more indebted to you for having given me this mark of your confidence in me than if you had made me a cardinal.'[25]

Orléans' attitude is more difficult to categorize. He understood and identified with the dynastic tradition, while sensing the need for an overriding, interlocking settlement. Hence his early interest in a *rapprochement* with the United Provinces and his support for a triple rather than a dual alliance (though at the end he was prepared if necessary to settle without the Dutch); hence his decision to communicate the Triple Alliance to Philip V immediately after the signing.[26] The peace of Utrecht had not altogether removed the problem of the various successions and had done nothing to reconcile the king of Spain with the Emperor. The Triple Alliance was a step in that direction, particularly when seen in the context of other diplomatic initiatives which linked the two protagonists with France's co-signatories: the Austro-Dutch Barrier treaty ratified in 1716, the treaty of Westminster of the same year between Britain and the Emperor, and the Anglo-Spanish commercial treaty of December 1715. Nor was the Triple Alliance disadvantageous to French interests. The abject failure of the 1715 Jacobite rebellion made it abundantly clear that support for a Stuart restoration was no longer politically worthwhile and similarly the sacrifice of France's old Baltic ally, Sweden, in deference to George I's electoral interests, seemed of little moment in view of that country's rapid decline. Even the destruction of Mardyk could be defended, as Orléans himself maintained, on the grounds of the excessive cost necessary to turn it into a military establishment, not to mention the risk of war with Britain which that enterprise – directly contrary to the spirit of Utrecht – would render more likely. That particular argument was in any case to be periodically resumed in the course of the eighteenth century and it would be difficult to prove that the maintenance or destruction of these installations seriously affected the balance between the two powers. At all events the regent extracted a unanimous acceptance of the Alliance from the regency council.[27]

Nevertheless, though the Triple Alliance provided a firm basis on which to build a European-wide settlement, it did not in itself ensure it. The Great Northern War persisted, complicated by the electoral interests of the king of England which made it a more central issue for the great powers than it had been before the Hanoverian succession. France's traditional alliance with Sweden and tsar Peter's interest in a Franco-Russian treaty made Orléans and Dubois particularly sensitive to the frail nature of the international settlement concluded at The Hague and caused them to view with little enthusiasm a visit which the tsar chose to make to Paris in May 1717. Peter's objective was a Franco-Russian treaty whereby the subsidies which had earlier flowed from Paris to Stockholm would be redirected to St Petersburg. Orléans was unwilling to offend George's Hanoverian sensibilities and hazard the Triple Alliance by adopting such a committed position in the Baltic in the wake of the tsar's abandonment of the Scania invasion plan which earned him the mistrust of the Hanoverian elector and the Danish king, and the treaty eventually signed in Amsterdam in August 1717 between France, Russia and Prussia was of a neutral cast. Nevertheless France profited from the Northern powers' guarantee of Utrecht and from their agreement in principle to bring the Northern War to an end through French mediation. Though of limited international significance it was another stabilizing factor.[28]

However, the most serious threat to the uneasy European equilibrium came not from the north but from the south, from Spain and Italy. Philip V and the Emperor, Charles VI, had refused to settle their differences at Utrecht: the latter continued to style himself king of Spain and sought to interfere in Spanish domestic affairs while the former tried to regain that part of his inheritance lost to the Emperor in Italy, particularly Sardinia and Naples. The dispute between them was essentially a dynastic one, yet it was becoming clear that if another full-scale European conflict was to be avoided the argument could not be settled along dynastic lines, but only by an agreement which took account of the interests of the other great powers, notably France and Great Britain. National interests were still posited in dynastic terms but international settlements had to satisfy a new criterion – collective security.

Stanhope and Dubois were well aware of the danger and even before the signing of the Triple Alliance, indeed as early as September 1716, the two men had come close to agreement on this delicate issue: the king of Spain should renounce his claims to the Spanish Habsburgs' Italian possessions with the assurance that one of his sons by his second wife, Elisabeth Farnese, who had a valid claim to the duchy of Parma, would be allowed to succeed there; to gain his support for adhering to the Utrecht settlement the Emperor would be offered Sicily – which under the terms of the treaty had passed to Victor Amadeus of Savoy – as well as Imperial suzerainty over Parma and Tuscany, the latter also the subject of legitimate Spanish interests. Intent on maintaining the fragile peace in Europe, Dubois pressed for Sardinia to be returned to Spain but Stanhope, who intended it for Victor Amadeus in exchange for Sicily, continued to resist that proposal. The Emperor accepted this solution in principle in January 1717 but Philip, whose chief concern at this time was regaining Naples, Sardinia and Sicily rather than the matter of the Farnese inheritance, rejected it.[29]

An unexpected *casus belli* now presented itself to Philip V with the arrest and imprisonment of the Spanish Grand Inquisitor by the Emperor's representatives in the Milanese in May 1717. A Spanish force sailed for Sardinia and by August the conquest of the island had begun. With Europe thus poised on the brink of a wider conflict Dubois set off for London to join with Stanhope in seeking a settlement to conclude the work only half finished by the Triple Alliance. This time the abbé travelled as the official envoy of the French government with the rank of ambassador extraordinary. Since the signing of the Triple Alliance his great influence at the centre of affairs had been acknowledged in part at least by his appointment to the council for foreign affairs in March 1717. Though his official position was secure his policy was by no means immune from attack. D'Huxelles as head of the council for foreign affairs gave the abbé his instructions: the Emperor should be persuaded to renounce his claim to the Spanish throne, 'article aussi important pour son altesse royale que pour le roi d'Espagne'; and every effort made to satisfy Spanish claims to Parma, Tuscany and even Sardinia. Yet d'Huxelles himself still hankered after a solution involving a Bourbon *rapprochement* between France and Spain in joint opposition to the Emperor and by implication at the cost of jettisoning the Triple Alliance. For his part, its author, Dubois, was prepared to envisage the use of French armed force against Spain as the ultimate sanction should Philip V prove to be intransigent: and this in spite of his official instructions.[30] Dubois met Stanhope in London at the end of September, to be joined on 1 November by the Emperor's envoy, Pentenrriedter.

After the abbé's departure from Paris Alberoni seized the opportunity afforded by his absence to rekindle the regent's interest in that Bourbon compact which d'Huxelles and the pro-Spanish party in Paris had always sought. The Spanish minister held out the prospect that Philip V might guarantee Orléans' rights to the French throne in return for French recognition of Philip's rights in Italy. Orléans' willingness to consider a policy at odds with the one so far pursued by Dubois is not altogether surprising. The regent, who had always wanted an accommodation with Philip V, was becoming aware of the fact that the abbé's current mission could lead to war with Spain. But a Franco-Spanish war against the Emperor would be much more popular in France than an unholy alliance of France with Great Britain, the Emperor and the Dutch against a grandson of Louis XIV. In addition, news reached Orléans late in October that Philip was dangerously ill and not expected to live; the possibility of his death inclined the regent to lend a more sympathetic ear to Alberoni's overtures.[31]

While Orléans was still weighing the merits of the respective policies, Dubois learnt of the pro-Spanish cabal and used all his influence to prevent the regent committing himself to Spain. However, Philip V's recovery reduced the likelihood of such a commitment, though it was not until Dubois' return to Paris on 5 December that it became clear that his argument had prevailed. By that time Orléans accepted that the European conflagration which he had worked to avoid was more likely to result from a Franco-Spanish alliance than from an enlargement of the Triple Alliance to include the Emperor. Yet he sought to resist British pressures favouring the Emperor at the expense of Spain which threatened to produce an unbalanced settlement. He wrote to Dubois in January 1718:

> All the difficulties would be resolved if there were a greater parity of treatment. I am well aware that my personal interest is not opposed to this inequality, and is indeed a kind of touchstone enabling me to recognize my friends at home as well as abroad. But I am regent of France and I must conduct myself in such a way that I cannot be reproached for having considered only my own interests.[32]

As a result the possibility of restoring Gibraltar to Spain entered fleetingly into the discussions, but the one genuine concession offered by Stanhope was the succession of the grand duchy of Tuscany to a son of Philip V and Elisabeth Farnese. This was a significant improvement for the Farnese prospects on those outlined in Stanhope's first plan, which had limited their expectations to the duchy of Parma. Otherwise his new proposals did not differ fundamentally from the original project: the Emperor would be asked for a definitive renuncaition of the Spanish crown in favour of the house of Bourbon, a more positive gesture than the mere recognition of the treaty of Utrecht (and one of the French aims formally stated in Dubois' instructions); to compensate for the eventual Spanish succession in Tuscany the Emperor would be offered a Tuscan enclave comprising Pisa and Leghorn as a vassal republic, while Parma and Tuscany would become Imperial fiefs. The king of Great Britain and the regent would guarantee to put the Emperor in possession of Sicily, transferring the incumbent Victor Amadeus of Savoy to Sardinia. Philip V would, of course, have to renounce his claims to the former Spanish-Habsburg possessions in Italy.

Orléans had persuaded Stanhope marginally to redress the balance of his proposals to take account of the Spanish point of view, in order to improve the chances of the general settlement which he sought. Such plans for international accord depend ultimately on the sanction of coercive power, and in their elaboration are unlikely to command universal and unreserved approval. Spain was to be deprived of Sardinia and Savoy of Sicily in order to preserve the peace and, if either chose to challenge that internationally guaranteed decision, they would be put down without the risk of igniting a European-wide conflagration. It was a concept to challenge rampant dynasticism and, though Orléans could be accused of disloyalty to the house of Bourbon in supporting these proposals, there was no surer way of preventing a far greater disaster for the dynasty.

Orléans was nonetheless acutely aware of the degree of animosity which these proposals would arouse in Spain, and he was not prepared to discount the strong feelings in France in favour of the elder Bourbon line, feelings truculently voiced at this time by marshal d'Huxelles. When Stanhope's envoy, Schaub, arrived in Paris in February 1718 he found the regent adamant that Tuscany in its entirety and Parma should revert to the children of Elisabeth Farnese. In the discussions with Schaub, therefore, a degree of diplomatic flexibility obtained and both parties secured desirable modifications to the agreement reached in London. The proposal relating to the division of Tuscany was erased; it was agreed that in the event of the extinction of the house of Savoy Sardinia would revert to Spain; and in deference to Schaub's advocacy of the Emperor's case, though without significant alteration, the words *in perpetuum* were removed from the Imperial renunciation of the Spanish kingdom.[33]

Charles VI accepted these proposals at the beginning of April. Orléans himself, prompted by d'Huxelles, showed signs of second thoughts until Stanhope's arrival in Paris in June 1718 with a draft convention for the regent's approval. The document, intended by Stanhope and Dubois to bring matters to a head, consisted of four short clauses providing for (i) Charles VI's renunciation of the Spanish crown, (ii) Spain's renunciation of Sardinia to the Emperor who would then trade it to the duke of Savoy in return for Sicily, (iii) the eventual inheritance of Parma and Tuscany by the children of Elisabeth Farnese and (iv) a three-month delay during which the Emperor and the king of Spain would be invited to accede to the first three propositions voluntarily; otherwise Great Britain and France would be committed to extract agreement by force from one or both of the recalcitrant parties. The proposed convention was in effect an ultimatum and a calculated risk. In binding close the two chief protagonists in the recent War of the Spanish Succession, it threatened to disrupt the victorious Grand Alliance and to divide the house of Bourbon. If challenged, the settlement of Utrecht and the Triple Alliance would be in ruins and a new war of the British, French, Spanish and Italian successions would appear inevitable. Yet at the same time it did offer a peaceful compromise solution to a complex range of international disputes.

Orléans was soon persuaded of the necessity to go through with the manoeuvre if the diplomatic structure built on Utrecht was to endure. He knew that the Emperor would accept the proposed convention's terms and he could get no better conditions for Spain. If it came to the worst Philip V could not hope to resist successfully an alliance of the great powers of Europe. However, Orléans needed firm support for a policy which would be most unpopular in France, leading, as it might well do, to the employment of French arms against the late king's grandson. On 17 July therefore he put the draft treaty before the regency council where only Maine and Villeroy raised serious objections. Even d'Huxelles, for all the bravado of his recent utterances, gave in without a fight.[34] The convention was signed on the following day and the treaty of London – the Quadruple Alliance itself – was signed on 2 August by Great Britain, France and the Emperor; the Dutch did not in the end adhere to the treaty though the accession of Savoy justifies the continued use of the title of Quadruple Alliance.

The Quadruple Alliance incorporated the terms of the Anglo-French convention, confirming the settlement reached at Utrecht and including an imperial guarantee of the orders of succession established there to the crowns of France and Great Britain.[35] It completed the work of Utrecht and The Hague (the Triple Alliance), and Dubois was quite correct in his claim that the alliance represented 'un projet qui pût achever le grand ouvrage que le feu Roi avait si fort avancé'.[36] What he did not point out was the late king's evident lack of enthusiasm for a settlement which had offended the dynastic principle on which he had been nurtured, though in fairness to the abbé there had been signs that Louis recognized the need to temper that principle to the realities of the international scene. The traditional view was reflected by president Hénault, a magistrate in the parlement of Paris but very much a man of the world and something of a literary lion, who expressed his surprise at this arbitrary division of Europe:

> A new and unexampled type of treaty was then hatched in Europe: this was the Quadruple Alliance concluded in London in 1718 between France, the Emperor and the King of England. . . . The three contracting sovereigns, confident of their own might and acting as if they had the authority of the other powers or as if they were the only powers in Europe, determined and dictated what the law was to be, composed the treaty between the Emperor and the King of Sardinia, disposed of the States of Tuscany whose Grand Duke was dying, and forced the King of Spain to acquiesce.[37]

The Quadruple Alliance was not well received in Madrid. In fact events had already overtaken the diplomats in London and Paris. On 17 June the greatest Spanish armada since 1588 left Barcelona for Sicily to undertake the reconquest of Spain's Italian possessions lost at Utrecht.[38] A landing was effected on 1 July but on 11 August, less than a fortnight after the signing of the treaty, the British Mediterranean fleet under admiral Byng destroyed this formidable force off Cape Pasarro. It was scarcely to be expected that Spain would recognize the three months' grace incorporated into the Quadruple Alliance, though Orléans and Dubois continued their efforts to persuade Philip V and Elisabeth Farnese to accept the treaty. They did succeed in persuading the British to offer to restore Gibraltar to Spain as an earnest of the Allies' pacific intentions. That was not enough for Philip even though Victor Amadeus's decision to accept the terms of the Quadruple Alliance removed any hope of the restoration of Sardinia to Spain.[39]

Philip's intransigence put Orléans in a delicate position: he was faced with the difficult task of persuading his government to make war on Philip V by the terms of the Quadruple Alliance. In the event, his task was facilitated by that ill-fated *drôlerie*, the Cellamare conspiracy, which enabled the faithful Dubois to mobilize opinion behind the regent and against Spain. The plot was maladroitly managed by the Spanish ambassador on behalf of a handful of inept political figures inspired by the duchess du Maine – bitter at her legitimate husband's loss of status during the regency – and including the marquis de Pompadour, cardinal de Polignac and the count de Laval. The plotters sought to reverse the policy leading towards an anti-Spanish alliance. They hoped to raise provincial noble support for the duke du Maine and to encourage some kind of Spanish intervention in France's domestic affairs, including a call for the re-convening of the states-general to replace Orléans. The abbé had been aware of Cellamare's involvement since June 1718 but he allowed the conspirators to pursue their relatively harmless machinations until the time was ripe for revelation. Then in December 1718, as international conflict threatened to break out, the arrests were made including those of the duke and duchess du Maine, and Cellamare was expelled from the country. Dubois wrote disingenuously to Destouches, his agent in London:

> I beg you to assure M. Craggs and milord Stanhope that all their suspicions about the delay in declaring war arise from no other reasons than those which I have raised with them in correspondence, particularly the recent revelation of the conspiracy and intrigues of the Spanish ambassador. We had reason to expect their discovery before long, and we felt strongly that after such an uproar our opponents would leave the field free for us.[40]

At this moment an influential voice was raised in justification of the regent's foreign policy, that of the marquis de Torcy, Louis XIV's foreign minister and an erstwhile supporter of 'old court' policies in favour of Spain and against the British alliance. Despite his connections with Orléans' enemies his expertise had been welcomed by the regent who instructed Dubois to co-operate closely with the marquis. In September 1718 Orléans went so far as to imply to Stanhope and Stair that in restructuring the government he might opt for Torcy to take the place of d'Huxelles in charge of foreign affairs.[41] Undoubtedly Torcy was the most experienced and professional of Orléans' foreign policy advisers and his view of French interests coincided with that of Dubois and the regent once it became clear that Spain did not intend to accept the general lines of the peace of Utrecht upon which Louis XIV had placed his hopes for a general pacification. Torcy retained his view of Great Britain as France's chief rival (their mutual opposition as natural as that between husband and wife, as one of Orléans' correspondents observed!)[42] and he feared the renewal of the Grand Alliance against

France. To prevent that happening – and to preserve the peace – Torcy accepted the need for a close relationship with Great Britain: for Spain to challenge the combined power of the Emperor, Great Britain and France and bring Europe once more to war was folly indeed. Torcy's views are instructive in the light of the hostile comments of such critics of the regent's policy as Emile Bourgeois. He distinguished strongly at this point between the interests of the regent and the kingdom, the latter sacrificed, so he maintained, to the former. It is possible that Torcy was adopting an accommodating, even a sycophantic line, in order to maintain his favour with Orléans and thereby increase his influence in the sphere of foreign affairs. However, the policy he was supporting on this occasion (December 1718) was that with which his great rival, Dubois, was closely associated.[43] Since the previous September Dubois' role as one of the regent's chief advisers had been publicly acknowledged by his appointment as secretary of state for foreign affairs. Supporting the abbé's policies would have been an odd way of challenging his supremacy; indeed a diplomatic silence would surely have served Torcy better in the event of the policy misfiring. His long-standing rivalry with Dubois and prolonged exposure to a different view of the European power system might well have suggested a hostile stance. In fact what Louis XIV's 'chiefest secretary' provided was a professional judgment; one which, coming from the most experienced diplomat in Europe, deserved to carry considerable weight.[44]

When it came the war was predictably short and one-sided. The campaign of 1719 was concentrated in north-western Spain where a French force under marshal Berwick won a series of siege victories and by the end of the year was poised for the conquest of Catalonia. Philip V was persuaded that his position was untenable and on 5 December Alberoni was ordered out of the country. On 17 February 1720 Spain acceded to the Quadruple Alliance.

There was, however, one final twist in the story of Franco-Spanish relations during the regency which paradoxically – for it involved the bringing together of the two powers – had the effect of completing Dubois' pacific design. To begin with, Orléans was dismayed to discover that the British offer to surrender Gibraltar to Spain, an offer to which the regent was publicly committed, had been withdrawn: Stanhope reported that the British nation would sooner wage a new war on Spain than cede the island.[45] This *volte-face* encouraged the old enemies of the British alliance at the French court to raise their voices in favour of an accommodation with Spain. Such a policy had always had its attractions for Orléans, who would have preferred to achieve his objective of maintaining the peace in co-operation with Spain. Since the latter's adherence to the Quadruple Alliance the prospects for co-operation between the two Bourbon states had improved. There were, moreover, additional reasons for a change in direction. By May 1720 Dubois was engaged in a struggle for power with John Law who, by advocating a strongly anti-British, pro-Spanish policy, had attracted into his camp members of the 'old court'.[46] At the same time the deteriorating domestic situation – with the long and intractable argument over Unigenitus coming to a head and Law's own financial System tottering on the edge of disaster – threatened serious public disturbances. Dubois had to work hard to maintain his grip on affairs. He appeared to have won his battle with Law by the end of May when the System began to disintegrate. On 9 June he was consecrated archbishop of Cambrai in the church of the Val-de-Grâce in Paris. Six days later a surprised Spanish ambassador learnt of the regent's desire for an entente with Spain.[47] By thus changing tack the new archbishop deprived the financier of his remaining influential supporters, members of the 'old court', and further consolidated his position.

The subsequent negotiations took place with British approval. This was partly because Stanhope was aware by now of another threat to the peace – in Italy – where the Emperor's intentions were causing him concern. It seemed that the latter hoped to side-step the stipulation in the Quadruple Alliance providing for the Spanish succession in Tuscany and Parma, and to establish a Habsburg hegemony in the Italian peninsula. Gibraltar was still a sticking point but Philip V was eventually persuaded by Stanhope's argument that the island would be restored to Spain within a year when the British House of Commons had been weaned from its current fierce attachment to it, a promise to be backed by the personal assurance of George I.[48] The Franco-Spanish convention was signed in Madrid on 27 March 1721. It was a defensive alliance of friendship and mutual guarantee, stipulating the two countries' support for the arrangements agreed at Utrecht and London. There were also clauses reaffirming the rights of French merchants in Spain and guaranteeing the return of Spanish territories captured by France in the war of 1719 (including the important port of Pensacola in Florida), promising Franco-Spanish support to the duke of Parma (Elisabeth Farnese's stepfather) for the maintenance of his states and rights, continuing French pressure on Great Britain in the matter of Gibraltar, and inviting the accession of Great Britain with a view to agreeing a new Triple Alliance. This last expectation was brought to fruition on 13 June 1721 when a Triple Alliance was indeed signed in Madrid. Despite some lack of enthusiasm in London

(Dubois' old friend and adversary, Stanhope, had died suddenly in February), the archbishop of Cambrai was determined not to lose the British alliance as a result of France's improved relations with Spain. The need to prevent a renewal of the Grand Alliance remained a central feature of the regent's foreign policy: the wider the range of interlocking guarantees the smaller the risk of polarization and war. Dubois was authorized, therefore, to buy the British signature at considerable cost to French and Spanish overseas commerce. Spain was persuaded to restore the rights of the *asiento* to Great Britain and to re-establish the commercial treaties of 1715 and 1716 favourable to the British at the expense of French traders. In return Great Britain acceded to the Franco-Spanish convention though she did not return Gibraltar to Spain.

French historians have tended to criticize this second Triple Alliance to be fashioned by Dubois on the grounds that it served the interests of the house of Orléans to the detriment of France. There is an element of truth in their strictures on this occasion: Orléans and Dubois were insensitive to the growing importance of the colonies and overseas trade and Dubois himself frankly acknowledged that the new arrangements 'donnent aux Anglais des privilèges et des avantages exclusifs, contraires aux intérêts des sujets du Roi'.[49] In the original Franco-Spanish agreement Pensacola, which would have given France an important hold over Spanish Florida, had been readily returned without any question of a *quid pro quo*.[50] Such an attitude was not uncommon in France – Louis XIV was likewise preoccupied with continental matters – yet, as the above quotation indicates, Orléans and Dubois were not unmindful of the sacrifice. They considered it worthwhile only because they were convinced of the overriding need to share in England's alliances. The prominence and successes of Dubois in international affairs disguised the fact that France was negotiating from a position of weakness after 1715. In the longer view some of the provisions of the Triple Alliance may seem short-sighted from the French side but the prospect of another full-scale European war was further diminished and France's first priority secured. The measure should be seen, therefore, as an extension of the principle of collective security in Europe, the culmination rather than the reversal of Dubois' policy.

A month after the signing of the Triple Alliance Philip V offered a double marriage alliance to cement the Bourbon reconciliation: his only daughter Maria Anna to be betrothed to Louis XV and the regent's third surviving daughter, Mademoiselle de Montpensier, to marry the heir to the Spanish crown, the prince of the Asturias. The regent was naturally delighted and flattered, and chose his friend Saint-Simon to lead an embassy to Spain to make the formal request for the infanta's hand and sign the marriage contract. No doubt Orléans was amused at the duke's keenness to undertake this ceremonial journey and add thereby to his family's honour and reputation.[51] The marriage between the prince of the Asturias and Louise Elisabeth d'Orléans took place at Lerma in January 1722; the three-year-old infanta, Maria Anna, who would return unmarried to Spain in 1725, made her solemn entry into Paris in March of the same year. Until his death cardinal Dubois, who had been raised to the purple in July 1721, continued his efforts to advance the cause of the Orléans dynasty and to preserve the general peace of Europe. Although this quest involved him mainly in the problems of southern Europe, there was a war still raging in the north which constantly impinged upon the wider diplomatic scene.

The connecting link between north and south was the electorate of Hanover, for France's overall commitment to the British alliance inevitably had repercussions in the north where George I took a very keen interest in the well-being of his Hanoverian territories. We have already seen how Orléans had felt obliged to temporise in 1717 when tsar Peter I was seeking French aid against Sweden. Once more in 1719 the French were forced to act as British agents in persuading their traditional ally, Sweden, to relinquish Bremen and Verden to Hanover, in providing the Swedes with subsidies to bolster their navy against the formidable Russian Baltic fleet, and in acting as guarantor of a defensive alliance between Great Britain and Sweden which came close to committing all three powers to an offensive league against Russia.[52] Great Britain's concern was to destroy the naval power of Russia and to protect her commercial interests in the Baltic, and for a time it did appear that France was to be used as a cat's-paw to achieve British objectives alone. However, Peter the Great proved to be a more formidable adversary in the north than Alberoni and Philip V had been in the south. The regent hesitated to commit himself to a northern war against Russia which the latter showed every sign of winning. Nor could he afford in the wake of the collapse of Law's System to provide subsidies for Prussia and Poland to stiffen their opposition to Russia. In the event the treaty of Nystad which brought the Great Northern War to an end in September 1721 was made possible as a result of French mediation. It represented a rebuff for British policies and a success for French diplomacy, in particular for M. de Campredon, France's ambassador at Stockholm, who had previously served as plenipotentiary at St Petersburg.[53]

On the morrow of this success Dubois opened negotiations with Peter with a view to substituting the new power of Russia for the declining power of Sweden as France's northern ally against the Emperor. He hoped to attract the tsar with the prospect of rivalling the Emperor as arbiter of the Empire. He asked Peter to guarantee French possession of all the provinces and towns ceded to France by the Habsburgs since the peace of Westphalia. Once more, however, French policy was calculated to take account of British reactions and the cardinal sought a triple alliance of France, Russia and Great Britain. The negotiations included yet another matrimonial proposal favourable to the house of Orléans: the marriage of the regent's son, the duke de Chartres, to Elisabeth Petrovna, daughter of the tsar and the succession of the former to the Polish throne. But Peter resisted entering into any formal agreement with his Hanoverian rival, and before that difficulty could be overcome cardinal Dubois died on 10 August 1723. In the remaining months of his life Orléans persisted with this enterprise and finally the tsar was persuaded to drop his opposition to British participation in the alliance, which would have been one of mutual defence and guarantee, based upon the treaties of Utrecht, the Triple and Quadruple Alliances of 1717 and 1718, and the treaty of Nystad. However, Orléans himself died on 2 December 1723 before a treaty could be signed and with his death this particular diplomatic initiative foundered.[54] The treaty which governed Russia's international relations for decades to come would be signed in 1726 not with France but with the Emperor.

Though French policy in the north as elsewhere during the regency was notable for its careful adherence to Anglo-Hanoverian interests, more prominent in this theatre was the evidence of traditional hostility to the Habsburgs which in the south was merged into the system of collective security. Critics of this policy could point to a cavalier indifference to the growing commercial predominance of Great Britain, a predominance actively promoted by French diplomacy. Yet French policy was essentially pragmatic. Neither Orléans nor Dubois aimed at establishing a permanent international system, but rather at arrangements which for some time to come would blunt the sharp edge of rival ambitions and thereby preserve the peace. Even in the crucial area of Anglo-French relations it is possible in this brief period to trace a changing emphasis. France's growing independence is clearly demonstrated by her *rapprochement* with Spain, and less obviously in the north where Orléans decided at the very end of his life to pursue the Russian alliance even at the risk of antagonizing the British.

Of course, it could be held that as Louis XV approached his majority so the regent's need for Great Britain's guarantee of his title to the French throne diminished. That would probably be the opinion of those French historians who view the regent's foreign policy solely in terms of his efforts to further the interests of his own house. Here we come up against the chief difficulty in interpreting Orléans' foreign policy: assessing the extent to which the interests of France were subordinated to the regent's dynastic ambitions. The dilemma is best resolved by refusing to couch the problem in either/or terms. Philippe was bound to take a strongly dynastic view of his situation, for that was still in every sense of the phrase the governing outlook in France and in most European states. It was to be expected, therefore, that he should take pride in the prospect of his son becoming king of Poland, of one of his daughters becoming queen of Spain and another the wife of Don Carlos, heir to the Italian duchies of Parma, Piacenza and Tuscany; most of all, of his own succession to the throne of France.[55] It is true that in times of regency it may be possible to distinguish between the regent's personal interests and those of the king, but only if the former are pursued by flouting what contemporaries see as the legitimate rules. Certainly, according to French fundamental law, Philip V of Spain should have followed Louis XV on the French throne if the latter died without heirs, but there were by this time other international considerations with which the dynastic principle had to reckon, and there could be no doubt that according to international law, as embodied in the peace of Utrecht to which Louis XIV had been a party, Philippe of Orléans was the rightful successor. There was a paradox at the heart of European affairs for the wide-ranging implications of dynastic rivalry were leading perforce to non-dynastic settlements: the dynastic principle was threatening its own eclipse. In that context there was nothing irregular about Orléans' policies. The question is not whether they served France badly and the regent well but whether, *tout court*, they served France well.

Orléans did succeed in preventing a recurrence of a serious international conflict. By substituting for the policy of polarized alliances one of collective security, he effectively insulated the danger points which the Utrecht settlement had left exposed. Nor could there be any doubt that France needed a period of peace after the prolonged, financially exhausting and increasingly unpopular wars of Louis XIV's reign. She had everything to gain and nothing to lose by a pacific policy. Not that this policy was pursued without reference to France's traditional security needs. Dubois remarked to his agent Chavigny, in relation to his efforts at securing a Russian alliance towards the close of the regency, 'Si je puis consommer ma négociation avec le Czar, j'aurai mis de tous côtés de furieuses entraves à la maison d'Autriche'.[56] There was a price to be paid for this success, however: the close alliance with Great Britain which helped to ensure the latter's international trading superiority over all her rivals, France included. Though the French emphasis upon continental military security was traditional, Orléans and Dubois should have paid more attention than they did to the implications of Great Britain's developing world-wide role.

The policies discussed and elaborated in this chapter should be ascribed jointly to the regent himself and to his tireless and ingenious representative, Dubois. The cardinal was an astute negotiator with a fertile brain who was undoubtedly responsible for most – perhaps all – of the major foreign policy initiatives undertaken by his master. He became a great expert, as Torcy had become in the previous reign, in the field of diplomacy and the regent leant heavily on his expertise. However, Orléans remained in command, and when he showed signs of uncertainty Dubois could do no more than put his case and hope that the regent would be persuaded by it. Invariably he was, for Orléans, who was both a dynast and a pragmatist, understood that Dubois' proposals made sound political sense.

IV

The Regent and the Parlement

The parlement of Paris was a sovereign court of appeal immediately subordinate to the king and his council. It was also a political body, for under the *ancien régime* politics was an aspect of judicial authority. The mechanism which gave this court an effective political role was its practice, dating from the first half of the fourteenth century, of registering royal enactments. Originally registration was a simple formality to ensure the publication and execution of the king's decrees, and to provide a record of past legislation. A century later the magistrates acquired the right to remonstrate, that is, to point out the inconsistencies or inequalities in any law sent for registration. The king might take account of the objections and modify the law or alternatively he might order the parlement to register it in its original form. This practice did not in itself constitute a threat to the king's authority in that the magistrates as royal counsellors had a duty to advise him on any matter about which he might seek advice; yet it did give them a significant influence in the government of the country. That influence waxed and waned according to the strength and weakness of the king's position. During the royal minorities of Louis XIII, Louis XIV and Louis XV the parlement played a leading role; it figured far less prominently in the great days of Henri IV and Louis XIV. When court and king were in dispute there was a grey area between the two of them which each would seek to exploit. Thus a dominant sovereign might assert that the parlement was essentially a court of law and must not interest itself in affairs of state, whereas a strongly placed parlement might claim that the king had to obey the law and laws were valid only when freely registered by the sovereign court. In practice, however, neither side chose to push its argument to the limit. The magistrates stopped short of challenging the king's ultimate sovereignty and the king, well aware of the legal basis of his authority, always sought the backing of his court in preference to confrontation with it. The French political theorist, Jean Bodin, had noted in the sixteenth century that there was a strong possibility that royal enactments registered by force would be badly observed.[1]

Thus it was to be expected that Orléans would seek the support of the parlement of Paris in order to bolster his shaky position at the commencement of the regency. It was also to be expected that, after such a lengthy period in the political wilderness, the magistrates would look for early opportunities to exploit the political authority restored to them on 2 September 1715.

The papal bull Unigenitus seemed likely to provide the first opportunity for the parlement to resume a political function. Its publication in September 1713 had not resolved the problem of Jansenism; on the contrary Louis XIV's handling of the issue had aroused a degree of opposition in the court, unexampled since 1673, thereby enabling the religious dissidents to rally widespread support under the Gallican flag. It is important for an understanding of later conflicts under the regency to appreciate the precise nature of the parlement's stand on this matter. Gallicanism formed part of the legal framework which supported French kingship, a fact acknowledged in 1682 with the publication of the four Gallican liberties as a law of the state. The magistrates were particularly angered by the king's subsequent policy of ignoring those liberties in order to satisfy the pope in the matter of Unigenitus. In 1705 they had willingly registered another papal pronouncement on Jansenism, Vineam Domini, because Louis himself had insisted that they should only do so if the bull accorded with the rights and pre-eminences of the crown and the liberties of the Gallican church;[2] in 1713, against the king's will, the magistrates added these qualifications to their reluctant registration of Unigenitus. The parlement's motives were to uphold a very important traditional aspect of French kingship – the Gallican liberties – and to assert the superiority of the law in general over the arbitrary wishes of an individual sovereign. There could be no doubting the legal correctness of the court's position; its political relevance, as the coming years would demonstrate, was quite another matter.

Orléans was aware that the French church was on the brink of schism. Such a division would indubitably have had serious implications for the stability of the political order. Thus it was necessary to act at once in order to dispel alarm as a first step towards a general pacification of the church. Nor could there be any doubt as to which camp would receive the regent's initial reassurances, for feelings were running highest among those, Jansenist or Gallican, who felt themselves threatened or affronted by Unigenitus. Consequently it was sound politics to seek to quieten their fears first. More to the point, however, Orléans needed parlementaire support to establish his authority as regent, and that fact alone dictated a pro-Jansenist policy. He was assisted in his calculations by a complete personal indifference to the theological niceties of the dispute: his scepticism held him aloof from either side's sense of commitment.

He embarked, therefore, upon a policy favourable to the Jansenist cause, though his assurance to pope Clement XI via the French ambassador in Rome that he was determined to bring religious conflict in the kingdom to an end, was a genuine expression of intent.[3] Cardinal de Noailles, leader of the episcopal opposition to Unigenitus, currently the idol of Paris and strongly favoured by the magistrates, was appointed – as we have seen – president of the *conseil de conscience*. He was joined there by three of the parlement's leading adversaries of the bull, d'Aguesseau, Joly de Fleury and the abbé Pucelle, while the abbé Dorsanne, a doctor at the Sorbonne and a zealous disciple of Port-Royal, was named as secretary. Louis XIV's Jesuit confessor, père Le Tellier, was exiled to Amiens, the handful of prisoners detained in the Bastille for alleged Jansenism were freed, and known clerical enemies of Unigenitus such as the archbishop of Tours and the bishop of Châlons made their reappearance in the capital.[4]

The new official attitude was reflected in the registers of the parlement. In January 1716 the court condemned a letter published in Rome supporting the absolute authority of papal bulls and denying the necessity of royal consent to make them lawful in France; in April an Instruction of the bishop of Toulon was condemned, not on doctrinal grounds (so Orléans was assured by the *gens du roi*), but in order to re-establish maxims of the kingdom which the bishop had abused. In May the parlement received appeals *comme d'abus* of six priests from the archdiocese of Rheims, excommunicated by their archbishop for refusing to adhere to Unigenitus. The court forbade archbishops and bishops to exact from their diocesan clergy signed affirmations of their acceptance of the bull without a decision of all the bishops on the matter and letters-patent registered in the parlement.[5] These decisions were entirely at one with the parlement's forensic tradition which tended to support secular jurisdiction against the spiritual, especially when the latter was exercised from Rome. In particular the device of the appeal *comme d'abus*, directed against an ecclesiastical judge who had allegedly offended against the Gallican liberties, had long provided the parlement, and through his sovereign court the king, with the means of overriding the spiritual jurisdiction. But enthusiastic implementation of such procedures in a controversial religious climate by a secular company whose voice had been muted for so long was likely to cause resentment among some bishops.

Indeed, Orléans soon found that the intransigence of the magistrates who opposed Unigenitus was matched by an equally unbending resolution on the part of its supporters, led initially by the archbishop of Rheims and the bishops of Toulon, Apt and Marseilles. Faced by such opposition, his hopes of an accommodation faded, and in March 1717 they were further diminished by the solemn appeal of four bishops, of Senez, Montpellier, Boulogne and Mirepoix, from the bull to a future general council of the church. The appeal, completely in accordance with Gallican doctrine, was not against papal authority as such but against the pope's refusal to provide explanations of Unigenitus which the French bishops could approve.[6] The effect of the appeal was to suspend the bull until an ecumenical settlement had been reached. The bishops received considerable support. The faculties of theology in Paris, Rheims and Nantes all followed their example and so did a number of individual clerics. Only the intervention of the regent prevented the Sorbonne from adhering to the appeal *en bloc*. Cardinal de Noailles himself drew up an appeal in April but did not publish it.[7] In May the parlement condemned as null and void the latest attempt by the archbishop of Rheims to force his clergy to accept Unigenitus.[8]

Orléans tried to moderate the storm: the offending bishops were ordered to retire to their dioceses, the faculty of theology in Paris, where the appeal had been published, was forbidden to assemble, and finally in October 1717 a royal declaration was issued suspending all disputes and contestations on the subject of the bull.[9] During the period of this imposition of silence negotiations between Paris and Rome continued in an attempt to draw up a core of doctrine which would provide an interpretation of Unigenitus acceptable to both sides. The silence was periodically broken: by the persistent archbishop of Rheims who, in a letter to the regent, criticized the very idea of suspending hostilities in this way; by the parlement's suppression of a decree published in Rome which condemned the appeal of the four bishops.[10] This decree was an indication of the pope's growing unwillingness to reach any settlement which did not presuppose the bishops' pure and simple acceptance of the bull. Although negotiations went on, rumours became more insistent that Clement XI was preparing a drastic measure. So indeed he was, for on 8 September 1718, the fifth anniversary of the publication of Unigenitus, he promulgated the letters Pastoralis Officii excommunicating all those who withheld their unqualified submission to the bull. The papal letters were denounced in the parlement by the *procureur-général*, Joly de Fleury, and the court accepted his appeal *comme d'abus* against the papal missives, thereby nullifying their effect. A complete stalemate had been reached.

By this time, however, relations between the parlement and the regent had changed dramatically; to discover how and why, it is necessary to review some other aspects of those first three years of the regency. The magistrates had lost little time in indicating that they did not subscribe to the view that the regent held the same authority and merited the same respect as the monarch himself, an idea with an irresistible pedigree but vitiated in practice by Orléans' debt to the parlement and his equivocal relations with Philip V of Spain. As one anonymous observer of the regency remarked: 'People set limits to the regent's authority according to their fancy, making a false distinction between a major and a minor king'.[11]

For his own security Louis XIV had adopted the policy on a grand scale of stripping possible noble rivals of all actual power, leaving them only the honours which formerly had reflected that power. The comparative weakness of the regent's position made possible attempts to reclaim lost authority, to marry the substance to the shadow. The *polysynodie* was one of the results and the *affaire du bonnet* also concerned the quest for political power. Much has been written about this curious affair which raged with great fury and bitterness over half a century.[12] Superficially the dispute was concerned with nothing more important than a matter of parlementaire etiquette. The trouble began when the first president, on addressing his fellow presidents, refused to extend the courtesy of doffing his official cap to the peers of the realm who were entitled to sit in the parlement. To make matters worse the presidents, but not the peers, were allowed to reply without uncovering. This and other disputes of rank and precedence, trivial and infantile as they now appear, did have real significance at the time.

A clear indication of this underlying importance is to be found in a memorandum of 1716 from the presidents of the parlement to the regent on the subject of the *bonnet*. Besides being a request for his support in their quarrel with the peers, it was an avowedly political document in which his debt to the magistrates was clearly stated. There was also a latent threat in the words: 'Monseigneur, you are not unaware of the esteem in which the parlement is held both in the capital city and throughout France, of the weight of its authority in the most important matters of State and of the influence of its example on the other parlements.'[13] The final reference, to the provincial courts, was an intimation of the later eighteenth-century theory of parlementaire solidarity whereby the magistrates were to claim that all the parlements together formed a united body.[14]

A more direct attack upon Orléans' position was made in August 1716.

Annually on the 15th of that month, the Feast of the Assumption of the Virgin Mary, a great procession took place through the streets of Paris. On this occasion the parlement claimed the right to take first place before the regent on the grounds that it represented the king. To prevent a quarrel Orléans accepted the magistrates' contention although when the time came he failed to appear. Saint-Simon, furious at the insolence of the magistrates, was correct in concluding that the parlement, by disputing a matter of precedence with the regent, was weakening his authority.[15]

Ten months later another long-standing quarrel, that between the princes of the blood and the legitimized princes, Maine and Toulouse, reached a climax. On 19 June 1717 the royal bastards formally protested in the parlement against any decision being reached in the affair except by the king upon reaching his majority or by the estates-general; and two days later the duke de Bourbon and the prince de Conti came to request the court not to receive the protest of Maine and Toulouse. The parlement resisted the temptation to intervene, deciding simply to inform the king of these visits though stipulating that the deputation should be to Louis XV, not to the regent.[16]

In all these matters there were important political implications behind the arguments about status and precedence, and in each case the parlement appeared to be vying with the regent for the dominant role. But explicit confrontation was most likely to come through the use of the newly restored right of remonstrance first employed by the parlement in May 1716. On this occasion the regent modified his proposals in the light of the magistrates' complaints – they were objecting to the cost and judicial influence of two offices which Orléans was proposing to re-establish – but was forced in the end to threaten them with *lettres de jussion*, royal letters demanding immediate obedience in order to secure registration without further remonstrances. The signs were that the judges would make matters difficult for the regent if a serious disagreement between them were to emerge.[17]

Increasingly that disagreement focussed upon the Scots financier, John Law, whose overall contribution to and significance for the regency are discussed elsewhere. He had established a private bank in May 1716 which had prospered to such an extent that in April 1717 the state was made solidary with the bank and banknotes were henceforth accepted in payment for all taxes. While he was enjoying this success, Law worked to establish a great commercial company which in time, financed by the bank, would take over the management of the whole of the state's industry and commerce. A declaration relating to the establishment of a new

trading company, the Compagnie de l'Occident, was duly sent to the
parlement on 28 August 1717, together with an edict designed to divert
state bills into more profitable channels for the government, and establishing in place of the *dixième* a tax on houses for the upkeep of the streets.

The mood of the magistrates was inflamed even before they received
this legislation. They were dismayed by the general financial embarrassment of the government and by three edicts in particular reflecting that
embarrassment, which had come before the court on 6 August. 'Il
paraît qu'aujourd'hui il y a bien du feu dans toutes les têtes', wrote one
observer, and Orléans himself was known to be apprehensive about the
possibility of civil disorder while the parlement was in this frame of
mind.[18] Nevertheless the declaration represented a major economic
measure which required the court's scrutiny and support.

When the magistrates debated the two measures submitted to them
on 28 August, they took the significant step of agreeing to ask the regent
to communicate to the court a comprehensive account of the government's financial situation. Though it might be argued that the parlement
needed the information to make an informed judgment on the legislation
before it, that was not how the regent interpreted the request. He saw it
as a challenge to the executive which, as he put it to the parlementaire
deputation, threatened to diminish the king's authority.[19] Shaken by
Orléans' unequivocal refusal, the moderate majority of the judges agreed
to withdraw the demand, substituting a request for additional financial
details only if they should prove essential to a proper examination of the
legislation before them. Orléans responded by summoning another
deputation from the parlement to hear the duke de Noailles, president
of the council for finance, explain his intentions and answer questions.
Subsequently, the parlement drew up remonstrances on the tax on
householders for the upkeep of the streets and on the decision to liquidate
state bills. They were argued with moderation, intended to remind the
regent of existing legal commitments. Orléans was persuaded to modify
the disputed clauses, yielding appreciably to the magistrates' point of
view.[20] The first protracted legal argument between the regent and the
court thus ended on a note of compromise and reasonableness without
hurt either to the parlement's pride or to the regent's authority. 'Le
Parlement est content et on est content du Parlement', wrote Dangeau,[21]
but the issue of finance, and particularly the growing influence of John
Law, now loomed as a source of serious friction between court and
regent in the near future.

The truce lasted for four months. During that time the government's
economic difficulties increased, and early in the new year of 1718 the

parlement was encouraged to take an active role in financial affairs by the example of the provincial parlement of Rennes, which drew up outspoken remonstrances on 3 January, arising out of the refusal of the Breton nobility to contribute the *don gratuit*.[22] These remonstrances went so far as to threaten that Brittany might secede from the French nation if the central government persisted in trying to dictate to the Breton estates. On 14 January the parlement of Paris, meeting to examine two minor financial edicts sent to it for registration, launched a broad attack on the government's fiscal policies unrelated to the legislation in hand, criticizing the expenses involved in the conciliar form of administration, the practice of duplicating offices in order to raise more government money by the sale of new posts, and the retarded payment of *rentes*; and calling upon the king 'de donner ordre à l'arrangement de ses finances'.[23] Discussion of whether to incorporate their criticisms into formal remonstrances, an innovatory proposal which implied an independent magisterial enquiry into affairs of state, was put off until the following day. The court's chief clerk, Gilbert, noted prophetically in the minutes of the day's session: 'thus ends a session which has set in motion matters which will have consequences of more than one kind; it would be possible to compose a moderately sized volume about it alone.'[24]

As a result of succeeding sessions which continued until 19 January, the magistrates agreed to draw up both remonstrances, which were always addressed to the king, and separate representations to the regent. Law figured prominently and unfavourably in the debates as a foreigner seeking to draw all the royal revenues into his bank without any guarantee that he would remain in the country; this despite the first president's protest that Law had obtained letters of naturalization. Remonstrances were drawn up on the non-payment of *rentes*, the dubious practice of duplicating offices, and Law's bank. The latter was not mentioned by name but the king was requested to restore the management of his revenues to the anciently established form and warned against 'une caisse nouvelle' and 'un genre de billets jusqu'à présent inconnus'.[25] The representations to the regent concerned the expenses involved in the running of the *polysynodie*. They were presented on 7 February, the remonstrances having been submitted on 26 January.

With these complaints the magistrates entered that uncharted region in which the frontier between the king's authority (or in this case the regent's, acting on the king's behalf) and that of the royal court was somewhere to be found. The first president feared that on this occasion the king's court had exceeded its powers. That was his view but in a jurisdictional no-man's-land there was room for more than one opinion.

The declaration of 1715 restoring the right of remonstrance had limited its application to legislative acts of the sovereign sent to the court for registration. This restriction invalidated the complaints of January 1718 which were remonstrances only in name. The term concealed the parlement's independent intervention on a political level. However, this independent action was by no means out of step with the court's political tradition, according to which the right of registration was only the starting point for a far wider political role. Indeed the regent himself had recognized that fact in his speech before the great assembly of 2 September 1715 when he assured the magistrates that he would welcome their advice *as well as* their wise remonstrances, and when later in the same month, in the declaration restoring the right of remonstrance, he made a similar promise in the king's name (though stipulating on the second occasion the need to obtain prior royal approval before the remonstrances were presented).[26] The fact that the king responded to these remonstrances and indeed tried briefly to answer them, though making the point that they did not conform to the precise stipulations contained in the declaration of 1715, suggests that Orléans was still willing to accept a broader interpretation of parlementaire influence than that made explicit in the declaration.[27] However, the path which the court was now following promised to lead to a more precise definition of the limits of its authority.

It is not difficult to sympathize with the court's point of view. John Law's schemes were novel and untried, and his reputation ill matched the sort of trust which Orléans was bestowing upon him. Nor was the parlement alone in its scepticism: opposition within the regency council and the council for finance was shared by merchants and bankers consulted by the government.[28] It is certainly true that a large number of magistrates were *rentiers*, fearful of what might befall their investments, and that self-interest provided the bitter edge to the debates and provoked some personal animosity towards Law himself. Yet there was far more to it than that: the remonstrances preached the regent's obligation to see that the government honoured its legal commitments, to conform with the law, and to eschew dangerous novelty. The parlement stood for the strict observance of legislation already recognized by the court; yet that stance which in the past had guaranteed the submission of the king's authority to the law, in changing circumstances risked rendering necessary government reforms stillborn.

Orléans gave an unencouraging reply to the representations and only answered the remonstrances on 21 February. Before that date he had made it clear, by removing the duke de Noailles from his presidency of the council for finance and by taking the seals from the chancellor, d'Aguesseau, that he did not intend to be intimidated. Both men had shown hostility towards Law's schemes, and d'Aguesseau in particular was a popular figure with the magistrates. The new president of the council of finance and keeper of the seals was the marquis d'Argenson, a former chief of police in Paris and a bitter antagonist of the parlement. In the words of the regency's most distinguished historian: 'D'Argenson ne se connaissait qu'un ennemi, le Parlement. . . . entre eux c'était une lutte sans pitié et sans merci.'[29]

On 21 February a deputation of magistrates was summoned to hear the royal reply to the remonstrances. From their point of view it was quite unsatisfactory since none of their demands was heeded. The parlement nominated commissioners further to scrutinize the reply but nothing came of that, and by 20 May it had become clear that the court's political tempo had slackened, restrained by its own rigid judicial procedure. There was a feeling among the magistrates that, having made their protest, it would not be easy or even desirable to take a new initiative.

The uneasy calm into which the parlement had drifted was dispelled by Orléans himself. During the preceding months the government had been systematically changing the value of money, a process that reached its climax on 20 May with an edict ordering a general recoinage. The edict was registered on 29 May, not in the parlement but in the *cour des monnaies*. It was this decision rather than the edict's contents which infuriated the parlementaires. Although the *cour des monnaies* was a superior court which gave the necessary publicity for the edict, it was generally recognized that in matters of public interest, especially where fiscal policy was concerned, it was the parlement's registration which provided the customary complement to legislation. Even Louis XIV had tacitly recognized that fact. Through by-passing the magistrates on this issue Orléans was threatening the very basis of their political authority. Later developments do not justify the suggestion that the regent was deliberately goading the court to bring about its downfall.[30] Probably he hoped to avoid conflict by ignoring the magistrates;[31] but he badly underestimated the strength of the court's reaction, and his misjudgment would embarrass him for several months to come. His determination to maintain his independence of action in the face of what he interpreted as the magistrates' incipient constitutional challenge blunted his sensitivity in dealing with the Paris parlement.

Once more the court appointed commissioners – the same ones in fact who had acted on the previous occasion – and their advice put to the court on 14 June was that deputies from the other superior courts in

Paris, as well as the capital's leading merchants and bankers, should be invited to join the parlement in order to discuss the edict in question. There was an historical significance attached to this proposed union of the courts, for in 1648 at the beginning of the Fronde these same bodies had united in the *chambre Saint-Louis* for the purpose of extracting economic reforms from the king. This precedent was to be found in the court's own registers though perhaps the recently published memoirs of cardinal de Retz, which were enjoying a great vogue at the time, provided the immediate stimulus.[32]

Prompted by Orléans, the other courts found it impolitic to send deputies and the replies from the merchants and bankers were vague and uninstructive. Ignoring this rebuff, the magistrates decided to ask the regent to suspend the coining and distribution of the new money until the court had been given an opportunity to examine the whole matter. Orléans refused but offered the alternative of remonstrances. This concession indicated his continuing desire to exercise royal authority in accordance with accepted legal practice; yet he also remained mindful of the need to protect the integrity of that authority against challenge from whatever quarter it might come, even from the king's own judges. It was a difficult balance for any regent to maintain: on 29 May Orléans had tried to circumvent trouble via the *cour des monnaies*; on 18 June he offered the magistrates a means of voicing their discontent though complaints such as those of January 1718 could not be called remonstrances, according to the letter of the 1715 declaration. On the same day he took the precaution of sending a troop of soldiers to mount guard over Law's bank.[33]

The magistrates responded with a deputation to Orléans to present formal complaints criticizing both the form of publication and the content of the money edict, though undoubtedly it was the former to which they gave priority. 'We have learned from our forefathers', they stated, that every law which contains a general government regulation affecting the whole kingdom, must be registered in the Parlement.'[34] Once more they were given no satisfaction and now the wilder spirits began to contemplate ways of projecting their dispute into the public arena. The demand was made that copies of the court's representations, and of the regent's reply, should be printed and distributed among the people. The first president refused to countenance this ploy since all correspondence between the court and the king or his representative, including remonstrances, was held to be secret. There was no indication at this time that such appeals would produce any response, for some of the more inflammatory speeches of individual judges were already circulating anonymously in the capital. 'I must tell you', noted the anonymous author of the *Gazette de la Régence* on 20 June, 'that the people are in no way inclined to co-operate with the Parlement in remedying the difficulty by resorting to force'.[35]

In order to pursue their dispute with Orléans the magistrates now decided to issue a direct challenge. Not only did they agree on remonstrances asking for royal letters-patent to revoke the controversial edict; they also produced their own *arrêt* forbidding the distribution and circulation of the new money. Thus the parlement was attempting to place its own legislative authority above the regent's. He responded with a decree from the regency council annulling the magistrates' ruling and ordering the execution of the financial edict. In addition he forbade the court to print its *arrêt*. Adopting a legalistic stance, the parlement refused to accept the council's decree, declaring that it would only obey royal letters-patent. The court's *arrêt* was ordered to be published in the accustomed places with copies to be sent to the other superior courts and to the inferior tribunals within the parlement's jurisdiction. On the same day, 21 June, a copy was posted defiantly in the Great Hall of the Palais de Justice where 'Il y eut grand nombre de personnes et de tout sexe à lire et copier ledit arrêt'.[36] Orléans' answer was to send soldiers to seize the printing press supplying the Palais, to countermand the attempt to circulate the court's decree and to express his willingness again to receive remonstrances. On 25 June a council decree evoked all matters dealing with the execution of the contentious edict to the king in his council. Orléans' offer of remonstrances was taken up by the magistrates, thus bringing to an end the parlement's paper revolt.[37]

It was not an end to the regent's difficulties, though remonstrances limited the danger, since the opposition neither dared nor wished to attack the king's sovereignty. The remonstrances duly presented on 27 June once more attacked the manner of the original edict's registration. The magistrates claimed with some justice that registration in the parlement, 'cette formalité nécessaire pour rendre une loi publique', could not be matched by any other tribunal. This was particularly so in the case of laws of general application where the maximum of solemnity and publicity was required to render them effective. They also hinted at a more representative role for themselves than Orléans would allow: 'in order to fulfil its most essential duty, your Parlement must bring to the foot of Your Majesty's throne the legitimate anxieties of all the orders of his kingdom.'[38]

The king's response on 2 July was a categorical statement of the monarchic theory of government. Speaking through the voice of the young king, Orléans took the opportunity to reassert his own authority. Laws subsist, he declared, only by the will of the sovereign and registration adds nothing to their validity. The parlement's authority was delegated to it by the sovereign and the court could not claim, therefore, to represent or speak for all the orders of the kingdom, nor was it entitled to unite with any other superior court.

This authoritarian reply was met by further remonstrances presented on 26 July, which stated in their turn an extreme parlementaire theory of government.[39] It was by far the most outspoken political document drawn up by the magistrates during the first half of the eighteenth century. They put forward the claim that according to what they called the principal laws of the state they had the right to examine freely all proposed legislation sent to them by the king, and that only royal enactments registered in the parlement were valid. By implication the parlement was claiming a role in law-making which was something more than passive, which seemed even to question the indivisibility of the sovereign's legislative power. The principal laws to which the magistrates referred, and which they claimed imposed upon them the duty of remonstrating if necessary, were not the fundamental laws of the French state. According to the parlementaire thesis, the court was obliged to safeguard the latter as well as the king's rights by means of these secondary laws. Yet it is difficult to resist the conclusion that laws devised to protect the fundamental laws must themselves be fundamental – a conclusion already drawn during the Fronde and noted by Claude Joly in his *Recueil des Maximes* where he classed the free verification of edicts as a necessary part of law-making.[40]

The magistrates also insisted that the court had always formed a link between king and people, that in some way they represented to the former the aspirations of the latter: 'c'est le seul canal par lequel la voix de vos peuples ait pu parvenir jusqu'à vous'. Likewise they claimed to be responsible to the king and to the nation for the exact observance of the fundamental laws. However, it is worth restating the caveat that the magistrates' position was based on a legal tradition, according to which the king's primary domestic obligation was to guarantee the multifarious judicial rights of his subjects. For some time the pressures exerted on the sovereign (especially external ones) had made it increasingly difficult for the king to abide by his traditional role: the power of the central government had to grow at the expense of the old liberties. The parlement's natural inclination – more than that, its only course – was to restrict its *imprimatur* to legislation which conformed with its own legal canons though it still recognized the king's ultimate right to have his wishes heeded. Thus, in remonstrances which seemed in parts to threaten the king's authority, the magistrates could still say with truth: 'nous reconnaissons que vous êtes seul maître, seul législateur'. Taken as a whole these remonstrances stated a theory of government in many ways comparable with the ideas to be elaborated three decades later by another magistrate, Montesquieu, who, in *De l'Esprit des Lois*, argued the parlement's obligation to do its utmost to counter what he called 'la volonté momentanée et capricieuse d'un seul', though he accepted that in the last resort that will had to prevail.[41]

These two statements – the king's reply on 2 July and the remonstrances of 26 July – elaborated mutually exclusive positions. Both sides bore some responsibility for seeking to enclose the common ground between them, risking thereby a constitutional crisis. Yet equally neither protagonist was committed exclusively to an inflexible position: the parlement acknowledged its ultimate dependence upon the crown and the regent had no wish to exercise royal power in an arbitrary fashion. He did believe, however, that the maintenance of that authority unchallenged justified coercive measures against the parlement, a belief which revealed itself in an increasingly cavalier treatment of the magistrates.

While awaiting the doubtless unsympathetic response from the regent, the court directed its attentions once more towards John Law. Outmanoeuvred by Orléans since the publication of the edict of 20 May and seeing no weakening in the regent's support for the financier, the frustrated magistrates allowed their deep-seated hostility towards Law to spill over into ill-conceived action. On 18 August the parlement published a decree ordering the reduction of Law's bank to the modest limits prescribed for it in May 1716 and, under the threat of legal summons, forbidding all foreigners, even if they were naturalized Frenchmen, to take any part in the administration of the royal revenues.[42] In a more comprehensive manner than before, this *arrêt* attempted to dictate policy to the government in defiance of the regent: independent legislation went far beyond the bounds indicated in the court's own most recent remonstrances. More than that, there was a vindictiveness about the court's attitude towards Law himself which Orléans could scarcely ignore. Rumours of the magistrates' desire to have him hanged at the first opportunity were persistent enough to make Law seek refuge in the Palais-Royal.[43] Stern reprisals duly followed. On 21 August Orléans was responsible for a regency council decree which drastically curtailed the parlement's political rights. Remonstrances upon laws sent to the court had to be presented within a week or the laws would be considered registered. The magistrates were forbidden to interpret edicts, to meddle in financial affairs without permission, to unite with other superior courts or to take cognizance of any matter of state unless the king asked for their advice. All acts of the parlement considered inimical to royal authority were annulled. At the time of the decree's publication Orléans was already considering a surer and more spectacular means of breaking the court's opposition. On the day it appeared Dangeau wrote, 'On parle d'un lit de justice sur la fin de la semaine.'[44]

The insecurity of the regent's position in the early months and years of the regency had made him unwilling to take extreme measures. If the *lit de justice* failed to contain the resentful magistrates, his best weapon would be lost and his authority dangerously undermined. By August 1718, however, encouraged by the signing of the Quadruple Alliance on the 2nd of that month, Orléans was ready for a *coup de force*. He decided, therefore, that Louis XV should hold his *lit de justice* on 26 August in one of the great antechambers of the Louvre. The parlement was not informed until the morning of that day, and upon hearing the news the magistrates decided to make their way on foot, choosing the longest route in the hope of arousing public sympathy. But Parisians watching on the quai des Orfèvres, on the Pont Neuf and over the river in the rue St Honoré showed no more than curiosity at the unusual spectacle.[45] At the *lit de justice* the decree issued five days earlier by the regency council was registered by the king's express command and the parlement was thus forced to assist at its own political eclipse.[46] On 29 August three of the court's most outspoken leaders were arrested and exiled in remote parts of the kingdom. Their colleagues, thoroughly overawed, merely petitioned for their release.

Twice within the space of two months in 1718 the parlement had dared to assume the mantle of supreme legislator in the state in defiance of the government; and it had sought to elevate registration of laws to the level of a supreme maxim of state. By registering his financial edict at the *cour des monnaies* the regent had committed a tactical error, laying himself open to the accusation of arbitrariness and provoking the excessive magisterial reaction which followed. However, Orléans held two decisive advantages over the court. One was the support of the king's authority which remained all-powerful and the other was the control of the army. 'Mon fils', the realist d'Argenson asked his son, 'votre Parlement a-t-il des troupes?'[47]

After the defeat of the parlement John Law was free to develop his financial schemes. By an edict of December 1718 Law's private bank was converted into a royal one to be administered in the king's name.

Following the policy adopted since the *lit de justice* the parlement refused to register the edict which, according to the council decree of 21 August, was held to be registered after a week had elapsed without remonstrances. Next Law turned to the other feature of his dual system – commercial expansion – and from May 1719 his Compagnie des Indes undertook to acquire the monopoly of maritime commerce. After hearing expert opinion on this matter the court decided to draw up remonstrances but Orléans refused to accept them, three weeks having passed since the parlement's receipt of the enactment.[48] From this time for almost a year he omitted to send any new financial measures to the court.

In the concluding months of 1719 Law's System reached its zenith. His company's shareholders acquired immense fortunes, progress was made towards reducing the national debt and the triumph of paper money seemed assured. The financier's personal prestige soared correspondingly and early in 1720 he was appointed controller-general of finance. However, the System was beginning to groan under the weight of growing inflation and the battle to preserve public confidence began. One of Law's measures, taken in March 1720, was to reduce the legal interest rate from 4 per cent to 2 per cent. Though this affected all shareholders, it particularly antagonized the *rentier* class, those people who bought government securities, whose *rentes* had been translated into company shares following the latter's takeover of the national debt. Many of the great *robe* dynasties of the capital had considerable investments of this kind and in their chief forum, the parlement, there were renewed signs of opposition. When Orléans sent this edict to the court, the magistrates, realizing that the System was faltering, were emboldened to present remonstrances in April 1720. They were not well received and Orléans ordered the parlement to register the measure without further ado.[49]

By this time the financial situation was critical, and on 21 May Law caused a decree to be issued which drastically devalued the bank-notes and the company shares. The publication of this decree heralding the breakdown of the government's fiscal policy, and the bankruptcy of a number of private investors, caused consternation in the capital.[50] The magistrates shared the general alarm and decided to present remonstrances to the king. Orléans was sufficiently perturbed by the financial crisis and the resulting public unrest to reverse his policy of the previous two years and consult the parlement in a political capacity. On 27 May the offending decree was repealed and the magistrates were invited to name a deputation to confer with the regent.[51] The subsequent meetings did not solve the grave economic problems facing the government but, from

Orléans' point of view, they did prevent the parlement from adding to his difficulties. For a while he co-operated with its envoys, reinstating d'Aguesseau as chancellor and dismissing Law from his post of controller-general. However, Law's dismissal was not an indication of his disgrace and a few days later he was again unofficially in charge of the country's ailing finances.[52]

The position steadily deteriorated during the month of June and the bank was forced to close because of the shortage of gold and silver. A new edict making the Compagnie des Indes perpetual in return for financial aid was sent to the parlement for registration. The government declined to elaborate further on this edict and consequently the magistrates agreed to ask the king to withdraw it.[53] Orléans' patience was at an end and on 18 July, at a meeting of the regency council, it was decided to exile the parlement as a body to the village of Pontoise some twenty miles north-east of Paris.

This was the culmination of the regent's hard-line policy towards the court: he had snubbed it from the time of the *lit de justice* in 1718 until the erosion of Law's System in May 1720 persuaded him of the need to adopt a gentler approach. Yet the change in emphasis then was slight and short-lived: not finding the court amenable he reverted abruptly to a coercive stance. Orléans faced a dilemma: whether to pursue a policy which he judged in the country's best interests but whose implementation required the exercise of strong central government authority, or to allow that policy to be swept aside by powerful centrifugal forces whose legal justification was to be found in the parlement's registers. While that policy was successful the regent was inclined to pay scant attention to the toothless opposition; subsequently, though he was no more willing to allow the king's authority to be questioned, he rediscovered the need to exercise it in a demonstrably legal framework: hence, for example, his decision to send to the court the March 1720 legislation reducing the rate of interest. Thus Orléans' anger at the court's intransigence and his decision to punish the recalcitrant magistrates by exile reflected not only his authoritarianism, but also his awareness of the necessity to secure the parlement's registration if the enactment relating to the Compagnie des Indes was to have its full effect. His attitude towards the magistrates had been inconsistent but not impolitic.

* * *

During the court's sojourn at Pontoise the issue of Unigenitus came once more to the fore. Throughout 1719 the parlement had continued its battle with the episcopal supporters of the bull of whom Languet, bishop of Soissons, had emerged as the most intractable. The level of acerbity on both sides grew, the parlement going so far as to fine the bishop and threaten the seizure of his property and revenues, until eventually Orléans intervened and forbade the quarrel to be pursued further.[54] He was still working for an accommodation which would satisfy both sides, and by May 1720 about a hundred prelates had indeed signed a body of doctrine interpreting the sense in which the bull's condemnation should be understood. However, the chief of the appellant camp, cardinal de Noailles, was wavering in a characteristic state of indecision, unwilling to confirm his adherence until a royal declaration embodying the explanations had been registered by the parlement. The regent recognized in this matter too that the court's registration would give the greatest possible weight to the compromise, and he also knew that Noailles' support was crucial. He decided, therefore, to send the draft declaration to the magistrates confined in Pontoise.

Orléans had no illusions about the difficulties involved in persuading the parlement to co-operate. The situation had not changed fundamentally since 1714 when the court pointed out that both the bull and its mode of acceptance by the bishops ran counter to the Gallican liberties. The government's hope was that the magistrates would compromise on a form of words, if not on the subsequent interpretation. The declaration was not intended to be a model of clarity. The threat of schism was to be averted by the use of ambiguous and equivocal language: the declaration was to be first and foremost a treaty of peace. The regent was also willing to allow the magistrates to qualify their registration so that it did not prejudice the Gallican liberties, the maxims of the kingdom in the matter of appeals to a future general council, and the jurisdiction of the bishops.[55]

The appellants promptly staged a counter-attack: the four bishops who had initiated the appeal in 1717 formally renewed it, adding a further appeal against the terms of the proposed settlement; and with the faculty of theology, the university of Paris and a number of curés from the same diocese, submitted their appeals to the court. The parlement began its debate on the royal declaration on 2 September and from the outset there was evidence of a strong lobby opposed to registration on the regent's terms.[56] On 7 September Orléans sent one of his secretaries to Pontoise with an ultimatum for the magistrates. They had either to register the declaration in its existing form or return it at once to the regent. The declaration was handed over unregistered and brought back to Paris.

Orléans now decided to adopt a harsh policy towards the court in an attempt to bring an end to the *affaire* Unigenitus. On 23 September the royal declaration was registered in the rival court of the *grand conseil* and letters-patent were issued granting it cognizance over all actions arising from the bull within the parlement's jurisdiction. By this time the magistrates had begun their long autumnal holiday which stretched from 8 September to 12 November, and Orléans took the opportunity of appointing his own *chambre des vacations*, none of whose members was a judge in the parlement. Only Noailles' persistent refusal to adhere to the declaration without parlementaire registration seemed to stand between the magistrates and further punitive measures. Yet even that safeguard proved to be double-edged for Orléans' suspicions grew that the cardinal was in collusion with the magistrates to force his hand.[57] Rumours began to circulate that the regent was on the point of taking vigorous action against the court either by reducing its numbers or by abolishing it altogether. On 4 November Le Blanc, one of Orléans' secretaries of state, warned one of the judges that the parlement was in imminent danger. On 10 November *lettres de cachet* were issued transferring the parlement to Blois where the new judicial year was to commence on 2 December.[58]

This more rigorous exile could be interpreted as the first step in a plan to suppress the parlement altogether, for the distance from the capital would make even the routine administration of justice difficult.[59] Leading members of the court now seeking to persuade the cardinal to publish his pastoral letter approving the declaration were met by what the *procureur-général* described as 'l'indécision si ordinaire de sa Eminence'.[60] At last on 16 November Noailles agreed to publish his Instruction. The order banishing the court to Blois was promptly rescinded; instead the magistrates were ordered to reassemble at Pontoise on 25 November when they would be given a second chance to register the royal declaration.

Since its withdrawal some ten weeks earlier Orléans had maintained a decisive advantage in his exchanges with the parlement and he now awaited the *dénouement* with confidence. Though he had allowed himself to be dissuaded by the first president from imposing further sanctions on leading opponents of Unigenitus within the court, the magistrates had no illusions about his willingness to take further stringent action if they did not conform.[61] They would certainly lose their jurisdiction over the bull if they again refused registration. The royal declaration was, therefore, duly registered, almost unanimously, on 4 December and ordered to be executed with the same conditions as had applied in 1714 and in conformity with the maxims of the kingdom on the authority of the church, on the power and jurisdiction of bishops, on the acceptance of papal bulls, and on appeals to a future council.[62] Immediately afterwards the parlement's jurisdiction over all actions arising out of Unigenitus was restored. Twelve days later, on 16 December, the magistrates received their official recall to Paris, two days after John Law had driven inconspicuously from the city and from the French scene. The juxtaposition of these two events was deliberate. Orléans had promised the first president an honourable return to Paris, an expression taken by the latter to refer to Law's banishment but there was no causal link between them:[63] the System had long been moribund and the reputation for clairvoyance which the magistrates acquired in the light of its collapse was largely unmerited, for their conservative view of economics did not allow them to see the potential in Law's grandiose scheme. Similarly, in the dispute over Unigenitus, the court had been compelled to bow before the regent's authoritarian methods. Yet the magistrates did not return entirely vanquished. The events of 1720 had strengthened the argument that laws of general public importance ought to be registered in the parlement, and had consequently reinforced the court's place at the centre of law-making. In addition the registration of the religious compromise, though it was to Orléans' satisfaction, was not a simple act of obedience: it maintained the parlement's self-respect by the inclusion of certain qualifications on behalf of the Gallican liberties. On the other hand the court in exile had been deprived of part of its jurisdiction, and for several days had lain under the shadow of total extinction. That it had emerged unscathed was due to the good sense of those leading members who appreciated the folly of further resistance before Orléans' unyielding application of the king's authority.

During the last two years of the regency there was comparative peace between Orléans and the parlement. The religious rift had been healed at least temporarily and Law's System, the other great source of friction, had vanished. Besides, the magistrates had no stomach for a further confrontation with a regent totally in command of affairs, especially since the king would reach his majority early in 1723. At the end of the period, therefore, as at the beginning, the parlement concerned itself more with external marks of honour and distinction and less with direct intervention in politics. In August 1721, at a *Te Deum* sung in Notre Dame in thanksgiving for Louis' recovery from illness, the court demanded in vain the pre-eminent place as representing the king's person; in March 1722 when the young infanta of Spain came to Paris as Louis XV's future wife, the magistrates claimed the right to participate in the marriage treaty since the king was still a minor.[64] Several other insignificant skirmishes took place before Louis XV celebrated his thirteenth birthday on 10 February 1723. Twelve days later a *lit de justice* marked the formal ending of the regency.

The relations between the parlement of Paris and the regent exemplify the basic dilemma of French government in the later days of the *ancien régime*. Kingship in France was legitimate in the sense that it was based on law, and that fact reinforced the sovereign's authority even, paradoxically, when it was exercised in defiance of accepted legal norms. There existed, therefore, a tension between the king's power to act and his right to act. As the supreme judicial body in the state whose registers provided a profile of its legal development the parlement had always to seek to limit royal arbitrariness, though by the same token it was bound ultimately to accept the imposition of the king's authority. With the growth of the power of central government, might was tending to oust traditional right though kingship had not lost its aura of legitimacy. Orléans was determined to protect both the absolute power and the legal image of the minor in his charge. He succeeded in handing on to Louis XV a royal reputation still revered and the opportunity to use his authority to reform the state along lines already beckoning during the minority. In particular, a reorganization of the kingdom's financial structure was of primary importance, and Orléans' imaginative support for John Law demonstrated his willingness to grasp the nettle. That particular scheme failed but the fundamental predicament remained: whether root and branch reform could ever be brought to fruition through the imposition of the king's will and in defiance of those very legal precepts upon which his authority was founded.

V

Economics and Finance during
the Regency

The War of the Spanish Succession had left the French crown heavily
in debt, underlining the fact that warfare on that scale was no longer
supportable on the old dynastic basis. The degree of commitment now
required was incompatible with the privileged hierarchical ordering of
society characteristic of the régime of patrimonial kingship. Louis XIV
had partly grasped that the situation was changing without attempting
a fundamental revision of the old order. In inheriting this state of affairs,
Orléans faced the immediate task of restoring order and stability to the
country's finances, as well as the longer-term problem of devising a
financial structure able to cope with the exigencies of the eighteenth
century.

At Louis XIV's death France's financial plight was worse than that
bequeathed by either Richelieu or Mazarin. The war had crushed the
revival in trade and industry which followed the restoration of peace in
1697: nearly two-thirds of its total cost had been obtained by one
expedient or another. These had included the employment of *billets de
monnaie*, first as a temporary measure to be substituted for hard cash
called in for recoinage and then exchanged for the new issue; later this
practice became a habit, an excuse to flood the country with bills which
led to massive inflation and a rapid decline in the value of the paper
currency. Other government contrivances included bi-metallic manipu-
lation of the currency, advances from tax farmers, the creation of new
offices, and forced loans levied on existing *officiers*. Between 1713 and
1715 the controller-general of finance, Desmaretz, pursued a deflationary
policy reducing both commercial activity and the availability of cash.
People began to hoard their money, and with decreasing circulation the
whole country began to feel the debilitating effects of the government's
efforts to counter inflation.[1] John Law's account of the situation inherited
by the regent tells a grim story of universal ruin, of the failure to culti-
vate the land, of farms crumbling for the lack of necessary repairs,

peasants badly nourished and clothed, indebted to the king, to their *seigneur*, to the usurers of the towns and villages; of manufacture coming to a halt, artisans without work, and merchants going bankrupt; of office-holders of robe and sword deprived of the payments owing on their investments; of troops mutinous over the lack of subsistence; of a multiplicity of debts between king and people and between subjects; and, most damaging of all, of fears that the decline was irreversible.[2]

Orléans was already acquainted with Law when the regency began and he found the latter's bold ideas for solving France's economic ills attractive. However, the weakness of his position dictated that he had to move cautiously at first in this as in every other sphere. Yet he did take Law's advice against declaring the state bankrupt. The Scotsman believed that such a course of action would have alienated and ruined a good many subjects, seriously damaged trade and manufacture and encouraged a reversion to subsistence cultivation.[3] Apart from this minor success, Law still awaited the opportunity to put his more elaborate schemes into effect.

Meanwhile Orléans concentrated on paying off the troops and the arrears of *rentes*. He could not risk an untrustworthy army nor did he wish to antagonize his new allies in the parlement, many of them substantial *rentiers*. So long as he eschewed Law's more radical solution he was forced to seek to improve the existing financial machinery as the only means of alleviating his government's difficulties, an approach successfully adopted by Colbert in the previous century. He was, for example, unhappy about the role of the collectors-general, each of whom was ultimately responsible for collecting the *taille* in his *généralité*. Because of these officers' practice of using government money raised locally to meet local or personal claims before dispatching the residue to the treasury in their area, it was very difficult to keep accurate and up-to-date accounts of the royal revenue available from the *généralités*. Orléans discussed with the council for finance the possibility of removing the collectors-general altogether and having all the local funds put straight into the royal treasury. This alternative was debated in the council on two successive days but on the grounds that it might alarm the people the decision was taken not to proceed with such a draconian measure as being something to be avoided in the first uncertain days of a regency.[4] Nevertheless, Orléans was determined to find a more effective means of establishing what funds were being deposited or not being deposited in the king's treasury. In June 1716 he approved a declaration elaborated by the duke de Noailles, president of the finance council, which set up a formal procedure to that end. The collectors-general were instructed to keep a daily record of the funds deposited in the treasury of each *généralité*. The provincial intendants were charged with seeing that copies of these records were regularly sent to Paris and with reporting any collector-general who was not adequately fulfilling his responsibilities. Once the money had been deposited it could not be withdrawn, except with the signed approval of the regent who had become the kingdom's sole *ordonnateur* in September 1715. An attempt was also made to distinguish between the various types of taxes being received and to establish how far payments were in arrears. Intendants were forbidden to raise taxes for military purposes simply on the authority of ministerial letters, a practice introduced by Louvois: henceforth such taxes were to be authorized by formal decrees which would indicate their precise purpose. The council for finance was instructed to work towards an up-dating of accounts so that an accurate picture of the current financial state of the country could be readily obtained. By 1717 Orléans was certainly better informed of the receipts and expenses connected with the various forms of direct taxation while the nation's accounts seemed likely to be up-to-date by January 1718.[5] Herbert Luthy has characterized the work of these opening years of the regency as representing 'un effort perseverant, et non sans succès, de remettre en ordre et en marche la machine déréglée de l'administration financière telle que le règne de Louis XIV l'avait léguée'.[6]

However, despite the increase in central government control represented by these reforms in financial administration the actual situation remained parlous. The various expedients undertaken – which included the auditing of the vast number of state bills and the attack in the *chambre de justice* on the financiers who had grown rich in exploiting government need – achieved little beyond raising the level of public vituperation against the unfortunate *traitants*.[7] Thus when Noailles made an important, detailed report to the regency council on 19 and 26 June 1717 he was not optimistic.[8] It was true that state borrowing had ceased, a number of debts had been paid off, expenses reduced and revenues increased. But that improvement simply followed the cessation of hostilities and in no way portended a permanent solution to the government's state of chronic insolvency. Noailles acknowledged the persistence of extraordinary taxation and an immense capital debt, and furthermore the government's inability in the face of an emergency to increase either. He conceded that the country remained vulnerable in the existing financial circumstances, and offered six general headings under which there was need for progress. First he called for proper procedures to be established in every area of state finance: there was still too much dilatoriness in collecting the revenue, and expenses did not wait upon the receipts. This was as important as augmenting the income and diminishing expenses, which were the next two points on Noailles' list; and he emphasized that the former could not be accomplished by establishing new taxes. Fourth came the need to re-establish trade and a sound currency, fifth, to relieve the people's fiscal burden and finally, to free the state of its debts. Here, quite simply, was a catalogue of basic prerequisites for a healthy economy; and the fact that they were all still lacking after almost two years suggested that a less conventional approach was now worth serious consideration. In fact two months before Noailles made his report to the regency council, Law's bank had been made solidary with the state (April 1717) and two months after (August 1717) the Mississippi Company was founded: the bold experiment of the System was already under way.

Another of Orléans' reforming endeavours during the early years of the regency was the introduction of a graduated *taille*, the *taille tarifée* or *proportionnelle*. The initiative was taken by the duke de Noailles and his project was approved by the regency council in October 1716.[9] The idea was not original: in 1675 the Sieur de Bresson, sometime assistant to the secretary of state for foreign affairs, had proposed a new, all-embracing, graduated tax, the *droit royal*, to be paid by all the non-privileged classes.[10] Noailles' proposal related only to the *taille* but he shared with Bresson the principle of payment according to means. It was a genuinely reforming measure even though there was no challenge as yet to the exemptions of the privileged groups. The intention was to introduce some rationality into tax-collecting so that the suffering of those subject to serious economic depression might be alleviated, the demands on the more affluent stabilized, and the collection of royal taxation facilitated. Boisguillebert's belief that agricultural prosperity was the key to the country's wealth was at the root of this measure which sought to give a boost to the circulation of money by providing greater incentives for production. An anonymous correspondent explained how he had conducted a pilot experiment on his own estate in 1716. Firstly, on the premise that the new method of collection would bring in ample funds the collectors in the parish concerned were asked not to demand expenses in advance. Then, in the presence of the local *curé*, the collectors and several of the leading residents, the writer took the most recent *taille* roll and divided the inhabitants according to property into three classes, the wealthiest, a middle group and the least well-off. It was then calculated that a tax of 30, 20 and 10 sous per acre when applied to each of these classes respectively would provide an adequate yield. A similar tripartite division and assessment was then carried out for day-labourers.[11]

Although theoretically there were certainly advantages to be gained for government and governed from the graduated *taille*, the practical problems were considerable as the above-mentioned scheme implies. The wealthier elements in the rural population would not willingly disclose their assets and the less wealthy might prefer not to prosper to the extent of being moved to a higher tax grade. Additionally the whole exercise required a level of literacy and expertise on the part of both the tax-paying population and the tax-collectors which was lacking. The idea was too sophisticated for its time, and the pilot scheme was much simpler than the *taille tarifée* actually adopted. There were some successes – in the *généralité* of Paris for example – but overall the expectations of its supporters were not realized.

In January 1718 Orléans approved a regency council decree inaugurating the *dîme royal*, another experiment intended to procure a more realistic, less arbitrary tax assessment and, therefore, a better return for the government, at the same time restoring economic vigour to the countryside. It was a much watered-down version of Vauban's famous project, for whereas the latter envisaged a single, though complex tax on privileged and non-privileged alike, this scheme, which was confined to Niort and La Rochelle, attempted simply to replace the *taille réelle* by a tithe on the produce of the land. The advantage of this measure, which was highly favoured by Orléans himself, over the *taille proportionnelle* was that it encouraged farmers to increase their productivity without the risk of translation into a higher taxation category. However, it threatened to be even more complex to administer. It enjoyed some success at Niort but failed at La Rochelle; by the end of the regency the experiment had been abandoned.[12]

Unsuccessful with these new initiatives, the regent did what he could to improve the standard of efficiency and the degree of rationalization in tax-collection. In November 1717 letters were sent out to the inspectors of finance instructing them to pick out some of the parishes from those *élections* most in arrears with their payments, and see whether the rules were being properly observed. In December 1718 a circular to the same inspectors of finance required them to see that by 20 January 1719 the collectors of the *taille* under their supervision forwarded to the central treasury in each *généralité* all the revenues amassed by them up to the 13th of that month: Orléans wanted the collectors-general to present their accounts for the second half of 1718 during the first ten days of February 1719. A year earlier the intendant at Poitiers was ordered to look into an anomaly in the assessment of the *taille* in the *élection* of Thouars where the parish of Vaudelinay was scheduled to raise 3,000 *livres* from a total population of 147 including 33 poor widows and many day-labourers. Yet the nearby parishes of Puy Notre-Dame with a population of 500 and Saint-Hilaire with a population of 130 had to pay only 4,800 or 4,900 *livres* respectively. Not surprisingly there was a residential drift to one or other of these more generously assessed parishes which made life difficult for the collectors of Vaudelinay. They brought the case to the regent's attention and he ordered the intendants of Poitiers and Tours (the latter's area of jurisdiction covering the two favoured parishes) to amend this disproportionate rating.[13]

Towards the end of the regency, in March 1722, Orléans made another major effort to regulate and systematize the flow of government receipts and expenses, this time taking into account the yield from taxes farmed out to financiers, the farmers-general, as well as the *taille*. These various sources of income were not paid in simultaneously nor did the periods of greatest state expenditure in the year necessarily coincide with the times of largest tax receipts. It was worth examining in detail, therefore, the timing of the annual influx and outflow of revenue to discover the extent to which supply and demand could be matched up. The efficiency of the government's financial machinery would be improved in proportion to the degree of correlation achieved. Orléans, who jealously guarded his role as *ordonnateur*, had already for some time been moving along these lines. Three months before the expiry of each year he called for a projection of the following year's income and then drew up a preliminary statement of distribution, assigning various royal revenues to meet various expenses. In issuing particular lists during the ensuing year, he was careful to adhere to the pattern of this original blueprint. However, although Orléans had been scrupulous in the maintenance and improvement of the central government's fiscal records, he had difficulty in checking whether the funds paid out by the government reached their intended destination. He fought to overcome this problem by careful monitoring. His regular authorization lists included instructions about the time in which payment was to be completed as well as detailing the source from which it was to be taken. Further payments would be withheld if the regent was not satisfied with the use to which the first had been put. In addition, payment was to be in funds already collected into the treasury, not in bills of credit. It was the particular charge of the intendants to see that the money owing from the *taille* was paid in when it was due; they were also responsible for the dispatch from the central treasury of their *généralité* on the 10th, 20th and 30th of each month of a statement of accounts indicating the balance at the time of the previous statement, the details of revenues brought in by each collector of the *taille*, and the precise number and dates of payments made in accordance with the regent's orders. A similar statement was required at the same ten-day intervals from the collectors responsible for gathering the proceeds due from the tax-farmers. This reform called for a fairly elaborate procedure under a centralized committee of the regency council. This committee received for approval the ten-day statements and with them proposals for withdrawals from one fund or the other; the proposals relating to the tax-farmers and to the *taille* were to be supervised separately. Similarly two distinct groups, one composed of collectors-general and the other of farmers-general, were appointed to report to the central committee on what had in fact happened to the funds earmarked for expenditure. If the committee was not satisfied it was empowered to summon any of the other collectors- or farmers-general to answer its questions.

However, like most bureaucratic developments under the *ancien régime*, it did not establish a clear chain of command. The relationship between the controller-general of finance, the central committee and the intendants was obscure; and all three depended heavily upon the personal initiative of Orléans himself. The regent supervised the drawing up of a central register which recorded the funds leaving the royal treasury, their intended use and their eventual destination. An anonymous memorandum of this time emphasized the financial system's dependence upon Orléans' careful and constant scrutiny of the claims for expenditure, the funds from which they were to be met, and the time in which payment was to be made. Only by such close control could the regent prevent a secretary of state or the controller-general from distributing funds 'à sa fantaisie'.[14]

Thus at the very end of the regency Orléans made significant progress in regulating the inflow and outflow of the royal revenues, so that the latter would be in cash and not in bills of credit, in monitoring the claims for expenditure made on the government, and in pursuing the authorized payments to their ultimate destination. This injection of method with its consequent embryonic bureaucracy increased the efficiency of the government's financial machine, and brought that much closer the concept of the overriding needs of the impersonal state. Yet Orléans' personal commitment remained the key to the whole enterprise, an indication of the possibilities then existing in France for a régime of enlightened absolutism.

However, in financial and economic affairs the regency is most closely associated with the ideas and projects of John Law. Law's economic theories were not new; and their practical application proved so disastrous that one might assume that they were also misguided. In fact the spectacular collapse of the System has served to obscure the importance of his achievement and the significant implications of his reforms. Though among influential government servants of the *ancien régime* he was the most radical, historians have so far failed to recognize his major role, preferring, like many of the Scotsman's contemporaries, to concentrate on the inadequacies of his economic theory or on the frenzied scenes in the rue Quincampoix. In the words of one observer he was 'one of those monsters which from time to time appear in human form so as to prey upon men and set themselves up as the scourges and public tormentors of nations'; and of another: 'This traffic in paper, which was indeed a snare and a chimera, has ruined the kingdom more than all the wars of Louis XIV'.[15] Such contemporary views help to explain the extent of the reaction following his downfall (and he is an important figure in subsequent French financial history for that negative reason alone); but they tell us nothing of the positive worth of his economic ideas nor of how close the government came under his influence to adopting a new and revolutionary political direction.

Law grew up in financial circles in Edinburgh, where his father was a goldsmith. He moved down to London in 1691 at the age of twenty and was still there in 1694 when the Bank of England was established. In debt and imprisoned for killing an opponent in a duel, he escaped to Amsterdam – home of another famous bank – in 1695 before eventually returning to Scotland. Although influenced by the Dutch and Italian examples – Law also investigated the Casa di San Giorgio in Genoa – the Bank of England, the only genuine 'banque d'émission' issuing bank-notes properly so-called, was his chief source of financial inspiration. And in the last years of Louis XIV's reign, when the Grand Alliance was putting the French armies to the sword, the political significance of the bank's role was becoming clear.

Law's interest in the use of paper money was evident from his earliest writings, though he preferred to base its value upon land rather than on precious metals. In this emphasis, upon agricultural rather than industrial production, he reflected the writings of Boisguillebert who in his *Détail de la France* of 1695 asserted that:

> ... the whole basis and foundation of all Europe's riches are grain, wine, salt and cloth which are to be found in abundance in France; and everything else may only be procured in proportion to the surplus available in those commodities. Therefore in dividing all wealth in France into two kinds, landed

property and that derived from industry, [one may observe that] the latter, which involves three times the number of people, increases or diminishes in proportion to the [productivity of the] former.[16]

Law accepted the basic premise that the foundation of a country's wealth depended upon the health of its agriculture rather than upon the amount of gold and silver stored in its treasury. He maintained too that land was not subject to the fluctuations in value which affected precious metals: its amount could not be increased, the demands for it were un- likely to diminish, and the products which it yielded could not be obtained in any other way. At first, therefore, Law proposed that land and not gold or silver should be the guarantor of paper money though he subsequently changed his stance and substituted bullion.[17] He shared another belief with Boisguillebert, namely that the circulation of money was far more important in enriching a country than the acquisition of capital, so that the more money in circulation the more flourishing would the agricultural base become and, therefore, the overall wealth of the country would grow. There was a crucial time-lag implied, how- ever, in this argument, the presumption being that an injection of paper money to a value in excess of the country's wealth would act as a catalyst and would in time stimulate the production of new wealth which, when added to existing resources, would truly reflect the amount of money in circulation. The money would be in the form of credit (bank-notes) and the whole inflationary mechanism would presumably be subjected to periodic pump-priming operations. It is not difficult to appreciate the ingenuity of the proposed mechanism nor its vulnerability should the timing go awry. One implication in particular deserves to be noted: new wealth in the form of gold and silver could only be acquired as a result of foreign trade; in the meantime, bank-notes would have to be conceived of and accepted as genuine money.[18]

These were the basic tenets of Law's economic theory, variously expounded in his writings and put into practice during Orléans' regency. In 1707, in a memorandum devoted to the proposition that paper money could be more valuable than gold and silver, he wrote:

> As it is in the interest of the king, landowners and people that the land should be used to encourage the employment of [paper] money, it rests with His Majesty and with the landowners to introduce this new currency into trade and other payment transactions without any constraints, and to exclude gold and silver coin by in future accepting payment of leases and other contracted debts in this new currency. The rest of the people would then avail themselves of it because it would not be possible to purchase the fruits of the earth with

gold and silver coin. The tenant-farmer will be obliged to exchange his produce for the money in which he has contracted to pay his lord and with which he has to acquit the *taille* or other dues owing to His Majesty. The money in which the landowners contract to be paid will become the money in which other contracts are authorized and the means through which trade is conducted. The manufacturer and the craftsman will sell their work to obtain this money, requiring it to buy their materials and to pay their workers who will themselves prefer this [paper] money to purchase the wherewithal to live. The rents of houses etc. will be paid with this money, because those who live off their rents are fed and clothed from the produce of the country and the people's toil. Similarly, manufacturing products will be bought with this new money.[19]

In his *Mémoire sur les Banques* of July 1715 Law indicated his belief that the abundant circulation of money in the state would improve the income of the king and the landowners, augment trade and industry, increase the population, and add wealth and power to the state. In the same month he addressed a letter to the controller-general, Desmaretz, in which he elaborated his doctrine of beneficent inflation:

> It is obvious that as money becomes more abundant in a State prices and incomes rise proportionately both as regards land, houses and other forms of real estate, and industry, trade and manufacture, because the value of everything depends upon the relationship between quantity and demand; with money becoming more plentiful and the amount of land remaining unchanged, the demand for land would grow, and more money would be paid for the same quantity of land. Equally, the fruits or produce of the land would be dearer, and the tenant-farmer better placed to pay his debts to the king and to the lord who owned the land, than if the sum total of money had remained unchanged.[20]

It has been remarked recently that Law's belief that the injection of money would stimulate the economy was not far removed from that of John Maynard Keynes; though understandably the latter paid more attention than Law to the related significance of full employment.[21]

Finally, in the *Idée Générale du Nouveau Système des Finances* (1720), John Law emphasized repeatedly the need to acknowledge paper money as true currency, although it did not precisely reflect the country's assets in terms of bullion. As the annual interest gave real value to the contracts of *rentes* so the immense profits emanating from domestic and foreign trade assured the value of paper money. He went further in asserting that:

> The State could never become bankrupt even if all the specie were to be forfeited; for just as the total loss of all precious metals would not destroy the

true value of the land and its products, so the lack of specie would not destroy the value of a paper-money which has this same land and its products for its surety.[22]

Once more, however, the idea of the land as the guarantor and producer of wealth is confused with the role of bullion by which that wealth may be measured; a confusion compounded by the substitution of paper money for precious metals.

Such economic theories bore important political implications, and indeed in his later writings Law made his radical views explicit. In particular his doctrines assumed a significant increase both in the state's interventionist role and in the subjects' reciprocal obligations. Since everybody's co-operation was needed in the effort to achieve national prosperity it was unreasonable, for example, to prohibit noble participation in trade. Equally the government must be in a position to regulate trade, 'to anticipate and put a stop to those branches of trade which do not produce profits for the State and the merchants; like the faithful shepherd it must be careful to prevent its flock from straying.' Since every member of the community had an obligation to contribute to the public good the state had to intervene if necessary to enforce that obligation upon those who resisted:

> As defiance grows it becomes necessary to resort to sanctions in order to persuade people to contribute to their own happiness and to make them perceive that if land, merchandise and commodities belong to them in such a fashion that sovereigns may not appropriate them to themselves without committing an injustice which sooner or later would entail the destruction of their power, so the money which causes goods to circulate and conveys them successively to every member of the State, belongs to the King and never to any citizen or individual; he may have only the use of it. This use is by means of circulation and since circulation gives life to the body politic, whoever halts it is guilty of parricide; anybody who saves his money without making use of it and thus puts a stop to the profit which proceeds from its circulation is a bad citizen and in such a case the sovereign can compel him to employ his money in the interests of the State. . . . As he can compel the indolent landowner to cultivate land which has been allowed to fall into neglect.[23]

In his halting French Law identified the chief obstacle confronting the successful implementation of his System: the need to fit it into an authoritarian political setting. It was unthinkable that traders should be free to furnish powder and shot to their enemies, as the Dutch were; yet was not the financial well-being of both the Dutch and the English closely linked with their political systems? In this context Louis Blanc's description of the Scotsman as an early state socialist carries conviction and serves to underline the hazards facing Law in seeking to introduce a subtle and complex credit structure into the world of divine-right absolute monarchy, where a different kind of public confidence was demanded.[24]

Law owed a good deal of his thinking to a Frenchman, Pottier de la Hestroye, an admiralty official at Dunkirk whose *Mémoires Touchant le Commerce de la France et les Moiens de le Restablir* was written in June 1700. Law borrowed extensively and verbatim from this work for one of his own publications, a memoir of 1715.[25] Pottier's concern was to increase the crown's effective control over all areas of the country's economic life by establishing intendants of commerce in all provinces to keep the central government closely informed of every aspect of commercial activity and to enable it to direct a national programme. He believed like Law that the state would flourish when all the people made their contribution and thus ensured the constant circulation of money.

> The gold and silver which a state must possess . . . should be in the hands of every subject without distinction. It is not even wise politics to have subjects who think only of accumulating great savings; it distinguishes individuals too greatly and renders them idle and idleness is almost always accompanied by vices pernicious to the state and to the authority of the sovereign. . . . All subjects must work; in the state everyone must be occupied. . . . The poor by hand and the rich by their purse, [spending] so as to make others work.

Pottier's concept of the state was an interesting one. 'The state is, properly speaking, a machine,' he maintained, 'the movements of which although different must be regulated without interruption; we cannot interfere with the movements without running the risk of destroying the state.' Or again, speaking of commercial intercourse, 'we must see it as the movements of wheels in a clock which must follow each other continually.' This view of the state as possessing a rationale which enabled it to continue to function smoothly and efficiently under the benevolent direction of the government instead of the Deity foreshadowed the mechanistic ideas of the German cameralists and the political doctrine of enlightened absolutism. The latter implied the subjugation of every private interest to that of the secular, materialist-orientated state, as expressed by the ruler, its chief servant. Under such a régime there would be no room for illogicality and inefficiency; logic and efficiency would for the first time have become the determining factors in *ancien régime* government.

John Law accepted the political implications of such ideas and in June 1719 wrote his *Mémoire sur le Denier Royal*, incorporating the most radical set of observations and proposals so far enunciated by an influential government figure under the *ancien régime*.[26] His argument revolved around two themes: the priority of the state's needs and the virtues of a rational, non-arbitrary approach to taxation. The serious business of balancing the country's finances should depend on a set of rules and principles, and the first general rule of sound financial administration was that taxes should be levied universally; exemptions and privileges were abuses contrary to the well-being of the state. A second rule was that taxes should be levied in proportion to the individual's ability to pay. It was necessary, therefore, to abolish the *taille*, the *capitation*, the *aides* and *gabelle*, and the various customs dues, replacing them with a single tax on goods. This standard tax would prove no more onerous to one group than to another since all would contribute at the same rate and, therefore, in proportion to their assets. Exemptions would be granted only to the very poor and to industry. In this way the king would exercise his undoubted right to impose whatever taxes he deemed necessary and to suppress those which he did not consider to be so. He would also thereby offer that universal incentive to work which Law considered to be the first prerequisite for a flourishing state.

In that last connection he was quick to point out that his single tax system would be simple to administer. It would not be necessary to employ the current army of some 40,000 tax-officials, the vast majority of whom could be re-employed in more profitable ways in trade or industry or on the land. In an unusually fierce attack upon them he permitted himself the following dialogue:

> What will become of the forty thousand men who are employed today on the King's business, who owe their own subsistence and that of their families to it? *Reply:* What will become of the rats which live in my granary if I remove the grain in order to store it in a better and more secure place?

His summing up of the reforms which he envisaged and believed necessary represented nothing less than the dismantling of the *ancien régime*:

> Immunities, privileges and exemptions must be regarded as abuses which cannot be abolished too soon. Clergymen, nobles or commoners [*roturiers*], we are all equally the subjects of the same King; it is against the essence of being a subject to claim to be distinguished from the rest by the privilege of not paying tribute to the Prince. What I am stating about comparisons between subjects applies equally to the relationship between provinces; in particular the clergy and nobility, as the two premier orders of the Kingdom, must seek to distinguish themselves by their eagerness to contribute to the expenses of

the State rather than by immunities and exemptions. Nothing is more important for the good order of a Kingdom than uniformity and it is to be wished that it may reign in the law and in taxation.

Here was an end to the régime of complementary estates or orders presided over by a king dedicated to the task of preserving the distinguishing characteristics of each; instead Law was formulating a doctrine of the corporate state in which all the subjects served without discrimination the dictates of the sovereign prince. To the objection that such a system was new and threatened to overturn the customs of the kingdom he retorted defiantly that novelty and tradition were equally irrelevant: the only significant question was whether it profited the king and the people.

The boldness of John Law's projects had undoubtedly intrigued Orléans for some time and, even before his elevation to the office of regent, it had seemed likely that the Scotsman would come to exercise an important influence on fiscal matters. Orléans and Law had first met in Paris in the late 1690s; the financier was there again in 1707, and in 1714 he acquired a house in the place Louis-le-Grand.*[27] It was significant that in January 1715 George I's newly appointed envoy-extraordinary to France, lord Stair, chose to receive Law before anybody else.[28] When he came to power, however, the regent was in no position to implement the untried and controversial ideas of a foreigner and, as we have seen, he settled at first for more conventional remedies. Yet he accepted many of Law's arguments, including the desirability of establishing credit and the prior need to create confidence. Law's suggestion to meet both requirements was that a bank should be established. The proposal was not generally well received though the duke de Noailles, who would later lose favour because of his opposition to Law, was not opposed to the setting up of Law's private bank, the *banque générale*, in May 1716. Indeed he spoke enthusiastically of the improved prospects brought about by the bank in his report to the regency council in June 1717:

> Finally, it appears that in all its workings so far the bank has shown itself to have no other designs than the general well-being of the kingdom and of trade, as well as to provide convenience and aid to individuals; and since in fact its interest cannot be separated from that of the State, far from this institution having any ill consequences it can indeed be said that there is every expectation that the bank will be successful and profitable.

At the same time he acknowledged that it had been the regent himself who had first foreseen the advantages to be gained.[29]

* Now the place Vendôme.

The Scotman's ambitions did not end there and, now that Orléans was prepared to give him firmer backing, he began to elaborate his grand design. In October 1716 he had persuaded the regent to issue a council decree ordering his tax officials in Paris to deal in bank-notes; in April 1717 the payment of taxes by bank-note was authorized; and by August of that year, still with the active collaboration of Noailles, Law was engaged in founding the Mississippi Company or the Compagnie de l'Occident to exploit the French colony of Louisiana. This venture ran into financial difficulties almost at once, and then into political difficulties with the parlement of Paris and with Noailles himself who began to see something of Law's fundamental purpose: the Mississippi Company was to be the first stage of a great national enterprise culminating in the establishment of a single banking and trading organization responsible for every aspect of government finance, and intended to enrich both shareholders and the nation at large. This was far more than had been in Noailles' mind in August 1717 when he had made his formal proposals to the regency council for the establishment of a trading company.[30] But Orléans was now solidly behind John Law, and at the end of January 1718 Noailles was dismissed and his office given to the marquis d'Argenson. The regent still preferred the Scotsman's policies to be implemented by a Frenchman for the foreigner was arousing a good deal of jealousy and animosity in high places. Law was not yet the complete master of the country's economic strategy; indeed d'Argenson, who had no talent for financial affairs, took his new job more seriously than Orléans had intended, even going so far as to appear in his carriage in the evenings with a lighted candle and papers in his hand to demonstrate the length of his working day! It was d'Argenson and not Law who proposed the controversial devaluation of May 1718, and though the latter accepted the measure he did not support it.[31] D'Argenson, like Noailles before him, began to turn against Law; but the financier's position was assured by Orléans' successful negotiation of the Quadruple Alliance and his *coup de force* against the troublesome parlement of Paris and his old rival, the duke du Maine, all of which took place in August 1718. By the beginning of September the regent was in a stronger position than ever before to prosecute Law's grandiose scheme.

The Compagnie de l'Occident had had mixed success in attracting shareholders, and Orléans decided in October to give it a sounder financial base than its so far limited overseas trade could provide by allowing it to take over the tobacco tax-farm. In December it acquired the Senegal Company, and in the same month Law's general bank became a royal one, *the* state bank owned exclusively by the sovereign.

Henceforth its issues would not depend upon the amount of cash deposited but upon council decrees, and its notes, equivalent to *livres tournois*, would presumably be subject similarly to devaluation.

Law was now making significant progress towards achieving his ambition of a vast monopolistic commercial empire, a company indistinguishable in economic and financial terms from the state itself. In May the East India and China Companies were absorbed into the Compagnie de l'Occident, in June those of Africa and Cap Nègre and in September the Saint-Domingo Company: thus the newly styled Compagnie des Indes had removed all its colonial trading rivals. Yet that was only a part of the Scotman's ambitions; he also wanted his company to play a decisive domestic role, by taking over the national debt and the collection of all the royal revenues. Initially, however, he faced a liquidity problem. Although the royal bank was free to print money as it wished, Law had first to overcome the opposition of the so-called Anti-System supported by d'Argenson. This was the syndicate of financiers responsible for the collection of indirect taxes. In the course of their work these influential tax-farmers acquired a considerable quantity of royal bank-notes which they could trade in at any time, demanding cash in return. Law, therefore, could not risk allowing the bank to print too many notes above the value of its cash holding. Orléans alleviated the problem of reserve funds in July 1719 by an ordinance granting the Scotsman the sole right to coin money. Then in the following month Law bought out his rivals and the Compagnie des Indes took over their tax-raising responsibilities. In return it took over the national debt, buying out the *rentes* and offering the *rentiers* company shares as an alternative investment, initially at the same rate of interest, 4 per cent. Finally, in October, the company was also charged with the task of raising direct taxes. One last adjustment was necessary to complete this ambitious System. In February 1720 the bank and the company were united, thus bringing into being what has been called an 'economic monster': a commercial company with a monopoly of maritime and colonial trade which was also a monopoly bank of issue empowered to raise taxes, to coin and print money.[32]

During 1719 and in the early months of 1720 Law's reputation grew along with the value of his company's shares, and on 5 January 1720 he was at last made controller-general of finance. In order to raise the capital necessary to drive the great financial machine he steadily increased the number of shares available for investors. In May 1719 an issue of 50,000 shares worth 500 *livres* each but actually to be sold at 550 *livres*, was announced; in July another 50,000 were made available which with an equivalent premium cost the investor 1,000 *livres* per share. Between September and October three more substantial issues were made, each of 300,000 shares sold at 5,000 *livres*. In order to make more money available for the purchase of these increasingly expensive shares and to bridge the gap still existing between the company's assets and liabilities, the bank increased the amount of paper money in circulation. From 1,000 million *livres* at the end of 1719 the issue rose to 1,200 million by March 1720, 2,700 million by May and ultimately to more than 3,000 million just before the System began to disintegrate. In January 1720 shares with a face value of 500 *livres* were selling for 18,000 *livres*.[33]

In this period of roaring inflation speculators abounded, and hard cash accumulated in the bank in exchange for a shoal of paper money with which to buy the company's shares. Besides, the public was convinced that it was a sounder policy to trade in notes, which, according to the council decree of April 1719, would not be subject to devaluation.[34] Thus the gap between the face value of the paper currency and the gold and silver reserves in the bank widened alarmingly and the crucial question of public confidence loomed. According to Law's theory the company's exploitation of its colonial monopoly would produce the wealth which, in the form of the dividends paid to its shareholders, would offer security *a posteriori* for the additional paper money. Such a delicate mechanism required time and a calm atmosphere in which to function. The frenetic activity around the rue Quincampoix had already destroyed the latter and threatened to limit the former.

Prices could not continue spiralling indefinitely and, as soon as speculators began to sell their paper holdings in return for bullion, the System appeared to be doomed. This process began towards the end of 1719 and gathered pace thereafter. In an effort to contain the disintegrative forces at work, Law resorted to force. A decree of 27 February 1720 forbade the holding of specie to a value of more than 500 *livres*: the bank's inspectors were authorized to search private houses and confiscate the gold and silver coins found there, and large fines were imposed on the culprits. As a means of inspiring confidence in paper money, the measure was predictably counter-productive.[35] Then in March Law opened an office at the bank for the buying and selling of shares in unlimited quantities at the fixed rate of 9,000 *livres*. Despite this 'pegging' of the price to check the rapid and demoralizing decline, sales greatly exceeded purchases in the new office so that the inflationary situation was exacerbated by the large number of additional bank-notes thus brought into circulation.[36] In the same month the controller-general was forced to introduce the measure reducing the interest rate payable upon the company's shares from 4 per cent to 2 per cent. The situation showed no sign of improving, however, and eventually Law decided to meet the crisis with a policy of massive deflation. On 21 May he had a decree published which ordered a staggered 50 per cent devaluation of both the royal bank-notes and the shares of the Compagnie des Indes.

This decision opened the flood-gates of protest and threatened to undermine the regent's government. In the words of Saint-Simon, 'There was a most violent disturbance. Every rich man thought himself irretrievably ruined, either immediately or in the not so distant future; every poor man saw himself beggared.'[37] Orléans sent a detachment of the Swiss guard to mount a twenty-four-hour watch around Law's house. At the same time he dismissed Law from the office of controller-general of finance so that his formal overlordship of the country's economy had only lasted for a little over four months. Orléans himself was shaken by the furious reaction provoked by the decree of 21 May and regretfully decided that it would have to be repealed; remarking that 'one pillar could not turn the current's direction'.[38] On 27 May he had another decree published which in theory restored the situation to that obtaining before the 21st. In fact public confidence was now totally lost and it was beyond the power of legislation to restore it.[39]

Following Law's dismissal responsibility for the state's finances was put into the hands of a commission. Far from being discarded by the regent, however, Law was appointed councillor of state, intendant-general of commerce and director of the bank, and it was his rival d'Argenson who was disgraced, on 7 June. The chancellor, d'Aguesseau, was restored to favour in order to contribute to the revival of public confidence in the government, a revival unlikely to be dramatic while the Scotsman retained his great influence at the heart of affairs. Law's policy now was to impose stringent restrictions on the circulation of paper money. The number of shares was reduced to 200,000; the *rentes* were re-established and the interest rate re-set at 4 per cent; and in return for guaranteeing to withdraw 600 million *livres* over a twelve-month period the Compagnie des Indes was to be given a perpetual charter. All this proved to be of no avail; the lack of gold and silver caused the bank to close its doors and by mid-July the parlement was again demanding Law's dismissal.

The mood in the streets of the capital was also becoming increasingly ugly. In the early hours of 17 July thousands gathered outside the entrance to the Palais Mazarin – now the Bibliothèque Nationale – which was the headquarters of the Compagnie des Indes. Some sixteen people died in the crush and these deaths incensed the crowd. Three of the corpses were carried to the Palais-Royal. There Orléans remained out of sight; and the mob did not carry out its threat to set fire to the palace in order to accelerate his appearance. Law's person, on the other hand, seemed to be in real danger. Though he reached the safety of the Palais-Royal, where he stayed for the next month, his coach was set upon and destroyed and his coachman badly injured.[40] News of this episode, when related to the parlement by the first president, drew great applause from the company, causing one serious-minded magistrate to record that on this occasion, 'the parlement lost the gravity which ought to accompany all its decisions and . . . the first president confirmed the universal opinion that his standards were considerably lowered.'[41] Undoubtedly the magistrates' undisguised hostility towards Law contributed to the regent's decision on the following day to exile the court.

A month later, on 15 August, a regency council decree announced that bank-notes with a face value of 10,000 *livres* would lose their currency on 1 October; while those valued at 100 *livres* and 10 *livres* would become worthless on 1 May 1721. This decision marked the final official repudiation of Law's ingenious enterprise, as the barrister Mathieu Marais observed, adding his own censorious gloss: 'Thus ends the system of paper money, which has enriched a thousand beggars and impoverished a hundred thousand honest men.'[42] On 15 September a further decree warned that from 1 November no payment would be considered valid if more than half the debt was paid in bank-notes; and with immediate effect the value of all current accounts in the bank was to be reduced by three-quarters. On 10 October much of the previous legislation was telescoped with the decision that from 1 November bank-notes could not be given or received in any sort of financial transaction: the young Voltaire sarcastically remarked that paper money was being reduced to its intrinsic value.[43]

Though the bank crashed the Compagnie des Indes was revived and would later play a vital part in French colonial commerce. For a time Law himself survived the venom of the Parisian populace until the reconciliation between the regent and the exiled parlement effectively sealed his fate. On Law's advice Orléans decided to appoint Le Pelletier de la Houssaye as controller-general, and one of the latter's first suggestions, resisted by the regent, was that the Scotsman should be sent to the Bastille, a view shared by many including d'Aguesseau, Villeroy and Villars.[44] However, he was to escape that fate thanks to the connivance of the regent himself and of the duke de Bourbon. The latter's mistress, the marquise de Prie, provided her post-chaise, the duke himself teams of fresh horses and the regent a passport. John Law left Paris on

14 December 1720, travelling first to Brussels and then into Germany and Italy. After a brief return to England in 1721, he settled finally in Venice where he died in 1729.

Orléans' refusal to sacrifice his friend during the death-throes of the System was characteristic, though not as disinterested as might at first appear. Early in the new year of 1721 the regent confessed at a meeting of the regency council that Law had considerably exceeded the permitted number of bank-notes in circulation, and that in order to protect him Orléans had issued back-dated council decrees authorizing the additional printing. Ironically this further indication of the regent's steadfast support for the Scotsman could have proved damaging to Orléans if discovered, making it that much more desirable that Law should not be apprehended. However, despite Orléans' embarrassed and blustering performance in the January session of the regency council at which the matter came to light, the balance of the evidence comes down in favour of the regent's temperamental preference to save rather than sacrifice his friend.[45]

John Law was a singular man. Throughout his life he was supported by two consuming passions, the intellectual challenge of macro-economic management and the gaming table. In both it was the excitement of the activity rather than the pursuit of wealth which motivated him. He used his money philanthropically and to invest in his own company. When the crash came, he offered to dispense most of his fortune amongst impoverished shareholders and he staunchly refused to establish a *cache* outside the country as a safeguard against just such a calamity. He rescued little himself from the disaster save the habitual gambler's optimistic instinct: Montesquieu visited him in Venice towards the end of his life and found him still imagining new projects, still making calculations, still hazarding his slender resources at the gaming table.[46]

Though Law was vilified by many of his adopted countrymen there were those who acknowledged his virtues. The regent's mother, the princess Palatine, thought him worthy and talented, though horribly ugly; no beauty herself, the old lady was impressed by his charm and good manners towards her, and she admired too the openness with which financial affairs were conducted under his aegis.[47] Saint-Simon also fell captive to the financier's beguiling manner, insisting that 'there was nothing greedy or knavish about Law'. His favourable impression, it must be admitted, owed something to Law's weekly visits to the duke, which he conscientiously kept up for four years between 1716 and 1720 and which were clearly designed to capture Saint-Simon's support for his schemes. The duke himself had serious doubts about the System's feasibility but he was impressed by Law's cleverness and, of course, flattered by his attentions. Characteristically, too, he approved of Law's relatively modest life-style: 'He was a good, kind, respectful man, whom excessive fame and good fortune had not spoiled, and whose bearing, coaches, table, and way of life were such as to offend no-one'; especially, he might have added, a *duc et pair* desperate for respect and obsessed with matters of status.[48] Nevertheless, for all the idiosyncratic subjectivity of the duke's view of John Law, his portrayal of a man more preoccupied with brilliant schemes than with personal glory, with calculating the odds than with amassing a fortune, carries conviction. A near-contemporary memorialist, Duclos, wrote in very similar terms, though his view may have been formed in part by Saint-Simon with whose writings he was familiar: 'Tall and well-made, he had an agreeable and noble countenance, much intelligence, conspicuous politeness and pride without insolence. His house was more remarkable for its order and neatness than for its luxury.'[49] Even more fulsome was the testimony of an intimate colleague, probably Angrand de Fontpertuis, a syndic of the Compagnie des Indes and after the regency a member of the council of commerce, who has left this generous though not imperceptive vignette:

> Law was a Scottish gentleman whose manners and appearance were noble, charming and attractive. . . . His intellect was lofty, penetrating, wide-ranging and exact; his imagination noble and resourceful, and perhaps too lively. His way of arguing was so persuasive that it made a deeper impression after reflection and scrutiny than it had done at the time. . . . He held truth as a principle and took the public good as his standpoint. He could not dwell on small matters and consequently was a little remiss in providing the details of how his schemes were to be executed, merely sketching the broad strategy and leaving the precise management to others. He was a proud and distinguished man, so noble as to make one doubt whether he felt injuries or disregarded them. He never took revenge on anybody and always sought to conciliate his enemies by kindnesses. His disinterestedness has had few parallels and will not be copied.[50]

During his final months in Paris Law's nerve broke and he appeared in a less attractive light. He was badly shaken by the violence of the hostility shown towards him on the streets, which transformed him, in the words of the princess Palatine, into a dead man, pale as a sheet. There had been some signs in 1718 that Law's resolution was vulnerable to the threat of physical attack, though the fact that an admirer like Fontpertuis should comment on his preference for conciliation over confrontation suggests only that he was not of a combative disposition.[51] However, under the strain of events a certain bravado began to emerge, as in his appearance in the regent's box at the opera in July 1720, an event recorded by Marais with the expostulatory if inaccurate comment, 'Impudence angloise'.[52] The same braggadoccio is apparent in a letter written by Law in February 1721: 'Am I not well avenged on the French? I have ruined them and enriched foreigners, I have made their king my subject, the regent my crony, the great noblemen my clerks, their women my whores and the first prince of the blood [a reference to the manner of Law's precipitate departure from France] my carriage-hirer.'[53] Even Saint-Simon reports that 'towards the end, finding himself obstructed everywhere while still valiantly seeking some means of procedure, he grew hard, ill-tempered and often rude in argument.' But the essential John Law, to whom the duke at once returns, was a man obdurately concerned with weighing the odds, 'and extraordinarily knowledgeable and learned in such ways, the kind of man who, without ever cheating, continually won at cards by the consummate art (that seemed incredible to me) of his methods of play.'[54]

In the event Law's private success at the gaming table was not matched in his public career, and the remainder of this chapter must be given over to an assessment of the System, its flaws, its accomplishments, its significance. There can be no doubt that a number of people lost heavily as a result of Law's System, and the frenzied scenes accompanying these losses have helped to instil a view of this period as one of collective madness, a time of economic deviation no more relevant to the norm than is a nightmare to reality. Law himself knew that there would be losers as well as beneficiaries. He wrote in May 1720 that when he promised to enrich the kingdom of France he did not mean that riches would be kept exclusively by those individuals who possessed them already.[55] In the arena of speculation there are no partial judgments in favour of wealthier investors; all must depend on their financial wits for survival. And like one of his mentors, Pottier de la Hestroye, Law was far more concerned with the introduction of money into circulation than with the fortunes of individuals. Aside from those who lost heavily on the stock exchange there were groups whose decline Law positively intended. His scathing metaphor of 1719, likening the tax-collectors to the rats in his granary, indicates one of his targets. With his company taking over responsibility for the gathering of direct and indirect taxation, he did succeed in reducing the number of tax-collectors and in abolishing the collectors-general, the results of which were to simplify the administrative structure and to improve the inflow of taxes to the central government; this in accordance with his expressed desire for a uniform, rational taxation system. By the same token Law succeeded in having a number of offices abolished; one ordinance alone, of September 1719, disposed of forty-eight of them.[56] The *rentiers* were another group adversely affected by the System. Their investment in government stock at 4 per cent, having been replaced by company shares following the latter's takeover of the national debt, was summarily reduced by the introduction of a 2 per cent rate of interest in March 1720. Law's justification lay in asserting the superiority of the public over the private domain. If it benefited the former to reduce interest rates then the king was entitled to act even though some of his subjects might be privately disadvantaged.[57] The general principle was well established in France though its application in the field of systematic economic management was novel.

Low interest rates were of prime importance in John Law's estimation. He believed that with the stimulus of credit more bullion would enter the country and that in turn would lead to the lowering of rates which would facilitate borrowing, lead to a higher level of employment, more cultivation, a rising population, and thus to the creation of more wealth. In this cyclical process more goods would be available for export in French ships and more bullion would be brought back in return to enable the economic miracle to continue. He practised what he preached, reducing the rate of his general bank to 4 per cent at the beginning of 1718; by October 1719 it was 2 per cent before finally dropping as low as $1\frac{1}{4}$ per cent. However, his commitment to low interest rates undoubtedly contributed to the inflationary crisis of 1719–20. When prices began to climb spectacularly during that period (caused primarily by monetary inflation through the over-issue of bank-notes), Law felt unable to reverse his earlier policy. Thus the alleviating deflationary influence of higher lending rates remained absent, the low rate simply adding impetus to the inflationary spiral.[58]

Law's concern to maintain low interest rates reflected the fundamental principle of his economic thinking upon which the whole System was posited, namely that the circulation of currency was the key to a country's wealth. Money in a state is like blood in the body, he maintained in his *Mémoire sur les Banques* (December 1715), and both suffer when the circulation is poor.[59] He viewed money as a means of exchange rather than as a measure of value, and exchange he saw as a social function which the State was obliged to encourage just as it was bound to frown on individual hoarding. The difficulty was to regulate the speed of the inevitably inflationary process and to correlate that with the overall economic strategy. The problem was of the chicken-and-egg variety. Law believed that the whole country must be involved *ab initio* in such a vast enterprise as the System if the latter were to fulfil its role as the generator of national wealth; and that, therefore, the foundation of the bank and the company must precede the development of domestic and colonial trade.[60] On the other hand, until there were positive signs of real wealth (which included a growing population, higher productivity, and more opportunities for employment) to match the readily available paper currency, there was a danger that the inflation of expectations would put the machine out of control. That is what in fact happened and it may be fairly argued that Law's handling of both the strategy and tactics of his inflationary policy was misguided.

Before we turn to that question, however, another caveat has to be made on the subject of circulation. Law failed to consider adequately the economic advantage to his System of some tendency to accrue savings which might have helped to stabilize the situation brought about by the massive injection of paper money. He also failed completely to take account of the natural human instinct to set aside resources to cope with future needs: the basic quest for security.[61]

By the end of 1719 the Compagnie des Indes seemed to be brilliantly placed with more than thirty large ships (excluding frigates and brigantines), more ships in fact than the British East India Company possessed. The growing prosperity of the western ports of Lorient and Nantes was reflected in the registration of vessels; 2,000 craft were registered at Nantes in 1721 compared with fewer than 1,350 in 1703. The re-establishment of the French Royal Navy began in July 1719 with the placing of an order for the construction of five ships at Brest and orders were also placed at Rochefort, Le Havre and Toulon. Although the collapse of the System slowed down the programme, it was not scrapped.[62] Similarly, the serious colonizing activities stimulated for the first time in the area of the Mississippi derived from the activities of the System and survived its fall. But the commercial advantages did not flow immediately from these preliminary ventures. In April 1720 Law himself admitted that the company had yet to draw any significant profit from its maritime commerce: there was bound to be a time-lag between the priming of the operation and the inflow of the returns. The financier appeared to misjudge the extent of this time-lag, or perhaps more accurately he believed it could be made irrelevant by maintaining the confidence of his shareholders at a high level. Hence his excessively optimistic estimate of the company's annual revenue from trade at 10–12 million *livres*; hence the double declaration in 1719 of future dividends, first at 12 per cent and then at 40 per cent per share; hence the rumour, for which he appeared responsible, that Louisiana possessed gold mines worth more than those of New Spain and Peru. He also appeared to confuse the increasing demand for paper money with an increase in real wealth, arguing that notes could not depreciate when issued in response to demand: this accounts for the traumatic effect on the public of the decree of 21 May 1720.[63]

Law failed to synchronize the expansion of the company's colonial trading activities with the growing expectations of his shareholders. The next question to be posed, therefore, is whether he succeeded in the domestic field. Undoubtedly the System did produce a boom. There was renewed emphasis upon the cultivation of wheat and a consequent reduction of the threat of famine. Land changed hands in favour of more go-ahead proprietors; owners paid off their mortgages and debtors their debts. More land was cleared and more building undertaken in the countryside. Large-scale construction projects, the building of roads, the Provence canal and the canal joining the rivers Loire and Seine, were set in motion. Paris in particular benefited. Some of the most elegant houses in the place Vendôme and the place des Victoires as well as the Palais-Bourbon owed their appearance to the System.[64] A source close to John Law painted a very different picture of France in the wake of the System than that favoured by most contemporary commentators: the consumption of meat in Paris and the provinces doubled; wine-drinking up by a third; wholesale merchants unable to keep retailers supplied; long-term provisions distributed in the provinces in 1720 promptly consumed; rural wages doubled and as a result taxes paid more promptly; the cultivation of land and the sale of produce made more profitable; luxury goods doubled in price.[65] This rosy view certainly requires qualification for Law did introduce a régime of steeply rising prices followed by a financial crash and it is unlikely that the only victims of his System would be the speculator, the tax-farmer and the *rentier*.

The economic historian, Earl J. Hamilton, whose reputation has come to be linked with the analysis of economic problems caused by the import of American treasure into Spain, has made two important contributions to our understanding of the System.[66] Looking first at the situation in the capital he was able to compile an index of commodity prices (with a 1716–17 base) comprising quotations of foods, raw materials, staple household supplies and building materials at wholesale rates. Prices remained relatively stable though the basic trend was upwards, from September 1718 when the index stood at 100·6, to July 1719 when it had reached 116·1. Thereafter it soared to its peak of 203·7 in September 1720. Prices just about doubled, therefore, over two years but in the two-month period of December 1719 to January 1720 they rose by 34·8 points or 25·5 per cent. Hamilton also compiled indices of money and real wages applicable to Parisian labourers over the same period. In

September 1718 money wages stood at 107·2; by July 1719 they had risen to 125·8 and they too reached their peak in September 1720 at 161·9. Though wages did increase, therefore, they did so by only some 50 per cent while prices were doubling. The most significant indication of the growing disparity comes from the December 1719–January 1720 figures which remained unchanged in the money wages index. Judged in terms of real wages, the deterioration in the labourer's position becomes abundantly clear, even though these figures indicate the considerable seasonal movement with increased living costs and reduced wages in the winter months: from 107·7 in September 1718 and 113·7 in July 1719 the figure slumped to 84·8 in September 1720 and was only 68·0 by the beginning of 1721. The crucial December 1719 to January 1720 movement showed a drop of 17 points, from 91·4 to 74·4.

Hamilton undertook a comparable investigation for Toulouse, Bordeaux and Marseilles with remarkably similar results. The index of commodity prices between September 1718 and October 1720 revealed an increase of 98·2 in Bordeaux and one of 132·6 in Toulouse. In Marseilles where the situation was exacerbated by the serious outbreak of plague during the summer of 1720, the rise was even more striking, 168·9 between September 1718 and September 1720. The September 1718 figures for Bordeaux, Marseilles and Toulouse respectively were 100·5, 101·2 and 105·5. There was a big leap in the Toulouse figure between December 1719 and January 1720 of 31·1 or 27·1 per cent. Hamilton was not able to unearth satisfactory wage figues for Bordeaux, but for Marseilles and Toulouse the lines of the money wage and the real wage graphs matched those of Paris. The fourth quarter of 1720 in Marseilles showed a money wage index rise from the same quarter of 1718 of 57·6, from 103·0 to 160·6, and in Toulouse one of 22·5, from 100·0 to 122·5. In the same period in real wage terms the index fell at Marseilles by 8·3, from 96·1 to 87·8, and at Toulouse by 9·0, from 91·2 to 82·2.

On the face of it, therefore, the labouring class were disadvantaged by the System and, according to this evidence, not only in the capital but across the country. However, there are several qualifications to be made. An examination of Hamilton's figures after the middle of 1720 demonstrates that the crisis was short-lived. In Paris by July 1721 commodity prices stood at 124·9, money wages at 124·7 and real wages at 115·1; in Marseilles by the third quarter of 1721 prices averaged out at 164·2, money wages at 169·1 and real wages at 124·1; in Toulouse over the same period prices were at 155·7, money wages at 115·4 and real wages 76·3 (in Toulouse the real wage figure marked the bottom of a trough after which there was a steady rise until the end of 1723).

Nor did the failure of John Law's System reduce the value of bank-notes to zero, a catastrophe which would have been dramatically reflected in the downward spiral of commodity prices over the ensuing months. Hamilton observes, 'I have found no evidence of a single commercial transaction in which bank-notes commanded only a small fraction of their face value.'[67] Thus paper currency apparently did not suffer a depreciation comparable with that of the *assignats* in 1796; in Paris the largest monthly drop in the commodity price index between the peak of September 1720 and the end of 1725 was that between November and December 1720, and that was only 17·4 per cent. A recent and original research approach, using notarial records in Paris and Versailles, tends to bear out Hamilton's findings. J.-P. Poisson concludes that:

> le répercussions du Système de Law dans la population même aisée aient été, mis à part un milieu étroit de financiers professionnels ou occasionnels, beaucoup plus limitées que les regards des nouvellistes de l'époque et des historiens fixés sur la rue Quincampoix n'auraient pu le laisser penser.[68]

There is a second qualification to be made. Because France did enjoy a period of domestic expansion under the System it is possible that for some the falling value of wages might have been offset by greater and more regular employment opportunities. There is no way of quantifying that hypothesis though it is a factor tending to cast further doubt upon what might be termed the 'catastrophic' interpretation of the System.

We return now to the question of the success or failure of Law's strategy in the domestic field. France's revival was real enough and appeared to be more capable of fulfilling John Law's ambitions than the slow-developing colonial side of his enterprise. There was a great deal of slack in the labour market to be taken up, land to be cultivated and capital to be invested. Consequently between the establishing of the general bank in May 1716 and November 1718 shortly before it became a royal bank, prices rose by only 8·7 per cent. Law was too impatient, however, and the promising but fragile revival was destroyed by the imposition of new and heavy burdens which it could not sustain: in August 1719 Law acquired the farm of all the indirect taxes; in October he took over responsibility for collecting direct taxation and the crippling weight of the national debt. As with his overseas operation, he had thrown the delicate mechanism out of balance. The financier made certain specific miscalculations too: the attempt to 'peg' the price of shares at 9,000 *livres* in March 1720 instead of allowing them to find their own level added fuel to the inflationary flame; the frequent manipulations in the value of the coinage – twenty-six in 1720 alone – and the promulgation followed almost immediately by the repeal of the deflationary edict of 21 May, seemed calculated to annihilate confidence. Indeed it was a fundamental failure of Law not to give the same attention to the practical step-by-step implementation of his project that he lavished on the theory. As his admirer Fontpertuis perceptively commented, 'He could not dwell on small matters and consequently was a little remiss in providing the details of how his schemes were to be executed, merely sketching the broad strategy and leaving the precise management to others.'[69]

Not that his economic theory was incapable of translation into reality. The need for a credit system had been painfully demonstrated to the French during the War of the Spanish Succession when the support of the Bank of England made the Grand Alliance such a formidable unit. Law wrote to the regent in December 1715, 'Before the introduction of credit the State which was richest in specie was the most powerful; now it is the one best served by its credit.'[70] Samuel Bernard had produced a scheme in 1709 for establishing a public bank to manage the state's debt, while from 1713 the English South Sea Company had been transforming some of the nation's creditors into company shareholders.[71] Law might have succeeded in making the state independent of its creditors through his Compagnie des Indes; he did succeed in establishing the first bank of issue in France and, by exploiting the country's credit potential, in giving a dramatic fillip to her domestic and colonial prosperity. His original belief that the French land and its produce securely guaranteed a paper currency was implicitly translated into his System in the form of company shares; though his view of the relationship between land, bullion and credit remained confused.

It was in the wider political setting that theory and practice proved ultimately irreconcilable, though Law was aware of the fundamental difficulty which faced him. He was at his most innovative in the field of politics, for he sensed, if he did not fully appreciate from the beginning, that the firm establishment of his System would depend upon the setting up of a new economic and political order. His aim was the creation of a rich and powerful state in which the interests of king and people would be inseparable and which would depend upon the contribution of every member – hence the need to abolish financial privilege – and on the significant reinforcement of the executive's power. Law was edging France towards a régime of enlightened absolutism. In such a reformed state even the daunting problem of marrying autocracy and credit might be overcome. Law acknowledged after the failure of the System that the two did not go together. Indeed he had said so some time before it was launched. Writing to the controller-general of finance, Desmaretz, in July 1715 he observed, 'Constraint is contrary to the principles upon which credit must be built.' But he did tend to fall back on it nevertheless. In his second letter on credit in 1720 he wrote of the System, 'Despotic power, to which we are beholden for it, will also sustain it.'[72] That such was not the case had been amply demonstrated by the ineffectiveness of the draconian decree of February 1720.

Orléans' lively and unconventional mind inclined him to favour Law's schemes, and as soon as he was able he gave them his full backing and the financier his personal loyalty. Indeed the two men were temperamentally similar and it was no hardship for the regent to back his friend's judgment. However, when the bubble burst, though Orléans ensured Law's personal safety, he does appear to have decided that the experiment had been a total failure and best forgotten. Had he been the ruler rather than the regent he might have been persuaded to test Law's ideas a little further; as it was, having survived the second great crisis of his regency and with the king's majority less than two years away, he was resolved to ensure that the young man in his charge should inherit the traditional authority of the Bourbons, secure and unchallenged. He preferred, therefore, at this stage of the regency, to play safe.[73] On the occasion of his first formal instruction to Louis XV concerning the affairs of the kingdom, on 26 August 1722, Orléans pointedly limited his remarks on Law's System to one brief and indirect observation:

During your minority various means have been employed to escape from this embarrassment [the debt left by Louis XIV] . . . and to support the indispensable expenses of the State, but since the chief [*les principaux*] of these means have not succeeded the immediate task is to pay off the remainder of these debts and make up what is lacking in funds to provide for current and necessary expenditure.[74]

VI

The Private Man and the Public Achievement

Before attempting to assess the achievements of the regency it is necessary to look beyond the policies of the regent in order to seek some understanding of the personality and enthusiasms of Orléans himself. Two contemporary men of letters have left assessments which, taken together, offer a convincing portrait. The elaborate picture painted by Saint-Simon deserves to be quoted at length since few observed Orléans from as close at hand as the *duc et pair*, and nobody matched his artist's eye, especially when his characters were not changed into caricatures by an obsessive animosity. With Orléans he begins cautiously, eschewing the bold black and white lines of a cartoon representation:

> Never in all my life have I met a man so conspicuously and perfectly inconsistent as M. le Duc d'Orléans. You will soon see that although I had known him intimately for many years ... yet I still did not know him; nor did he fully understand himself.
>
> M. le Duc d'Orléans was of medium height, at most, stout without being obese, with a bearing that was easy and extremely noble, a large pleasant countenance, a high colour, black hair, and a wig to match. ... he possessed so much natural charm of manner that it enhanced his every action, even the most commonplace. ... He conversed lucidly and fluently on any subject, never feeling for his words, and often remarkably interesting. What is more, he could be just as sensible and as eloquent on the abstract sciences, State affairs, finance, the law, military matters, and the doings of the Court, as in polite conversation, or in the discussion of engineering or the arts. He had read the histories and memoirs of great men, and put them to excellent use. He was familiar with the lives of the leading personalities in other periods, and with the intrigues in ancient courts as well as in those of his own day. To hear him talk, you would have thought him vastly learned. Not so, indeed, for he was a skimmer; but his memory was so uniformly good that he forgot nothing, not even names and dates, which he quoted accurately. His grasp was so complete that in glancing through a book he took in as much as though he had read it carefully. ...

No one was more respectful in speech and manner, no one more noble in his attitude towards the King and the Sons of France; for he had inherited Monsieur's inordinate pride in his royal ancestry. . . . He was accused of most brutal crimes, yet I never met a man more violently opposed to murder, or even to causing pain. You might say that he carried kindness and even tolerance too far, for I maintain that he made a vice of the sublime virtue of forgiving one's enemies, and that such indiscriminate generosity verged on blindness to crime. . . . He was born bored. . . . Never was there a man born with so many gifts, such facility and eagerness to use them, never one whose private life was so idle, so much given up to dullness and boredom. . . . he broke so many pledges that his word ceased to have any meaning, for he many times promised to several people what he could grant only to one. Many were discontented and he ceased to be respected. In the end, no one believed him, even when he spoke in good faith, and his glibness in speech greatly discredited him. Finally, the low and knavish company which he kept, and from among whom he chose those boon companions, whom he openly referred to as his *roués*, drove better men from his side. . . .[1]

Voltaire provided a characteristically acute and epigrammatic summing up: a man of few scruples but incapable of crime.[2]

Orléans' private life was characterized by self-indulgence on a gargantuan scale: mistresses enough to inspire a sizeable volume in the nineteenth century, and a daily routine of gluttony, drunkenness and licentiousness calculated to undermine the most robust of constitutions.[3] It is at this point indeed that the historian must take cognizance of Philippe's standards of personal morality, for though his unrelenting pursuit of pleasure did not generate any specific political crises, there were indications towards the end of the regency that it very well could;[4] and in a general way his behaviour detracted from his credibility as regent and heir to the throne, and thereby weakened his political authority. It drained him of ambition, impaired his health, and must certainly have contributed to his death. The serious flaw in his character has thus quite properly assumed a significance for historians, as it did for contemporaries, which it would not otherwise have had. Yet it must not be allowed to overshadow other aspects of his personality. Orléans was a remarkable character precisely because his incorrigible conduct hid as much as it revealed of the true man.

When he entertained his friends at the Palais-Royal, *roués* like Canillac, Nocé, Brancas and Broglie, and ladies more or less in favour, 'les maîtresses en titre, en sous-titre, triomphantes ou congédiées',[5] like mesdames Parabère, Sabran, d'Averne and Falari, the regent did succeed in remaining silent on affairs of state. He also distinguished clearly between those upon whose service he relied as regent and those who helped a friend to keep boredom at arm's length.[6] Dubois and Law were not of this latter circle and, conversely, few of those who were obtained posts of any political importance. They were ephemera attracted to the source of power yet accustomed to keep their distance; if, like Nocé, they strayed too close they could not expect to survive unscathed.[7]

Philippe had no illusions about the fragility of his relationship with his supper guests but towards some members of his family, including the young king, he revealed a strong sense of personal loyalty and affection. It is true that he had resented his enforced marriage to Louis XIV's youngest illegitimate daughter, Françoise-Marie, Mademoiselle de Blois, and was constantly unfaithful to her. For her part the duchess, who never forgot, or allowed anybody else to forget, that she was a king's daughter, displayed a degree of arrogance towards her husband which would have taxed the patience of a less tolerant and easy-going man. Orléans amused himself on occasion by calling his wife Madame Lucifer, though he habitually treated her with respect and courtesy, and if their relationship was never close it was at least tolerable.[8] The duchess bore him eight children, seven of whom were daughters. For whatever genetic reason, that generation was plagued by mental instability, though through Philippe's only son, Louis, the male line would produce the citizen king, Louis Philippe, the regent's great great-grandson.

The eldest of Orléans' daughters to survive to adulthood was Marie Louise Elisabeth, who was married in 1710 to the king's grandson, the duke de Berry. She was Philippe's favourite child and became as notorious as her father. She profited from his bad example to indulge her precocious and ungovernable appetites, and did not live long enough to reveal many compensatory virtues. Perhaps she was deranged before her death in July 1719, on the twenty-fourth anniversary of her birth. Because of the unattractiveness of the duchess de Berry's personality her father's fervent devotion to her seems remarkable and was much remarked upon. The amiability, the unwillingness to inflict hurt or disappointment, which normally characterized Orléans' relationships, was transformed in dealings with his neurotic daughter into unedifying displays of weakness. His deep affection for her made it easy to spread rumours of incest between these kindred spirits. No valid foundation for such reports has ever been adduced, and there is no reason whatever to doubt the naturalness of the deep bond between father and child. Philippe's mother adequately explained her son's distress at his daughter's death in the simple phrase, 'C'était son enfant chéri'.[9]

Though the regent's relationship with his other daughters was not close the Palais-Royal does appear to have exercised a malign influence on at least two of them despite their convent education away from Paris – Mademoiselle de Valois who married the duke of Modena, and Mademoiselle de Montpensier who became princess of the Asturias. Their elder sister, Louise-Adélaïde, was of a more amiable disposition. She entered the religious life, and in 1719 was enthroned as abbess of Chelles in the presence of Orléans. The regent's son, the duke de Chartres, lacked his father's intelligence and charisma, and Orléans was not fond of him. It is not to the regent's credit that he was apparently responsible for introducing his son to a life of debauchery with the assistance of girls from the Opéra.[10]

It is impossible to be dogmatic about the number of Philippe's illegitimate offspring. Among those who reached maturity were two sons, the chevalier d'Orléans and the abbé de Saint-Albin, and a daughter whom he married to the marquis de Ségur. The chevalier became grand prior of France in the Order of Malta and was one of Philippe's bastards to be legitimized. Such preferential treatment is explained by the identity of his mother, countess d'Argenton, who retained a special place in Orléans' affections. Saint-Albin's mother, Florence, a celebrated dancer at the Opéra, had left no such emotional mark but his cause was taken up by the princess Palatine, his grandmother, who maintained that 'de tous les enfants légitimes ou illégitimes de mon fils, c'est celui qui m'aime le mieux.'[11] Eventually the regent succumbed to her promptings and recognized him. The abbé's career was ultimately crowned with the archbishopric of Cambrai.

The regent's attitude towards his mother, that formidable old lady with the figure of a Swiss guard and the language and bearing to match, was one of affectionate respect. He visited her regularly when she was staying in Paris and stayed with her at St-Cloud during her last illness, in December 1722. They both appeared to derive pleasure from their conversations, which were concerned with private, not public matters. Madame was proud of her son and content with their relationship:

> Although he is the regent he never appears before me or leaves me without kissing my hand before I embrace him; he never takes a chair in my presence; in other respects he does not stand on ceremony but chatters briskly with me. We laugh and joke together like true friends.

And, at a time of illness:

> My son is on good terms with me; he shows me great affection and would be broken-hearted to lose me. His visits do me more good than quinine; they rejoice my heart and do not give me pains in the stomach; he always says something funny which makes me laugh; he has wit and expresses himself with

great charm; I would be a most unnatural mother if I did not love him from the bottom of my heart; if you knew him well you would see that there was no ambition or malice in him. Good Lord, he is only too kind, he forgives everything undertaken against him and merely laughs about it.[12]

The most important member of Orléans' family was the king himself. The regent treated him rather as he treated his own mother, with exemplary respect lightened by an air of gaiety, and in each case he established a relationship of mutual warmth. One of Philippe's pre-occupations during the last six months of the minority was the super-vision of the king's political education. In his will, Louis XIV had named Fleury, the bishop of Fréjus, to be his great-grandson's tutor and the regent had honoured that wish. Though the personnel responsible for instructing the king changed over the years, Fleury remained and would later become Louis' chief minister. The king's academic instruction gradually veered in a more political direction, history and geography joining with the study of military campaigns and the art of waging war. His political education proper, however, began on 26 August 1722 with a formal session conducted by Philippe and Dubois, and was mainly concerned with the organization of the state's finances. Although Dubois played an important part in arranging this programme for the king – he had just become first minister and had one eye on his own and on the regent's future after the royal majority – and although much of the material was prepared by experts, the tuition evidently took place in a series of private sessions confined to Louis and Orléans alone. We owe that information to Philippe's *valet de chambre*, Cangé, who also reports seeing his master reading Richelieu's political testament and other memoirs, before going off to instruct the king. In his meetings with Louis the regent acted decorously, never taking advantage of his influence over the shy young king to browbeat him or undermine his regal authority. Louis responded by calling the regent 'uncle', and trusting him. He remembered Philippe with affection long after the grief which he felt at his passing had faded.[13]

As well as the close relationships which he established within his own family and his twilight world of revelry in the Palais-Royal, there was a third dimension to Orléans' life, that of the intellect. We have already seen something of his enthusiasm for patronizing artists and collecting paintings, and his own intellectual range and capacity were outstanding. His mother remarked fondly if indiscriminately that he had studied a great deal and could express himself well on many subjects.[14] Barbier was more specific: '... he had received the best possible education and had a knowledge of everything: besides mechanics, chemistry, history, matters of ceremonial and public law, he could paint quite pleasingly and had a perfect understanding of music.'[15] He received instruction in mathematics from Joseph Sauveur, the most distinguished French mathematician of his day, whilst in the field of science his early links with Homberg became notorious as the result of rumours marking Orléans as a poisoner. At the beginning of the regency Philippe became superintendent of the Académie des Sciences and encouraged research into such topics as the possibility of obtaining gold from French rivers on a commercial basis, and methods of improving the precision of map-making. His scientific interest brought him into contact with René-Antoine Ferchault de Réaumur, a scientist of protean genius whose work on the conversion of iron to steel undertaken between 1720 and 1722 Orléans followed eagerly, even being present to hear a paper delivered by Réaumur on the subject.[16]

The regent's links with men of letters were similarly close. Mention has been made of his regard for Fénelon and Fontenelle, and of his patronage of Jean-Baptiste Rousseau and La Motte. Nor was his relationship with literary figures limited to material support: he was a perceptive critic, unerringly ranking Rousseau before La Motte, and introducing Voltaire to the works of Rabelais.[17] The youthful Voltaire was himself becoming a considerable literary figure during the regency, particularly after the spectacular success of his tragedy, *Oedipe*, which opened at the Comédie-francaise in November 1718. However, because Voltaire's interests were also political, his relationship with Orléans was by no means straightforward. The writer found himself imprisoned on one occasion and exiled from Paris on two. He was subsequently reconciled with the regent who showed considerable interest in the construction of Voltaire's epic poem on Henri IV, Philippe's favourite ancestor. Though both men were doubtless aware of the political implications of the *Henriade*, that is no reason for discounting the genuineness of the regent's literary curiosity in this case.[18]

Two final and related examples may serve to emphasize Orléans' concern with intellectual matters. At the outset of the regency the *bibliothèque du roi* was inadequately staffed and housed; by 1723 it had been transferred to a more spacious site in the rue de Richelieu (where, as the Bibliothèque Nationale, it still stands) and its staff considerably increased, 'providing salaried posts for a score of men of letters and an impetus to intellectual activities in general'. The library's contents were classified and sub-divided, and the basis laid for the later national library. Philippe played a leading part in this transformation in support of the librarian, the abbé Bignon. He was also responsible for instigating the classification of the Bastille archives, ordering papers of the chief of police to be deposited there in the care of two permanent officials. Thereafter the archives began to be used as a library.[19]

In sum, to undervalue the stimulus and satisfaction which Orléans derived from artistic and intellectual activity would be no more equitable than to deny his part in the lubricious proceedings at the Palais-Royal.

Philippe d'Orléans set and reflected a regency style which was in part a reaction against the measured classicism and tight-reined conformity of Louis XIV's later years, and the expression of a new and increasingly influential set of values. During these years an aura of sensuousness, profanity and inventiveness radiated from the Palais-Royal which encouraged cynics to mock existing gods, though not, as we shall see, to reject them out of hand. Libertine at its least refined, in the image of the buxom duchess de Berry flaunting her uncorseted *négligé* at La Muette and the Luxembourg, that spirit was most perfectly expressed in the canvases of Watteau, one of which, *Le Bal Champêtre*, formed part of the regent's own collection. The pursuit of love, often sacrificed to wantonness, was not as idyllic as the *Embarquement pour Cythère* suggested; but it was already being expressed with a new abandon by authors like Robert Chasles, whose *Illustres Françaises* of 1713 heralds the more famous comparable works of Prévost and Marivaux.[20]

When Louis XV came to reside in the Tuileries palace close to the Palais-Royal, Paris regained the prestige lost to Versailles in the preceding reign. The new town houses which celebrated that fact also reveal the subtle changes which French architecture was undergoing as the classical values of Hardouin-Mansart's day gave way to freer and more intimate forms. The Palais-Bourbon (1722) was pulled down to accommodate the present National Assembly but the Hôtel d'Evreux (1718), now the Elysée Palace, the Hôtel Matignon (1720), and its near neighbour in the rue de Varenne built for Orléans' mistress, the actress Charlotte Desmares, are only the most spectacular architectural pointers in the direction of the new rococo style.[21]

This predominantly ornamental style – *le goût moderne* to contemporaries – defies precise definition. Most suggestive is the analogy with the crest of a wave caught at the instant of its unfurling. Characteristically mobile, its curved lines embody subjects largely abstracted from nature, a cascading profusion of shells, vines and foliage. Rococo is chiefly associated with interior decoration, and with embroidery, painting and furniture. But it also introduced a sense of lightness and elegance into aristocratic salons by a reduction of scale to more intimate proportions and by the use of mirrors, of light pastel colours, white and gold.[22]

Besides providing a dramatic setting for his superb collection of paintings, Orléans' first-floor apartments in the Palais-Royal, re-designed by the architect, Gilles-Marie Oppenord, offered a brilliant example of the new fashion. So did the magnificent furniture which they contained, the work of Charles Cressent, who was principal cabinet-maker to the regent. Cressent's work remains outstanding for its rich combination of bronze and marquetry in coloured woods. He was one of the first *ébénistes* to construct the commode, a piece of furniture characteristic of the eighteenth century which made its *début* as the commode *à la Régence*.[23]

However, although the rococo did reflect something of the regency's exuberant challenge to existing orthodoxies, we should beware of pressing ideas of novelty too far in either art or politics. Orléans was an enlightened aristocrat, not a political radical, and the art-form with which he was associated was likewise aristocratic, not popular. There was no *avant-garde* break with the traditions of the *grand siècle* though the death of its most influential representative made inevitable experiment and innovation which stimulated the process of change. It would be gratuitous to deny the importance of those genuine shifts in attitude which did occur or to discount the modernity in the regent's own approach. Yet a sense of discipline and order continued to regulate the regency style: the derogatory implication attached to the word 'rococo' comes from the later eighteenth century; and the persistent influence of classical values may be plainly seen in the still formidably symmetrical façade of the Hôtel Matignon. In politics, Orléans' imaginative and enterprising backing of John Law's financial projects and Dubois' schemes for an international settlement have to be judged in the context of his prior determination to defend and maintain the king's authority, the motive which also made him, a sceptic, take very seriously the religious quarrel over Unigenitus which he had inherited from Louis XIV. Indeed, Orléans was dynast enough himself to ensure that his legitimated sons became clergymen, so that the legitimate line would not be vitiated by unwelcome grandsons.[24] Finally, it should be remembered that the organization of government in the regency years was far less removed from that of the previous reign than was at first apparent.

Though the technique of *trompe-l'oeil*, which so delighted the artists who decorated Versailles, was not favoured by exponents of rococo, there is undoubtedly an air of illusion surrounding the regency as a whole. This derives from the power of the emotional reaction against the crabbed longevity of the previous régime which has led to a blurring of the strong underlying element of continuity linking the two reigns;

and to a view of the regency as a period frivolous and frothy, incapable of maintaining anything more substantial than wit. Even that cool magistrate, Montesquieu, encouraged the latter deception and ironically, because he could not resist a good aphorism, associated himself with it: 'C'était le siècle des bons mots: il [Orléans] se conduisait par un bon mot, et on le gouvernait par un bon mot.'[25]

*   *   *

The political profile of the regency may be readily adumbrated: a tentative beginning, when Orléans' primary concern was to establish his authority in difficult circumstances, followed by the first critical period, in the second half of 1718; a high plateau while the country enjoyed the benefits of John Law's System before the second major crisis which began and ended almost exactly two years after the first; and a quiet *dénouement* leading towards the king's majority. The minority had not been quite the stormy time which the keeper of the seals suggested at its conclusion; indeed the remarkable fact was that from such an inauspicious beginning Orléans had fashioned a régime capable of defeating the various combinations of his opponents without bloodshed, even without much difficulty. In doing so he handed on to Louis XV a secure throne and the opportunity to govern as he wished. There were aspects of the regent's political legacy which the young king might have pursued and developed with profit; unfortunately for the house of Bourbon that quest for private pleasure which so vitiated Orléans' public role was in the end to enslave his protégé too.[26]

The starting point, therefore, in any attempt to summarize the achievements of the regency must be the question of how much credit Orléans himself deserves for the smooth transition from Louis XIV's death to his great-grandson's majority. In the first place, he gave his unswerving loyalty to the young king. Despite the gossip and his well-known – on the basis of Utrecht well-founded – ambitions to succeed to the French throne himself, he showed no inclination whatsoever to anticipate that claim. What he clearly could not do was ignore the possibility of a disputed succession in the event of Louis XV's premature demise, and particularly in his foreign policy that factor figured prominently. Yet the regent, through Dubois, did not pursue a policy geared exclusively to the interests of his house; rather he sought, and so did all European statesmen, short-term solutions to long-term problems. If the king had died before his majority and Philip V had claimed the crown by right of the French law of succession, it is highly unlikely that Orléans would have acted so unrealistically as to demand support from the British and the Dutch to place him on the throne against the wishes of most Frenchmen. But the fluid international situation of late-1715 made it essential for a weakened France to secure a breathing space and allies; the policy leading to the Triple and Quadruple Alliances was the only way of acquiring both. Together with the later *rapprochement* with Spain and the success of French diplomacy in the north, these initiatives left Louis XV with a far stronger hand to play in Europe than Louis XIV had bequeathed him.

In his handling of the king's domestic affairs the regent's wholehearted loyalty was similarly allied to an instinctive pragmatism. He knew that, so long as his own will was subject to challenge, the king's authority which he exercised would risk being diminished. Therefore, he acted with caution, seeking to gain time while his authority in the kingdom was made proof against assault, and with craft so that the assaults might be few in number. Generally speaking, *de facto* arrangements tended to precede their formal confirmation: Dubois had to wait until September 1718 to become foreign secretary and until August 1722 to be first minister; Law was only appointed controller-general in January 1720 and, though his dismissal from that office in May 1720 signified the effective end of his career in France, he was not finally jettisoned by Orléans until the following December. The *polysynodie* survived the combined hostility of Law and Dubois from the spring to the autumn of 1718. Before then, far from being a doctrinaire implementation of the governmental ideas of the abbé de Saint-Pierre, the *polysynodie* had masked the manner in which government was effectively conducted.[27]

In the potentially explosive situation provoked by Unigenitus Orléans acted with similar circumspection, first packing the *conseil de conscience* with some of its most influential opponents while aiming ultimately at a settlement with Rome, later imposing silence on the rival camps. The regent's choice of confessor for Louis XV was the abbé Claude Fleury who, like Orléans, was committed to neither side in the dispute.[28] In his relations with the parlement Orléans was for a time prepared to give way over issues which did not compromise the king's authority: in the August 1716 wrangle over precedence when the magistrates challenged the regent's place in the procession in honour of the Assumption, he found a way of avoiding a confrontation. Likewise, in his response to their remonstrances in 1716 and 1717 the magistrates found him willing to modify his legislative proposals, though only when he was satisfied that royal authority was not at risk. When he thought otherwise his tone and his actions acquired a more autocratic ring.

From the beginning of 1718, with his position increasingly well established, the regent's determination to maintain his own and the king's absolute power (which he quite properly refused to separate) was less subject to disguise. So that John Law might have scope to develop his financial schemes Orléans' old ally, the duke de Noailles, was sacrificed, and the influential and much respected chancellor, d'Aguesseau, disgraced. Shortly afterwards he announced to a deputation from the parlement of Paris that, since the king's authority had been entrusted to him, he would not allow it to be demeaned during his regency; it would be handed on to the king in precisely the form in which he, Orléans, had received it.[29] His chief domestic rival, Maine, was first humiliated by the deprivation of his royal rank and the office of superintendent of the king's education and then arrested for his part in the comic-opera Cellamare conspiracy. The conciliar system was disbanded; and the political authority of the parlement, so recently regained, was drastically curtailed once more. From 1718 the regent was prepared to threaten force, and use it, to command the magistrates' obedience. His authoritarian attitude to the court wavered briefly in mid-1720 when John Law's System was on the point of collapse. However, though d'Aguesseau, one of the heroes of the parlement, was reinstated as chancellor, the court as a body was soon bundled into exile at Pontoise (July–December 1720) for its unhelpful response to Orléans' efforts to restore the financial situation. Despite the parlous state of affairs in the country resulting from the breakdown of the System, Orléans' own position was secure, and away from the capital the parlement felt the full weight of his absolute authority as he extracted its support for his proposals to settle the Unigenitus dispute. After the traumatic events of 1720 the regent was content to leave the faithful Dubois to regulate affairs of state on his behalf, though he abdicated nothing of his power as regent.

Orléans' various manoeuvres then were chiefly concerned with securing the king's authority – the primary obligation, after all, of any regent – rather than with the pursuit of particular policy lines of his own. He cared little how the religious dispute was settled so long as its divisive effects were brought to an end and, though in both foreign and financial affairs he adopted far more positive and original policies, he never lost sight of the pre-eminent need to bequeath a position of strength to Louis XV: hence the final total break with the System and the *rapprochement* with Spain. That is not to deny his own shrewd grasp of France's needs nor to underestimate the possibilities offered by his approach to a sovereign successor: it is simply to recognize his order of priority.

One potentially serious threat to the king's authority, which should be mentioned at this point, was the revolt in Brittany. A number of Breton noblemen had been complaining since 1715 against having to pay their contributions to two royal taxes, the *dixième* and the *capitation*. Matters came to a head in December 1717 in a meeting of the Breton estates at Dinan when, despite the governor's announcement that the *dixième* was to be suppressed, and his warning that the regent 'would not suffer any attack against royal authority nor would he allow the least distinction to be made in the matter of the obedience owed to a minor king',[30] the deputies refused to vote the expected *don gratuit*. The governor, marshal de Montesquiou, was forced to suspend the session without an agreement. This defiance led the regent to issue a council decree permitting the levying of certain ordinary taxes in lieu of the *don gratuit*; in Rennes the parlement of Brittany refused to register the decree and instead, as we have seen, dispatched its remonstrances to Paris.[31] Their presentation to Orléans on 24 January 1718 was undoubtedly a factor in his decision to take a harder line towards the parlement of Paris and its allies, beginning with the disgrace of d'Aguesseau four days later.

The parlement of Rennes subsequently backed down and the regent reconvened the estates of Brittany on 1 July 1718 to resume their suspended session. This meeting too ended in deadlock and once more the parlement of Rennes remonstrated on behalf of the estates' rights in matters of taxation. The unrest in Brittany was now quite serious and the duchess du Maine, who was engaged at this time in her efforts on behalf of the Cellamare conspirators, met a number of Breton noblemen seeking support for their opposition from Spain. In Brittany itself a league of noblemen was formed in September 1718, and some of its wilder spirits did attempt to exploit the king of Spain's hostility towards Orléans. Their aim was to make Philip V regent in Orléans' stead. The latter was accused of preparing to take the crown for himself from the head of his charge, hesitating only until he had amassed an adequate fortune to support his treacherous design. Thus was character assassination of the regent neatly joined with condemnation of John Law's financial régime. In looking to the king of Spain to help them redeem their lost cause the conspirators naturally assumed that the new regent would agree to guarantee the liberties and privileges of the Breton nobility! The government reacted firmly. A number of arrests were made and an extraordinary jurisdiction, the *chambre royale*, was set up to try the accused. Eventually in March 1720 four Breton noblemen were executed for the crime of *lèse-majesté*, and over a hundred more sentenced to a variety of lesser penalties. The opposition dissolved before this demonstration of force, the effectiveness of which was noted by Dom Leclercq: 'La noblesse de France comprit la leçon salutaire et jamais plus, jusqu'à sa destruction, elle ne conspira contre son pays.'[32]

The ease with which Orléans contained and then put down the Breton revolt is indicative of the personal authority which he had established over the kingdom by 1718. It was thought possible that his generosity of spirit might persuade him to pardon the guilty noblemen but, as ever, Orléans came down in favour of the need publicly to assert the king's authority. Other examples may be cited. When the abbé de Saint-Pierre wrote his *Polysynodie* he depicted Orléans as an enlightened ruler against the backcloth of Louis XIV's authoritarianism, but the regent reacted sharply against the book's critical view of the monarchy, ordering the suppression of all copies and the arrest of the printer, and supporting the abbé's expulsion from the Académie francaise which took place in May 1718. Similarly, Orléans showed himself to be extremely sensitive to the vicious libel printed in La Grange-Chancel's scurrilous verses known as the *Philippiques*, to the effect that he was planning to have Louis XV poisoned. 'I have never seen a man more outraged, more deeply hurt, more overwhelmed by a sense of injustice', recalled Saint-Simon, who went on to note La Grange-Chancel's subsequent arrest and incarceration on the Ile Sainte-Marguerite.[33] The author of a recent critical examination of the regency from a literary standpoint quotes these episodes along with a third, the draconian punishment meted out to Voltaire, who was confined to the Bastille between May 1717 and April 1718 and subsequently forbidden to return to Paris until October of that year for publishing libellous verses against the regent and his daughter. Dr Waller points out that Voltaire's alleged offence did not appear to match the sentence, which was comparable with those imposed on the Cellamare conspirators. He suggests that Orléans' harsh response was prompted by that section in the *Puero Regnante* which inferred that Louis XV's life was threatened by the regent's design to have him poisoned. Orléans would not tolerate any undermining of his official relationship with Louis. He carefully separated his own opinions and life-style, and criticisms of his conduct as a private individual, from his public role in which he stood as surrogate king of France. This freethinker's official attitude to Protestantism, for example, differed not a jot from that of Louis XIV; nor is there any real evidence that a more liberal attitude was adopted towards censorship during his period in office. On the other hand, he does not appear to have been concerned by innuendo and invective directed at him personally, such as the allegations of an incestuous relationship between himself and his daughter, the duchess de Berry.[34]

It appears therefore – in answer to the question posed above – that Orléans himself does deserve considerable credit for the relative tranquillity of the regency years. His shrewd assessment of the politically possible allied with his determination to yield nothing of substance enabled him, at first behind a façade of apparent novelty and later more directly, to preserve the king's authority and, by insisting upon that priority, to maintain his own position.

There were, however, two significant factors working in his favour. The first was the success, viewed retrospectively, of Louis XIV's régime. His efforts over more than half a century to create a professional government system, without in the end provoking the kind of upheaval which had marred his own childhood, had evidently succeeded. Whatever qualifications must be adduced to limit the scope and effectiveness of his measures – and there are many – it does seem beyond doubt that the failure of the nobility, both of robe and sword, to mount an effective challenge when tradition as well as the political realities of 1715 suggested that the central authority was vulnerable, owed something to the new government ethos inculcated by Louis. We now know enough about the incipient bureaucratization of the later years of Louis' reign to understand how that could be: the establishment of various departmental depositories for foreign affairs, war, the navy and the colonies, to cope with that surest harbinger of government by committee – paper; the creation of a school to train diplomats in the formal ways of European diplomacy; the periodic dispatching of officials from the capital to enquire into the economic well-being of the provinces; the re-creation of a council of commerce (in 1700) in order to allow a proper concentration upon an area which previously had been the joint preserve of the secretary of state for the marine and the controller-general; the infrastructure of bureaux and commissions giving depth to the conciliar structure.[35] Yet it must be borne constantly in mind that this increasingly elaborate régime still depended for its effectiveness upon the dynamism of the ruler: as with the more highly systematized enlightened absolutist governments which followed, the crucial relationship was that obtaining between the king and his administrators. The second factor contributing to the regent's success was the contrasting and complementary roles of the abbé Dubois and John Law.

Orléans had long appreciated the talents of his two friends, and it was to his credit that he allowed both of them so much freedom in the elaboration of their projects, the one in financial, the other in diplomatic affairs. The fact that both men leant so heavily upon the regent's personal support made them rivals; it also practically guaranteed that the eventual triumph of the one would encompass the disgrace of the other. In the end Dubois won through to become first minister because his policies succeeded whereas Law's failed. However, the spectacular disaster which ultimately overtook John Law did not cancel out his positive contribution to the regency years when the promise of his System carried Orléans' government along on a great wave of new-found optimism. Nor was that optimism unjustified for subsequently the government was persuaded by the example of the Compagnie des Indes' control of indirect taxation that the amount paid out to tax-farmers was excessive; considerable reductions in that area from 1726 produced a near-balancing of the budget.[36]

Indeed, Dubois' own position was far from secure for much of the period up to June 1720. At the end of 1717, for example, the abbé had been forced to return post-haste from London fearing that his foreign policy had been discredited; while some eight months later we find him anxiously seeking the support of his British associates in his pursuit of government office. Not surprisingly, therefore, in these early years he was prepared to treat Law as an ally and the latter, who was even more vulnerable, was anxious to reciprocate. Thus, in the course of 1716 and 1717 a liaison was effected between the two men: Dubois assisted Law in his efforts to establish a general bank and offered his support against the increasingly hostile duke de Noailles. Even during his London embassy from the autumn of 1717 he maintained close contact with the Scotsman whose influence in Paris was continuing to grow.[37] Although Dubois duly obtained his brevet as secretary of state for foreign affairs in the government reshuffle of September 1718, his personal authority was soon to be challenged by the success of Law's System and his rival's appointment as controller-general of finance in January 1720.

Law's success impinged upon Dubois' policies in a specific area: the fear was expressed in Great Britain that the Mississippi venture might ultimately threaten British colonial possessions. The British ambassador in Paris, lord Stair, was particularly hostile to his fellow countryman, Law, and early in 1720 Stanhope was forced to have Stair recalled. In response to this attack Law increasingly favoured a French foreign policy opposed to the British alliance and in favour of a *rapprochement* with Spain and friendly relations with Russia which, under Peter the Great, was threatening both Hanoverian and British interests in the Baltic. This line brought him into head-on conflict with Dubois who was further irritated by Law's friendship with Torcy, his great rival in the foreign policy field, who, despite his support for the Quadruple Alliance, remained in favour of a reconciliation with the Bourbons in Spain. For the rest of the year Law and Dubois fought each other for political survival. At first the ominous cracks in the System appeared to favour Dubois and his advantage was confirmed in May when Law was dismissed from the office of controller-general. But his disgrace proved to be of short duration and, with his authority restored, Law once more posed a threat to his rival. The latter, however, had already gained a significant advantage by recourse to his supporters abroad who, in February 1720, had pressed the regent to bestow upon Dubois the vacant archbishopric of Cambrai. Since Philip V had just indicated his readiness to accede to the Quadruple Alliance, thereby bringing the abbé's major foreign policy initiative to a satisfactory conclusion, Orléans was disposed to grant the request. The new archbishop next concentrated his attention on Law's supporters among the 'old court' who approved of his pro-Spanish policy. By announcing his determination to mend the rift between France and Spain he was able to detach Maine and Toulouse, Torcy and d'Huxelles, and effectively cut the ground from under his rival's feet. That ground was in any case breaking up under the tremors announcing the collapse of the System. Although John Law held on until December 1720, he had lost his battle with Dubois by the middle of June. On the 19th of that month the new archbishop wrote confidently to Destouches, his agent in London, 'L'Intérieur est encore plus parfait que les apparences.'[38]

The in-fighting between Law and Dubois during these months had, therefore, one significant political effect: it quickened, though it was by no means solely responsible for, the move towards restoring friendly relations between France and Spain. Otherwise events and policies at that time were dominated by the irreversible decline of the System and governed in the last resort by the regent's fiat. Policies were not, in other words, merely the products of powerful rivalries: they stemmed from the often brilliant perceptions of three exceptional men. By temperament Orléans was closer to Law than to Dubois. The shared originality of approach and willingness of these two men to take risks were allied to some uncertainty of touch in matters of detail, an area in which the cautious cleric was at his most assured. Yet there was originality too in the shape of Dubois' foreign policy and understanding in depth in Orléans' appreciation of John Law's complex schemes. Theirs was a talented if unholy trinity rendered no less formidable by the inner tensions which characterized their relationship.

How, finally, may one sum up the political character of the regent himself? As a politician Orléans was sometimes indecisive, as in October/November 1717 in Dubois' absence in London when he was almost persuaded to support d'Huxelles' arguments in favour of a Spanish alliance; and in May/June 1718 when, again in the absence of Dubois, Stanhope's arrival in Paris was necessary to stiffen his support for a Quadruple Alliance. The regent was inclined to be won over to a new opinion by an argument powerfully made: hence the remarkable recovery of Law's fortunes shortly after his dismissal from office in May 1720. This trait was compounded of Orléans' readiness to see the virtues in conflicting points of view and a certain moral cowardice which led him to avoid personal confrontation whenever possible. As the barrister, Barbier, reported in his Journal, 'He had all the qualities necessary to be First Minister though he had some faults too including . . . saying yes to the one and in the very next moment no to the other.'[39] His political virtues tended, therefore, to be obscured by the low-key nature of his performance, something which was noted by that same shrewd observer of John Law's character to whom reference has already been made. He remarked on how profoundly some of Orléans' ministers misjudged him:

> . . . he was pliant and they thought him weak as indeed he appeared to be in trivial matters though always strong in important ones; he was a man of great intellect, penetrating, rational, profound and they thought him superficial and frivolous; . . . they did not believe that he possessed any of the qualities necessary to govern yet he had almost all of them; an elevated and fertile mind, the ability to dissemble, shrewdness, consistency, the ability to work quickly; they took him for an adventurer.[40]

A further contributory factor to the somewhat dilettante political image which Orléans projected was his propensity for boredom. This arose partly from the situation into which he was born, not close enough to the throne to succeed but too close to be allowed to outshine his cousins, and partly from the cast of his mind, which allowed him to master problems readily and then to lose interest in them forthwith. He admitted as much to his mother who recorded the fact in her correspondence: 'Although he talks of learned matters it is easy to see that they bore rather than please him. I have often taxed him about this and he has told me that it was not his fault, that as soon as he understood something it ceased to give him any pleasure.'[41]

Nevertheless there were those who did acknowledge his political skills: the abbé de Saint-Pierre, for example, who professed to having never witnessed so many essential qualities combined in a single person; even the bishop of Angers, whose less than enthusiastic oration at Orléans' funeral was not printed, confessed in his correspondence that Orléans had been a man of superior intellect, capable of learning from his own mistakes and better equipped to cope with the problems facing the government than any newcomer would be.[42] Saint-Simon's testimony was predictably favourable though, since he chose to represent the opinion of foreign diplomats, the most professional element at the French court, his observations are especially interesting.

> The death of M. le Duc d'Orléans [he wrote] made a great stir both at home and abroad; but in foreign countries he was far more highly esteemed and far more deeply mourned than by Frenchmen. . . . foreigners . . . learned by experience to recognize the breadth and soundness of his understanding, the nobility of his mind, his remarkable sagacity, his skill and wisdom in statecraft, the dexterity of his manoeuvres in constantly changing circumstances, his superiority to his ministers and to the ambassadors of foreign powers, the delicate perception he brought to the unravelling of State affairs, and the consummate skill with which, when he was pleased, he could swiftly answer questions of all kinds. These are rare talents in government and caused him to be feared and treated with respect by foreign envoys, and his gracious ways that could lend charm even to refusals made him still more agreeable to them.[43]

Yet the political and intellectual qualities which equipped him so admirably for presiding over an enlightened régime were offset by other characteristics pointing in the opposite direction: the flaw in his make-up which rendered him so easily bored and which undoubtedly lay close to the root of the hedonistic philosophy by which he lived and died; his unwillingness to inflict the smallest hurt even upon his enemies; and the total lack of ruthlessness or vindictiveness in his nature, which was reflected in his treatment of the Cellamare conspirators, of the magistrates of the parlement during their exile at Pontoise, even of the author of the *Philippiques* during his incarceration on the Ile Sainte-Marguerite.[44]

All this is to judge Orléans as though he had been king instead of regent. Had he inherited the crown himself who can say what sort of man and ruler he would have turned out to be? Within the narrower limits of the regent's office, acting as custodian of the king's authority, he achieved remarkable success. However, it may be instructive to examine some of the underlying implications of Orléans' policies, not least because the last two monarchs of *ancien régime* France seemed quite unaware of their importance.

Philippe was not, even conventionally, a religious man, a fact of the utmost political significance for it meant that for him the idea of divine-right monarchy carried no conviction. His firm defence of royal authority was justified by a deeper commitment to the state than that of dynastic self-esteem, and based on canons of reason and efficiency. He was, in other words, a proto-enlightened absolutist. He did possess a pride in his house which inevitably coloured his foreign policy since the dynastic configuration of Europe was still the natural starting point for diplomacy; but it did not dominate him. He had no vision of a permanent international order – that was not in the mind of his generation – but he did favour short-term collective security as an antidote to the imminent dangers of rampant dynasticism. Through his understanding of the changing political realities in Europe he served well both the French state and the house of Bourbon.

Particularly in domestic politics Philippe's determination to maintain the royal prerogative, coupled with his awareness of the need for radical reform, pointed towards a régime of enlightened absolutism. Even before the introduction of John Law's System the regent had tried to bring some order and rationality into the administration of finance so that the royal treasury might be more regularly and efficiently replenished, with the subjects' ability to pay taken more seriously into account, at least in a limited way. His measures increased the degree of central government control: indeed such rationalizing concepts presupposed a heightened sense of the state's interventionist role. That regulatory function was dramatically extended with Law's System which, developed to its ultimate limits, would have led to the abolition of fiscal privilege and allowed the prince unrestricted control over a wide range of his subjects' activities. Orléans' interest in reintroducing free instruction at the University of Paris may be cited as illustrative of his desire to provide the country with the sort of right-minded subjects (i.e., those uninfluenced by Jesuit ultramontanism) whose service to the French state would be of most value. The *Mercure de France*, commenting on this particular measure in April 1719, observed that 'this new arrangement should contribute substantially to the progress of Letters and yield a greater number of subjects useful to the State.'[45]

There was a fundamental difficulty, however, in the way of such developments. The king's authority to act legally depended upon his maintaining the traditional social and political order by the exercise of a quasi-spiritual, quasi-judicial power which was itself embedded in that same tradition. Orléans had no respect for the prop of divine-right monarchy, yet how could the king act legally without that justification? Similarly, how could the crown introduce necessary reforms without overturning existing and long-established rights, thereby calling into question its own legality? In everything he did Orléans maintained the final absolute authority of the executive, whether in his methods of financial control, in his relationship with the parlement, or in his organization of central government. Thus he gave Louis XV the opportunity either to pursue his predecessors' traditional path or to build on the new possibilities which Orléans had perceived but not pushed to the point at which there might have been a risk of compromising the king's jurisdiction. The regent was a political realist who sensed the shifting nature of contemporary values; he deserves credit for bequeathing to his successor the prestige and stimulus to capitalize upon that intuition.

When Louis XV reached the end of his minority, in February 1723, he intimated his desire that Orléans should remain at his right hand and that cardinal Dubois should be the first minister. When Dubois died in the following August Orléans added that formal title to the authority which he was exercising already. His influence with Louis would probably have remained strong for some time for this shy and withdrawn thirteen-year-old was no more than an apprentice king and he was genuinely fond of his kinsman. However, that was not to be, for Orléans himself died at Versailles on 2 December 1723, some eight months short of his fiftieth birthday, and his place was taken by the premier prince of the blood, the talentless duke de Bourbon. Though death came suddenly, as he hoped it would, it was not altogether unexpected: his complexion, which was ruddy for many years, had changed to an unhealthy purple, and there were other indications that prolonged excess was beginning to threaten his life.[46] Doubtless he would have derived some sardonic pleasure from the shocking manner of his passing, in the arms of his latest mistress, the duchess de Falari. The recollection of his scandalous private life loomed large at that moment: in contemplating this 'visible and terrible hammer-blow of divine justice', the bishop of Angers mused on how cardinal Dubois, the servant, had been given time, had he chosen to profit from it, to make his peace with God before entering eternity, whereas his master, Orléans, had been denied even a minute's reflection.[47] That judgment on the 'fanfaron de crimes'[48] was the one which, by and large, posterity has chosen to echo. Yet with eyes fixed firmly on the mundane political arena it is possible to infer, from the evident distress which Orléans' death aroused in the popular young man now successfully embarked upon his majority, a more favourable valediction.

Chronology

1712	18 February	Death of the duke de Bourgogne
	8 March	Death of the duke de Bretagne
1713	April	Treaty of Utrecht signed
	8 September	Publication of the papal bull, Unigenitus
1714	4 May	Death of the duke de Berry
	29 July	Duke du Maine and count de Toulouse given the right to succeed to the French throne by Louis XIV
	August	Louis XIV draws up his will
1715	26 August	Contents of Louis' will revealed to Orléans
	1 September	Death of Louis XIV
	2 September	Orléans proclaimed regent
	15 September	Right of remonstrance restored to the parlement of Paris
	September–December	Establishment of the *polysynodie*
	December	Anglo-Spanish commercial treaty
1716	May	Law's private bank established
	June	Treaty of Westminster between Britain and the Emperor
	July	Dubois' mission to the Hague
		Failure of Louville's embassy to Madrid
1717	4 January	Triple Alliance of the Hague
	March	Dubois appointed to the council for foreign affairs
		Appeal of the four bishops against Unigenitus
	May	Tsar Peter I in Paris
	July	Maine and Toulouse lose their right of succession to the French throne
	August	Spain begins the conquest of Sardinia
		Treaty signed between France, Russia and Prussia
	October	Declaration imposing silence in the dispute over Unigenitus
	December	Estates of Brittany refuse to vote the *don gratuit*
1718	January	Duke de Noailles replaced by d'Argenson as head of the council for finance. D'Argenson also takes over as Keeper of the Seals after d'Aguesseau's disgrace
	29 May	Edict ordering a general recoinage registered in the *cour des monnaies*
	2 August	Quadruple Alliance
	18 August	Parlement of Paris forbids foreigners to take any part in the administration of royal revenues
	26 August	Maine and Toulouse reduced to the status of peers
		Parlement's opposition crushed at a *lit de justice*

	September	Dubois made secretary of state for foreign affairs; councils for religion (*conscience*), war, foreign affairs and the interior suppressed
		League of Breton noblemen formed against Orléans
	November	Voltaire's *Oedipe* opens at the Comédie-française
	December	Law's bank becomes a royal one
		Cellamare conspiracy broken
1719	February	Appearance of the *Philippiques*
	April	Council decree proclaims that bank-notes will not be subject to devaluation
	26 May	Compagnie des Indes established
	July	Law given sole right to coin money
		Death of the duchess de Berry
	August	Compagnie des Indes made responsible for collecting indirect taxation
	October	Compagnie des Indes takes over responsibility for the collection of direct taxes
1720	5 January	Law appointed controller-general of finance
	February	Union of the bank and the company
		Council decree forbids the holding of specie to a value of more than 500 *livres*
		Spain adheres to the Quadruple Alliance
	March	Legal interest rate reduced from 4 per cent to 2 per cent
		Share prices pegged at 9,000 *livres*
		Four Breton noblemen executed for *lèse-majesté*
	21 May	Drastic devaluation of bank-notes and company shares
	27 May	Edict of 21st repealed
		Law dismissed as controller-general
	June	Dubois consecrated archbishop of Cambrai
	July	Parlement of Paris exiled to Pontoise
	September	Declaration incorporating the compromise on Unigenitus registered in the *grand conseil*
	October	International conference at Cambrai in the wake of Spain's accession to the Quadruple Alliance
	4 December	Declaration on Unigenitus registered by the parlement
	14 December	Law flees from Paris
	16 December	The parlement recalled to the capital
1721	March	Franco-Spanish convention signed at Madrid
	June	The convention becomes a triple alliance with Britain's accession
	July	Dubois becomes a cardinal
	September	Treaty of Nystad

1722	January	Marriage of Orléans' daughter, Louise Elisabeth, to the prince of the Asturias
	March	Orléans makes a major effort to systematize the flow of government funds
		Office of intendants of finance restored
	June	Council of commerce converted into a bureau
	August	Dubois becomes first minister
1723	15 February	Louis XV reaches his majority
	10 August	Death of Dubois at Versailles
	2 December	Death of Orléans at Versailles
1729	21 March	Death of Law in Venice

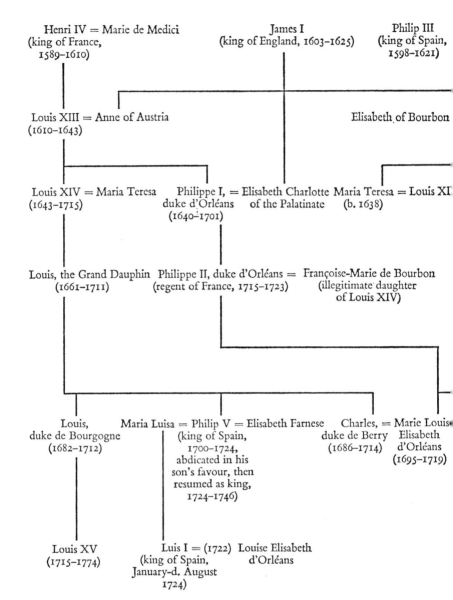

Margaret of Austria

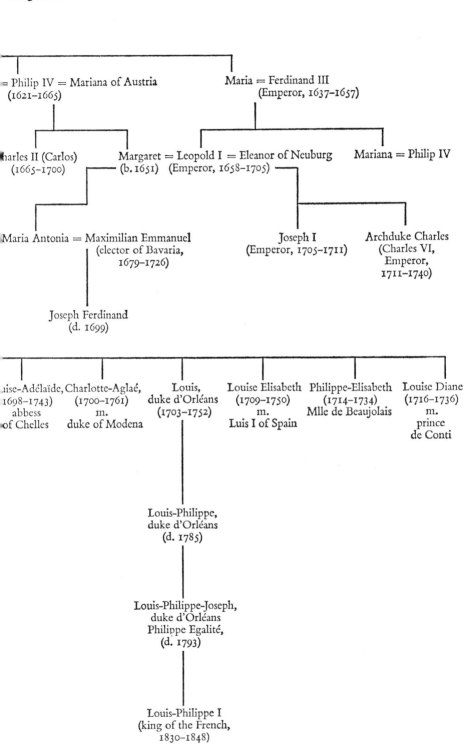

= Philip IV = Mariana of Austria
(1621–1665)

Maria = Ferdinand III
(Emperor, 1637–1657)

Charles II (Carlos)
(1665–1700)

Margaret = Leopold I = Eleanor of Neuburg
(b. 1651) (Emperor, 1658–1705)

Mariana = Philip IV

Maria Antonia = Maximilian Emmanuel
(elector of Bavaria,
1679–1726)

Joseph I
(Emperor, 1705–1711)

Archduke Charles
(Charles VI,
Emperor,
1711–1740)

Joseph Ferdinand
(d. 1699)

Louise-Adélaïde,
(1698–1743)
abbess
of Chelles

Charlotte-Aglaé,
(1700–1761)
m.
duke of Modena

Louis,
duke d'Orléans
(1703–1752)

Louise Elisabeth
(1709–1750)
m.
Luis I of Spain

Philippe-Elisabeth
(1714–1734)
Mlle de Beaujolais

Louise Diane
(1716–1736)
m.
prince
de Conti

Louis-Philippe,
duke d'Orléans
(d. 1785)

Louis-Philippe-Joseph,
duke d'Orléans
Philippe Egalité,
(d. 1793)

Louis-Philippe I
(king of the French,
1830–1848)

Bibliography

Philippe d'Orléans has long presented an enigmatic countenance to would-be biographers. His surviving correspondence is inconsiderable in volume and significance – so that his motives and objectives must often be inferred – and he chose to project a public image more readily caricatured than understood. Similarly, his period of office is all too easily drained of significance in the afterglow of his uncle's brilliant reign. However, both Orléans and his regency deserve fresh consideration on their own account, and there is evidence enough available for such an undertaking.

MANUSCRIPT SOURCES

This volume is based in approximately equal proportions upon archival material, contemporary printed sources, and secondary works. Every historian of the *ancien régime* who has worked in the Parisian archives will be aware that the available manuscript material is shared out among a relatively large number of institutions. Though the Archives Nationales and the Bibliothèque Nationale are vast storehouses, no student of French history can afford to ignore the smaller collections with which the capital is well endowed, where important, sometimes unsuspected, manuscript funds may be unearthed.

Archives Nationales

There are many guides, catalogues and inventories to assist readers in the national archives, the most important of which are listed in the brief *Guide du lecteur* (1966), pp. 10–12. Much of the material gathered from this collection is judicial and financial. The best introduction to the former section is provided by the *Guide des recherches dans les fonds judiciaires de l'ancien régime* (1958), and the much older *Répertoire numérique des archives du parlement de Paris* (1889). Series X contains the official records of the parlement, among which the registers of the *conseil secret*, X1a, relate to the court's political debates. But from this source we learn only of final decisions, nothing of the discussions which preceded them. An exception is X1a 8299 *bis* (registres de la troisième chambre des enquêtes) which provides an unofficial record of one of the court's chambers. Series U, Extrait de diverses juridictions, offers more informative material: U357–366, collection Delisle: Extraits du conseil secret du parlement entremêlés de lettres-patentes, d'arrêts, de mandements épiscopaux et autres imprimés, 1715–23. Delisle was a clerk in the parlement and his notes from the *conseil secret*, unlike the finished article in Series X, contain accounts of the speeches of individual magistrates. U416, also from the collection Delisle, is entitled Journal du parlement pendant l'année 1718. U420 and U421 come from a different source: Premières minutes des séances du conseil secret du parlement, rédigées par le greffier, Gilbert, 1718–22, and U747 and U748 revert to the collection Delisle: Journal du parlement séant à Pontoise, 1720. The relevant financial material is located in Series G7, contrôle général des finances: especially 23–30, 774–86, 1849; and in Series E, *conseil du roi*, 3649–53, Registres contenant l'analyse des matières de finance rapportées et décidées au conseil de régence, 1715–18. In addition the following registers and cartons should be noted: K, monuments historiques, 544, 696, which both relate to the events surrounding the death of Louis XIV and the very beginning of the regency; L, monuments ecclésiastiques, 18, pièces relatives à l'histoire de la bulle Unigenitus; M, mélanges, 784, papiers Mirabeau; KK 820 and 1321–25, the latter containing some of Orléans' correspondence relating to his scientific interests.

Bibliothèque Nationale

H. Omont's *Catalogue des manuscrits français de la bibliothèque nationale* (1895–1918), 13 vols, is an indispensable guide to the manuscript collection housed in this great library. The fonds des anciens manuscrits français (ms. fr.) contain the official records of the regency council, 23.663–23.673, besides the following valuable material: 6931, 6935, 6942 (lettres du duc d'Orléans et du duc de Noailles, 1715–17) (copies); 7765 (recueil de mémoires sur la réforme et le rétablissement des finances, 1715–17); 7769 (mémoires pour les finances, adressés au régent, 1715–17); 10231 (pièces diverses, titres, règlements, mémoires, etc., concernant les charges de la cour, du conseil, du parlement et autres, et touchant divers points d'administration); 10362 (mémoire sur la régence); 10543 (entreprises des parlements sur l'autorité de l'église); 10907 (livre secret . . . du parlement de Paris – actually the unofficial registers of one of the court's chambers, the 5th enquêtes: cf. A.N., X1a 8299 *bis*, above); 10908 (extrait des choses les plus importantes qui se sont passées au parlement); 13683–90 (journeaux historiques); 13732 (mémoires de la régence); 17044 (portefeuilles du docteur Vallant, which contains a copy of an important letter written by Orléans).

A separate series also housed in the Bibliothèque Nationale is the nouvelles acquisitions françaises (n.a.f.) which includes 9644; 23.929–23.937 (mémoires du duc d'Antin). It also contains a voluminous fund entitled, Collection du parlement: copies et extraits de registres du parlement de Paris . . . provenant des présidents de Lamoignon. This collection Lamoignon, as it is generally known, is more manageable than the official material in Series X in the Archives Nationales, providing an edited version of the records of the *conseil secret* which make it a valuable source of reference. Volumes 8158–8170 were consulted for my study.

Finally, two smaller collections located in the Bibliothèque Nationale further reward the researcher in this period. The collection Joly de Fleury contains material on legal, political and religious matters, gathered together by various members of the family to which the *procureur-général* during the regency, Guillaume-François Joly de Fleury, belonged: mss. 8, 9, 14, 17, 18, 2476 and 2553 are of particular value. The collection Clairambault includes in ms. 529 (histoire de la régence … depuis 1715 jusqu'en 1723) a manuscript attributed on the frontispiece to Angrand de Fontpertuis, an official of the Compagnie des Indes. Copies of the same document are to be found in ms. fr. 10361 and n.a.f. 1431, as well as in the Bibliothèque de l'Arsenal, ms. 3857. In his introduction to John Law's complete works P. Harsin concludes that the Scotsman himself was the author of this particular piece, an opinion supported by M. Giraud in his *Histoire de la Louisiane Française*, vol. 3. However, though much of the content may well have been written by Law, or at least represents his views, the internal evidence makes it clear that another hand was also at work and there is no reason to doubt that it belonged to Angrand de Fontpertuis.

Archives du Ministère des Affaires Etrangères
The archives at the Quai d'Orsay provide a salutary reminder of the fact that *ancien régime* sources are not always susceptible of clear categorization. Because leading ministers like Cardinals Dubois and Fleury strongly interested themselves in the field of foreign affairs, much of the material concerning their régimes has found its way to the Foreign Office, including documents relating to matters of domestic policy. The following manuscript volumes proved especially profitable: mémoires et documents, France: 311, 445, 1218, 1220, 1233, 1235, 1236, 1251, 1252, 1253; mémoires et documents, Hollande: 300; correspondance politique, Espagne: 143; correspondance politique, Angleterre: 226, 334.

Bibliothèque des Amis de Port-Royal
This small collection – a shrine to Jansenism – preserves the eighteenth-century library of Adrien Le Paige, a barrister in the parlement and a noted disciple of the movement. The collection came into the hands of the great Jansenist historian, Augustin Gazier, whose handwritten summary at the head of each tome provides the only indication of its contents. In the absence of a formal catalogue the wealth of printed and manuscript material relating to the religious crisis of the regency years is but slowly revealed. Those volumes of the collection Le Paige which proved of particular value to this study were numbers 412, 413, 415, 416, 417, 422, 424 and 425. Vol. 424, no. 3, is a diary by the abbé Couet, a magistrate in the parlement, recording details of the court's exile at Pontoise in 1720.

The best printed guide to the following four libraries is the *Catalogue des manuscrits des bibliothèques publiques de France*.

Bibliothèque de l'Arsenal
Besides ms. 3857 mentioned above, this pleasant little library, whose Bastille

archives offer a direct link with the regency (see pp. 131–32), contains the following useful sources: 3968 (recueil historique sur la régence); 3724 (recueil de Fevret de Fontette); 4492 (recueil de mémoires sur les finances).

Bibliothèque du Senat

There are some relevant sources here, though fewer than might appear from a first glance at the catalogue since two manuscripts, 424 and 799, are both copies of B.N., ms. fr. 10908, mentioned above. The secret registers of two more of the parlement's chambers, the first and second enquêtes, mss. 721 and 732, are to be found here, the former being the most detailed of all the secret registers. Mss. 792–93, 796 add little, but mss. 422–23 (Journal historique du Palais, 1711–25), by another parlementaire, Moreau de Nassigny, is a valuable document which does not duplicate other sources. The official records of the *conseil de conscience*, mss. 224–25, are also deposited in this library.

Two additional sources are worth noting: in the **Bibliothèque Mazarine**, ms. 2497 (recueil de pièces imprimées et manuscrites sur la bulle Unigenitus), and **Bibliothèque Sainte-Geneviève**, ms. 2084 (pièces sur l'histoire de France, XVII*e*–XVIII*e* siècles).

Finally, I am deeply indebted to the authors of two unpublished doctoral theses who have allowed me to cite their work: E. R. Briggs, *The Political Academies of France in the Early 18th Century* (Cambridge Ph.D., 1931); and R. E. A. Waller, *The Relations between Men of Letters and the Representatives of Authority in France, 1715–1723* (Oxford D. Phil., 1971). I am especially grateful to Dr Waller for allowing me the leisurely perusal of his own copy; the value of his work to this volume may be judged by reference to the footnotes.

CONTEMPORARY PRINTED SOURCES (the place of publication is Paris except where otherwise indicated)

Letters, Journals, Memoirs

There can be few periods of French history richer in such material. Dominating the scene is the monumental work of Louis de Rouvroy, duc de Saint-Simon, *Mémoires* (ed. A. de Boislisle), 41 vols, 1879–1928; and in a recent attractively abbreviated form, ed. L. Norton, 3 vols, London 1967–72. Saint-Simon's acute eye, dramatic sense and envenomed pen translated the scandalous tittle-tattle of courtiers, as well as their triumphs and tragedies, into a literary masterpiece. Life in the streets of the capital and around the palais de justice was reflected in the diaries of two barristers: E.-J.-F. Barbier, *Chronique de la régence et du règne de Louis XV, 1718–63*, 8 vols, 1857, and M. Marais, *Journal et Mémoires* (ed. M. de Lescure), 4 vols, 1863–68. Useful for chronology and for the additions by Saint-Simon but otherwise almost a court circular is P. de Courcillon, marquis de Dangeau, *Journal* (ed. E. Soulié and M. L. Dussieux), 19 vols, 1854–60. Also reflecting the work of Saint-Simon is C. P. Duclos, *Mémoires secrets sur les règnes de Louis XIV et de Louis XV*: vol. 34 of *Mémoires relatifs à l'histoire de France* (eds J. F. Michaud and J.-J. F. Poujoulat), 34 vols, 1854. R. L. de V., marquis d'Argenson, *Journal et Mémoires* (ed. E. J. B. Rathéry), 9 vols, 1859–67, written by the son of the keeper of the seals, deals only fleetingly with the regency period, whereas J. Buvat, *Journal de la régence* (ed. E. Campardon), 2 vols, 1865, concentrates on the rumours pullulating in the Parisian streets during those years. The *Journal*, 2 vols, Rome 1753, of abbé Dorsanne, secretary to the *conseil de conscience*, provides an exhaustive, if palpably one-sided account of the Jansenist controversy. Other, more prestigious, royal servants have likewise left accounts of their stewardships: A.-M., duc de Noailles, *Mémoires politiques et militaires*: vol. 34 of *Mémoires relatifs à l'histoire de France* (eds J. F. Michaud and J.-J. F. Poujoulat), 34 vols, 1854; J.-B. Colbert, marquis de Torcy, *Mémoires*, 3rd series, vol. 8 of *Nouvelle collection des mémoires pour servir à l'histoire de France* (eds J. F. Michaud and J.-J. F. Poujoulat), 34 vols in 32, 1836–39; C. L. H., duc de Villars, *Mémoires*: vol. 33 of *Mémoires relatifs à l'histoire de France* (eds J. F. Michaud and J.-J. F. Poujoulat), 34 vols, 1854. The judges of the parlement are represented by C.-J. F. Hénault, *Mémoires* (ed. F. Rousseau), 1911; and G. de Lamoignon, *Journal historique, 1713–18* (ed. H. Courteault and published in the annual bulletin of the *Société de l'histoire de France*), 1910. The *Gazette de la régence, 1715–1719* (ed. E. de Barthélemy), 1887, and P. Narbonne, *Journal des règnes de Louis XIV et Louis XV* (ed. J. A. le Roy), 1866, should also be noted. Among letter-writers, *Les correspondants de la marquise de Balleroy* (ed. E. de Barthélemy), 2 vols, 1883, supply some useful comments on the early years of the regency but nothing so revealing as the robust *Correspondance complète de Madame, duchesse d'Orléans* (ed. G. Brunet), 2 vols, 1855. The views of an appellant bishop may be gauged from J.-B. Gaultier, *La vie et les lettres de messire Jean Soanen, évêque de Senez*, 2 vols, Cologne 1750.

Documentary collections

R. Cerveau (ed.), *Nécrologe des plus célèbres défenseurs et confesseurs de la vérité du XVIIIᵉ siècle*, 7 vols, 1760 – a handbook dealing with famous Jansenists. J. Flammermont (ed.), *Les remontrances du parlement de Paris au XVIIIᵉ siècle*, 3 vols, 1888–98. P. Harsin (ed.), *John Law: œuvres complètes*, 3 vols, 1934. F.-A. Isambert, (ed.), *Recueil général des anciennes lois françaises*, 29 vols, 1821–33. L. Mention (ed.), *Documents relatifs aux rapports du clergé avec la royauté*, 2 vols, 1893–1903. E. Raunié (ed.), *Chansonnier historique du XVIIIᵉ siècle*, 10 vols, 1879–84 – a barometer to the fickle favours and dislikes of popular opinion.

Other printed sources of the seventeenth and eighteenth centuries

J. Bodin, *Six livres de la république*, Geneva 1629 ed. E. Daire (ed.), *Economistes financiers du XVIIIᵉ siècle*, 1851, prints both P. le P. de Boisguillebert's *Détail de la France* and S. le P. de Vauban's *Projet d'une dîme royale*. C.-J. de Ferrière, *Dictionnaire de droit et de pratique*, 2 vols, 1740. J.-B. Gaultier (ed.), *Les oeuvres de messire Charles Joachim Colbert, évêque de Montpellier*, 3 vols, Cologne 1740 (pro-Jansenist). C. Joly, *Recueil des maximes*, 1653. P.-F. Lafiteau, *Histoire de la constitution Unigenitus*, Besançon 1820 ed. (anti-Jansenist). L(a) M(othe) D(e) L(a) H(ode), *La vie de Philippe d'Orléans, petit-fils de France, régent du royaume pendant la minorité de Louis XV*, 2 vols, London 1736. C. de S., baron de Montesquieu, *Oeuvres complètes*, ed. D. Oster, 1964. C.-I. de Saint-Pierre, *A discourse of the danger of governing by one minister*, London 1728. (*Discours sur la polysynodie*.) *Testament de Charles II, Roy d'Espagne, fait le 2 d'Octobre 1700* (with Louis XIV's reply to the newly established junta in Spain, 12 November), Paris 1700.

Secondary works

It may be helpful to divide more recent historiography into groups, beginning with works forming a useful or necessary introduction to the regency period: H. Brocher, *Le rang et l'etiquette sous l'ancien régime*, 1934; E. Carcassonne, *Montesquieu et le problème de la constitution française au XVIIIe siècle*, 1926; A. B. Cobban, *A History of Modern France*, vol. I (Pelican ed.), London 1957; F. L. Ford, *Robe and Sword*, Cambridge, Mass. 1953; P. Goubert, *Louis XIV and Twenty Million Frenchmen*, London 1970; A. Grellet-Dumazeau, *L'affaire du bonnet et les mémoires de Saint-Simon*, 1913; A. Lemaire, *Les lois fondamentales de la monarchie française*, 1907; M. Marion, *Dictionnaire des institutions de la France aux XVIIe et XVIIIe siècles*, 1923; L. Rothkrug, *Opposition to Louis XIV*, Princeton 1965; J. C. Rule (ed.), *Louis XIV and the Craft of Kingship*, Ohio 1969 (the articles by Rule himself, 'Louis XIV, Roi-Bureaucrate' and H. G. Judge, 'Louis XIV and the Church', are mentioned in the footnotes); J. H. Shennan, *The Origins of the Modern European State, 1450–1725*, London 1974; J. B. Wolf, *Louis XIV* (Panther ed.), London 1970.

As for the regency itself, the magisterial opus of Dom H. Leclercq, *Histoire de la régence*, 3 vols, 1921, commands the field. It is a work of dedicated and exhaustive scholarship and one need look no further for information about the regency years; yet it is oddly lacking in interpretative form and conceptual consistency. Volumes concentrating on the regent himself include the perceptive C. E. Engel's *Le régent*, 1969, and the rather older biography by P. Erlanger, *Le régent*, 1938; while M. de Lescure, *Les maîtresses du régent*, 1860, deals with one aspect of the regent's private life. J. D. Hardy, *Judicial Politics in the Old Régime*, Baton Rouge 1967, and the composite work *La régence*, 1970, produced by the *Centre aixois d'études et de recherches sur le dix-huitième siècle*, examine widely differing themes. The contributions to the latter are much concerned with the artistic, literary and intellectual life of the period, as are G. Atkinson and A. C. Keller, *Prelude to the Enlightenment*, London 1971; L. Hautecoeur, *Histoire de l'architecture classique en France*, vol. 3, 1950; *Index biographique des membres et correspondants de l'académie des sciences*, Paris 1954; *Louis XV: un moment de perfection de l'art français*, Hôtel de la Monnaie, Paris 1974; A. G. Palacios, *The Age of Louis XV*, London 1969; J. H. Shennan, 'Louis XV: Public and Private Worlds', *The Courts of Europe* (ed. A. G. Dickens), London 1977; R. E. A. Waller, 'Voltaire and the regent', *Studies on Voltaire and the eighteenth century*, CXXVII, 1974.

The structure of central government under Orléans is brilliantly dissected by

M. Antoine, *Le conseil du roi sous le règne de Louis XV,* Geneva 1970; note also his *Inventaire des arrêts du conseil du roi, règne de Louis XV,* vol. I, 1968. M. Benoit, *La polysynodie,* 1928, is a little known analysis of the regent's conciliar system. The following recent contributions on administrative developments span the period between Louis XIV's last years and his great-grandson's majority: M. Bordes, 'Les intendants de Louis XV', *Revue Historique,* CCXXIII, 1960; Vivian R. Gruder, *The Royal Provincial Intendants,* Ithaca N.Y. 1968; H. M. A. Keens-Soper, 'The French Political Academy, 1712: the School for Ambassadors', *European Studies Review,* II (4), 1972; T. J. Schaeper, 'The Creation of the French Council of Commerce in 1700', *European Studies Review* (to appear); C. C. Sturgill, *Claude le Blanc: Civil Servant of the King,* University of Gainesville, Florida 1975; C. C. Sturgill, 'Le conseil de la guerre (1715–1718)', *Revue historique de l'armée,* March 1969.

The family background and social and economic status of the judges in the parlement of Paris have been brilliantly and painstakingly established in two books by J. F. Bluche, *L'origine des magistrats du parlement de Paris au XVIIIe siècle,* 1956, and *Les magistrats du parlement de Paris au XVIIIe siècle* (1715–1771), 1960. Their political actions during the regency is the subject of an article by J. H. Shennan, 'The Political Role of the Parlement of Paris, 1715–23', *Historical Journal,* VIII, 1965; see also by the same author, *The Parlement of Paris,* London 1968. An older treatment is provided by E. Glasson, *Le parlement de Paris. Son rôle politique depuis le règne de Charles VII jusqu'à la révolution,* 2 vols, 1901. The following volumes should also be noted: R. Bickart, *Les parlements et la notion de souveraineté nationale au XVIIIe siècle,* 1932; J. Egret, *Louis XV et l'opposition parlementaire,* 1970; and A. Renaudet, *Les parlements. Etudes sur l'histoire de la France, 1715–89,* 1946.

Religious issues which frequently informed the parlement's political role were dominated by the problem of Jansenism. J. Carreyre, *Le jansénisme durant la régence,* 3 vols, 1929–33, offers a scholarly path through a veritable thicket of partisan opinion. Most distinguished among pro-Jansenist historians is A. Gazier, *Histoire générale du mouvement janséniste,* 2 vols, 1922. An introduction to this complex theological dispute is to be found in N. Abercrombie, *The Origins of Jansenism,* Oxford 1936; R. A. Knox, *Enthusiasm,* Oxford 1950; and J. Orcibal, *Les origines du jansénisme: Jean Duvergier de Hauranne, abbé de Saint-Cyran et son temps,* Louvain 1947. J. Parguez, *La bulle Unigenitus et le jansénisme politique,* 1936, brings us back to the political ramifications of the quarrel, as does J.-F. Thomas, *La querelle de l'Unigenitus,* 1950. On a wider canvas the excellent series edited by J.-B. Duroselle and E. Jarry, *Histoire de l'Eglise,* provides us in vol. 19 (1) with E. Préclin and E. Jarry, *Les luttes politiques et doctrinales aux XVIIe et XVIIIe siècles,* 1956. Finally the article by G. Rech, 'Daguesseau et le jansénisme', *Le chancelier Henri-François Daguesseau, 1668–1751,* Limoges 1953, which analyzes the legal implications of Unigenitus; and A. Leroy, *La France et Rome de 1700 à 1715,* 1892, are worthy of attention.

A small group of historians, writing around the turn of the last century, have contributed a number of seminal works in the field of foreign affairs. Between them, they have undertaken a comprehensive investigation of the relevant sections in the English, French and Spanish archives and their works still provide the best starting point for research in this area. They include A. Baudrillart, *Philippe V et la cour d'Espagne*, 5 vols, 1890–1910; E. Bourgeois, *La diplomatie secrète au XVIIIe siècle*, 3 vols, 1909–10, in particular *Le secret du régent et la politique de l'abbé Dubois*, and *Le secret de Dubois, cardinal et premier ministre*; A. Legrelle, *La diplomatie française et la succession d'Espagne*, 4 vols, 1888–92; L. Wiesener, *Le régent, l'abbé Dubois et les anglais*, 3 vols, 1891–99. Bourgeois takes a hostile view of Orléans' diplomacy, Wiesener a favourable one. Among other works consulted in this field are the following: A. Bailly, *Le cardinal Dubois*, 1944; W. Coxe, *Memoirs of the Life and Administration of Sir Robert Walpole*, 2 vols, London 1798; *Hardwicke State Papers*, 2 vols, London 1777–78 (containing extracts from the Journal of Lord Stair, British ambassador in Paris at the beginning of the regency); Ragnhild Hatton, *Diplomatic relations between Great Britain and the Dutch Republic, 1714–21*, London 1950; Ragnhild Hatton and J. S. Bromley (eds), *William III and Louis XIV: Essays 1680–1720 by and for Mark A. Thomson*, Liverpool 1968; C. Hippeau, *L'avènement des Bourbons au trône d'Espagne*, 2 vols, 1875; H. Kamen, *The War of Succession in Spain, 1700–15*, London 1969; G. Murray (ed.), *Letters and Despatches of John Churchill, First Duke of Marlborough*, 5 vols, London 1845; H. L. Snyder (ed.), *The Marlborough-Godolphin Correspondence*, 3 vols, Oxford 1975; P. H. Stanhope, *History of the War of the Succession in Spain*, London 1836 ed.; A. Vandal, *Louis XV et Elisabeth de Russie*, 1882; B. Williams, *Stanhope*, Oxford 1932; note also the article by M. A. Martin, 'The Secret Clause: Britain and Spanish Ambitions in Italy, 1712–31', *European Studies Review*, VI (4), 1976.

The last group of titles relates to economic and financial matters. M. Giraud, *Histoire de la Louisiane*, vol. 3: *L'époque de John Law (1717–1720)*, 1966, deals with the overseas aspect of the System, while E. J. Hamilton has contributed two valuable articles on the domestic effects of Law's System: 'Prices and Wages at Paris under John Law's System', *Quarterly Journal of Economics*, LI, 1936; and 'Prices and Wages in Southern France under John Law's System', *Economic Journal* (Economic History Supplement), 1937. Besides editing John Law's collected works P. Harsin has published *Les doctrines monétaires et financières en France du XVIe au XVIIIe siècle*, 1928, and *Crédit public et banque d'état en France du XVIe au XVIIIe siècle*, 1933. H. M. Hyde, *John Law*, London 1948, is a competent though by no means definitive biography. Two useful wide-ranging works which cover this subject are F. Braudel and E. Labrousse (eds), *Histoire économique et sociale de la France*, vol. 2: *1660–1789*, 1970, and H. Luthy, *La banque protestante en France*, vol. 1, 1959. In conclusion, three further articles may be cited, all of them concerned with aspects of John Law's System: E. Levasseur, 'Law et son système jugés par un contemporain', *Séances et travaux de l'académie des sciences morales et politiques*, CLXXI, 1909; J.-P. Poisson, 'Introduction à une étude quantitative des effets socio-économiques du système de Law', *Journal de la société statistique de Paris*, 1974; and M. A. Sallon, 'L'échec de Law', *Revue d'histoire économique et sociale*, XLVIII, 1970.

Notes to the Text

Prologue

1 In that year Louis had decreed that royal enactments were to be registered by the parlement before it submitted remonstrances against them. See below, pp. 24–26.

2 On this question see below, pp. 19–20.

Chapter I

1 Saint-Simon, *Historical Memoirs*, ed. and transl. by Lucy Norton, II, 428–29. This edition of the famous *Mémoires* is a most readable version though in a much reduced – and therefore manageable – form. Reference will also be made to the magnificent 41-volume standard edition by A. de Boislisle.

2 Archives Nationales, Paris [hereafter A.N.], Series M784, no. 69.

3 J. B. Wolf, *Louis XIV*, p. 424.

4 L(a) M(othe) D(e) L(a) H(ode), *La Vie de Philippe d'Orléans, petit-fils de France, régent du royaume pendant la minorité de Louis XV*, I, 9–13, 33.

5 On the subject of Philippe's many paramours see M. de Lescure, *Les maîtresses du régent, passim*.

6 Saint-Simon (ed. Norton), *op. cit.*, I, 333.

7 L(a) M(othe) D(e) L(a) H(ode), *op. cit.*, I, 65–78.

8 See below, pp. 16–17 ff.

9 A. Bailly, *Le cardinal Dubois*, p. 19; R. E. A. Waller, *The Relations between Men of Letters and the Representatives of Authority in France, 1715–1723*, pp. 173–203; *Index biographique des membres et correspondants de l'académie des sciences*

du 22 décembre 1666 au 15 novembre 1954, p. 250.

10 C.-E. Engel, 'Le régent collectionneur', in *La Régence*, pp. 58–65. The art historian G. F. Waagen, writing in the mid-19th century, provides a slightly different, though no less impressive list: cf. Waller, *op. cit.*, pp. 174–75.

11 Lescure, *op. cit.*, pp. 64 ff.

12 *Correspondance complète de Madame, duchesse d'Orléans* (ed. G. Brunet), II, 164–65.

13 Saint-Simon (ed. Norton), *op. cit.*, II, 441–42.

14 Cf. below, p. 126.

15 *Testament de Charles II, Roy d'Espagne, fait le 2 d'Octobre 1700*, article XIII; the original Spanish version of the will is printed in A. Legrelle, *La diplomatie française et la succession d'Espagne*, III, 712–37.

16 *Testament de Charles II*, Louis XIV's reply, p. 71.

17 Cf. the genealogical table, p. 150.

18 C. Hippeau, *Avènement des Bourbons au trône d'Espagne*, II, 322–24.

19 A. Baudrillart, *Philippe V et la cour d'Espagne*, II, 21.

20 Wolf, *op. cit.*, p. 707; cf. Legrelle, *op. cit.*, IV, 72–73, 664; M. A. Thomson, 'Louis XIV and the Origins of the War of the Spanish Succession', in *William III and Louis XIV. Essays by and for Mark A. Thomson* (ed. Ragnhild Hatton and J. S. Bromley), pp. 147–48.

21 P. H. Stanhope, Viscount Mahon, *History of the War of the Succession in Spain*, pp. 261 ff. and Appendix, pp. lxix–lxxi.

22 Saint-Simon (ed. Norton), *op. cit.*, I, 370; H. Kamen, *The War of Succession in Spain, 1700–15*, p. 49.
23 Baudrillart, *op. cit.*, II, 75.
24 Legrelle, *op. cit.*, IV, 462–63; cf. Marquis de Torcy, *Mémoires*, Part II, pp. 619–27.
25 Saint-Simon (ed. Norton), *op. cit.*, I, 463.
26 *Ibid.*, I, 462; Kamen, *op. cit.*, p. 49.
27 *The Marlborough-Godolphin Correspondence* (ed. H. L. Snyder), III, 1200; also Marlborough's letter to Stanhope, 26 January 1709, printed in *Letters and Despatches of John Churchill, First Duke of Marlborough* (ed. Sir G. Murray), IV, 409.
28 Stanhope, *op. cit.*, Appendix, p. lxxxiv, Stanhope to the earl of Sunderland, 20 December, 1708; also cf. Baudrillart, *op. cit.*, II, 99.
29 Baudrillart, *op. cit.*, I, 692–95; II, 88.
30 Legrelle, *op. cit.*, IV, 663–64; E. Bourgeois, *Le secret du régent et la politique de l'abbé Dubois*, p. 25.
31 Baudrillart, *op. cit.*, I, 670–72; II, 211.
32 Saint-Simon (ed. Norton), *op. cit.*, II, 354; cf. also the remarks of Orléans' mother, *Correspondance complète de Madame*, *op. cit.*, I, 271–72. The terms of the king's will are printed in H. Leclercq, *Histoire de la Régence*, I, 107–14.
33 Leclercq, *op. cit.*, I, 75–77.
34 J. Flammermont (ed.), *Remontrances du parlement de Paris au XVIIIe siècle*, I, 165.
35 Bourgeois, *Le secret du régent*, pp. 29–30.
36 F. L. Ford, *Robe and Sword*, pp. 226–28.
37 Vauban's *Projet d'une Dîme Royale* and Boisguillebert's *Le Détail de la France* are both printed in E. Daire (ed.), *Economistes financiers du XVIIIe siècle*, pp. 33–148, 163–247.
38 L. Rothkrug, *Opposition to Louis XIV*, p. 144.
39 Rothkrug, *op. cit.*, pp. 392 ff.; but cf. T. J. Schaeper, 'The Creation of the French Council of Commerce in 1700', *European Studies Review* [to appear].

Schaeper rejects Rothkrug's view that the council was forced upon the government by the merchants' offensive.
40 P. Goubert, *Louis XIV and Twenty Million Frenchmen*, p. 281.
41 Bibliothèque de l'Arsenal, Paris [hereafter Arsenal], ms. 4492, p. 351.
42 F. Braudel and E. Labrousse (eds), *Histoire économique et sociale de la France*, II, 270–76.
43 H. M. A. Keens-Soper, 'The French Political Academy, 1712: the School for Ambassadors', *European Studies Review*, II, 4 (1972), *passim*; see also below, p. 137.
44 J. C. Rule, 'Louis XIV, Roi – Bureaucrate', in *Louis XIV and the Craft of Kingship* (ed. Rule), p. 40. On the growth of the impersonal state idea in France see J. H. Shennan, *The Origins of the State in Early Modern Europe*, pp. 104–6.
45 L. Mention, *Documents relatifs aux rapports du clergé avec la royauté de 1682 à 1789*, I, 27–31.
46 J. Carreyre, *Le Jansénisme durant la régence*, I, 3–5.
47 Abbé Dorsanne, *Journal*, I, 101–2; G. Rech, 'Daguesseau et le Jansénisme', *Le Chancelier Henri-François Daguesseau, 1668–1751*, pp. 122–23.
48 Dorsanne, *op. cit.*, I, 103; Carreyre, *op. cit.*, I, 7.
49 *Bibliothèque Sainte-Geneviève*, Paris, ms. 2084, fo. 11ʳ.
50 Dorsanne, *op. cit.*, I, 190.
51 (L)a (M)othe (D)e (L)a (H)ode, *op. cit.*, I, 121.
52 E. R. Briggs, *The Political Academies of France in the Early 18th Century*, pp. 220–24; Leclercq, *op. cit.*, I, 27; Bourgeois, *Le secret du régent*, pp. 11–12.
53 *Hardwicke State Papers*, II, 543; Leclercq, *op. cit.*, I, 55–56; L. Wiesener, *Le régent, l'abbé Dubois et les Anglais*, I, 34–36, 43–44.
54 Leclercq, *op. cit.*, I, 99–100.
55 The most famous description of this dramatic occasion is in Saint-Simon (Boislisle ed.), XXIX, 12–33; see also Flammermont, *op. cit.*, I, 1–30. An account by d'Aligre, a president in the parlement, which covers the last days of Louis XIV and the opening of

the regency, A.N. Series K 696, 1, has been printed in *Revue Rétrospective*, 2nd series, VI (1836).
56 L(a) M(othe) D(e) L(a) H(ode), *op. cit.*, I, 127–29.
57 Bibliothèque Nationale, Paris [hereafter B.N.], *nouvelles acquisitions françaises* [hereafter n.a.f.], Collection Lamoignon, 8160, pp. 751–52.

Chapter II

1 See, for example, A. B. Cobban, *A History of Modern France*, I, 16–26: 'The regent fails to put the clock back.'
2 M. Antoine, *Inventaire des arrêts du conseil du roi. Règne de Louis XV*, I, viii–ix.
3 M. Antoine, *Le conseil du roi sous le règne de Louis XV*, pp. 28–29.
4 *Ibid.*, p. 79.
5 Flammermont, *op. cit.*, I, 40–41.
6 Antoine, *Le conseil du roi*, pp. 79–84; *Inventaire des arrêts*, I, ix–x.
7 B.N. manuscrit français [hereafter ms. fr.], 17044, fos 7–14.
8 Waller, *op. cit.*, p. 137.
9 See below, p. 136.
10 Saint-Simon (ed. Norton), *op. cit.*, III, 22–25, 93–94, 110.
11 Antoine, *Le conseil du roi*, 80–83; Leclercq, *op. cit.*, I, 148–51.
12 L(a) M(othe) D(e) L(a) H(ode), *op. cit.*, II, 142–43.
13 Saint-Simon (ed. Norton), *op. cit.*, III, 22.
14 M. Benoit, *La polysynodie*, pp. 134–35, 168; Saint-Simon (ed. Norton), *op. cit.*, III, 62.
15 Archives des Affaires Etrangères, Paris [hereafter A.A.E.], mémoires et documents, France, 1233, fo. 226ʳ.
16 Leclercq, *op. cit.*, III, 262–63, 432.
17 A.A.E., mémoires et documents, France, 1233, fo. 166ᵛ.
18 J. F. Bluche, *L'Origine des magistrats du parlement de Paris au XVIIIᵉ siècle*, pp. 192–93; Antoine, *Le conseil du roi*, pp. 86, 107–8; J. F. Bluche, *Les magistrats du parlement de Paris au XVIIIᵉ siècle*, p. 167; for a recent assessment of Le Blanc's career under the regency, see C. Sturgill, *Claude Le Blanc: Civil Servant of the King*, pp. 146 ff.
19 Antoine, *Le conseil du roi*, p. 93; C. Sturgill, 'Le conseil de la guerre (1715–1718)' in *Revue Historique de l'Armée* (March, 1969), blames its president, Marshal Villars, for the failure of this particular element in the polysynodie.
20 Benoit, *op. cit.*, p. 141; cf. Leclercq, *op. cit.*, I, 491.
21 B.N. mss. fr., 23.665, 23.670, 23.673.
22 Antoine, *Le conseil du roi*, pp. 84–85.
23 B.N. ms. fr., 23.663, *passim*.
24 Antoine, *Le conseil du roi*, p. 86, f.n. 149.
25 Bailly, *op. cit.*, p. 83.
26 Saint-Simon's account of this session of the regency council is justly famous: in the Norton ed. it is to be found in vol. III, pp. 188–97; Benoit, *op. cit.*, p. 173.
27 Saint-Simon (ed. Norton), *op. cit.*, III, 197; see below, pp. 65–66.
28 Both returned to their home in the palace of Sceaux during 1720.
29 M. Marais, *Journal et Mémoires*, I, 430.
30 A.A.E., mémoires et documents, France, 1233, fos 166–67.
31 Antoine, *Le conseil du roi*, pp. 103 ff.
32 *Ibid.*, p. 103; A.A.E., mémoires et documents, France, 1233, fos 202–3, 215–16.
33 L. Wiesener, *op. cit.*, II, 262, 264.
34 A.A.E., mémoires et documents, France, 1233, fo. 194.
35 *Ibid.*, fos 166–67; Leclercq, *op. cit.*, II, 225.
36 Arsenal, ms. 3724, fos 169ᵛ–170ʳ; Antoine, *Le conseil du roi*, p. 114.
37 See below, pp. 100–1.
38 Saint-Simon (ed. Norton), *op. cit.*, III, 456.
39 The question of Orléans' role after the majority had exercised Dubois at least since the first half of 1718: see Bailly, *op. cit.*, p. 83.
40 See below, p. 128.
41 A.A.E., mémoires et documents, France, 1252, fos 17–20.

42 *Ibid.*, fo. 67; see also fos 47–48, 74.
43 Antoine, *Le conseil du roi*, pp. 107 ff.; A.A.E. mémoires et documents, France, 1252, fos 50–51.
44 Cf. footnote above.
45 A.A.E., mémoires et documents, France, 1252, fo. 124^r.
46 Vivian R. Gruder, *The Royal Provincial Intendants*, p. 9.
47 *Ibid.*, Appendix IV, pp. 246–52.
48 M. Bordes, 'Les Intendants de Louis XV', p. 52; A.N., G^{7}28, fo. 266; G^{7}23^{90}, fos 23, 37, 74^v–75, 76^v–78^r.
49 A.N., G^{7}23^{90}, fos 22^v–23^r, 71^v–72; G^{7}23^{91}, letter dated 24/9/18; G^{7}23^{94}, letter dated 19/12/18.

Chapter III

1 For Dubois' relations with Orléans before the regency see Bailly, *op. cit.*, pp. 15 ff.
2 Saint-Simon (ed. Norton) *op. cit.*, III, 449–50.
3 Kamen, *op. cit.*, p. 299.
4 Wiesener, *op. cit.*, I, 9–10.
5 For the political uncertainties surrounding the Hanoverian settlement see J. H. and Margaret Shennan, 'The Protestant Succession in English Politics, April 1713–September 1715', in *William III and Louis XIV*, pp. 252–70.
6 Wiesener, *op. cit.*, I, 112.
7 *Ibid.*, I, 30–39.
8 B.N., ms. fr., 23.663, fos 14, 57. At Utrecht the French agreed to expel the Pretender from France and not to assist him in his efforts to acquire the English crown.
9 Baudrillart, *op. cit.*, II, 209.
10 B.N., ms. fr. 23.663, fo. 129^r; Leclercq, *op. cit.*, I, 269–93; Ragnhild Hatton, *Diplomatic Relations between Great Britain and the Dutch Republic, 1714–21*, p. 91.
11 W. Coxe, *Memoirs of Sir Robert Walpole*, I, 154.
12 See M. A. Thomson, 'Self-determination and Collective Security as Factors in English and French Foreign Policy, 1689–1718', *William III and Louis XIV*, pp. 271–86.
13 Leclercq, *op. cit.*, I, 232, 237.
14 *Ibid.*, I, 256.

15 *Ibid.*, I, 240–43.
16 *Ibid.*, I, 337; Wiesener, *op. cit.*, I, 129–31, 195, 226–28.
17 Leclercq, *op. cit.*, I, 347, 352.
18 *Ibid.*, I, 368.
19 Hatton, *op. cit.*, pp. 125, 133–34; cf. Bourgeois, *Le secret du régent*, p. 148.
20 Orléans expressed his own anxiety to secure a triple, not a dual, alliance in a letter to Dubois dated 30 October 1716: A.A.E., mémoires et documents, Hollande, 300, fo. 165.
21 Details of its eight articles may be found in Leclercq, *op. cit.*, I, 413–15.
22 Leclercq, *op. cit.*, I, 417; Bailly, *op. cit.*, p. 66; Bourgeois, *Le secret du régent*, pp. 173–74.
23 Baudrillart, *op. cit.*, II, 272.
24 E. Bourgeois, *Le secret de Dubois*, pp. 438–40.
25 Bailly, *op. cit.*, p. 66.
26 A.A.E., mémoires et documents, France, 311, fos 38^r, 46^v.
27 Bourgeois, *Le secret du régent*, pp. 112, 168.
28 Leclercq, *op. cit.*, I, 421–47; Hatton, *op. cit.*, p. 162.
29 Bourgeois, *Le secret du régent*, pp. 194–95; M. A. Martin, 'The Secret Clause: Britain and Spanish Ambitions in Italy, 1712–31', p. 413.
30 Bourgeois, *Le secret du régent*, pp. 229–30, 240.
31 *Ibid.*, pp. 254–55; Leclercq, *op. cit.*, I, 477–80.
32 Leclercq, *op. cit.*, I, 500.
33 *Ibid.*, I, 502–5.
34 B.N., n.a.f., 23.933, fos 24–26, Mémoires of the duke d'Antin; Bourgeois, *Le secret du régent*, p. 341; Baudrillart, *op. cit.*, II, 297.
35 Details of the Quadruple Alliance may be found in Leclercq, *op. cit.*, II, 17–20.
36 *Ibid.*, II, 21–22.
37 *Mémoires du président Hénault* (ed. F. Rousseau), p. 37.
38 G. C. Gibbs, 'Parliament and the Treaty of Quadruple Alliance', *William III and Louis XIV*, p. 298.
39 Bourgeois, *Le secret de Dubois*, pp. 10–13.
40 Leclercq, *op. cit.*, II, 272; Bourgeois, *Le secret de Dubois*, 21–42; a copy

of the confession of the prime mover, the duchess du Maine, is in A.A.E., mémoires et documents, France, 1235, fos 171–96.

41 Wiesener, *op. cit.*, pp. 263, 270.

42 A.A.E., mémoires et documents, France, 1236, fo. 381ᵛ.

43 Leclercq, *op. cit.*, II, 15, 284; for Torcy's strong support of the Quadruple Alliance at the regency council meeting of 17 July 1718, see B.N., n.a.f., 23.933, fo. 24ʳ; cf. Bourgeois, *Le secret de Dubois*, pp. 43–44.

44 J. C. Rule, 'King and Minister: Louis XIV and Colbert de Torcy', *William III and Louis XIV*, p. 236.

45 Leclercq, *op. cit.*, III, 46–47.

46 Bourgeois, *Le secret de Dubois*, pp. 192–96.

47 Bailly, *op. cit.*, pp. 120–21.

48 Baudrillart, *op. cit.*, II, 446–48; B. Williams, *Stanhope*, pp. 345–50.

49 Baudrillart, *op. cit.*, II, 463; see also Bourgeois, *Le secret de Dubois*, pp. 286–90.

50 For the significance of Pensacola see M. Giraud, *Histoire de la Louisiane Française*, III, 300 ff.

51 Saint-Simon (ed. Norton), *op. cit.*, III, 311–12.

52 Leclercq, *op. cit.*, III, 33; Williams, *op. cit.*, pp. 378–79.

53 Bourgeois, *Le secret de Dubois*, pp. 127, 135–39, 364–65.

54 Leclercq, *op. cit.*, III, 257–60; Bourgeois, *Le secret de Dubois*, pp. 373–77; A. Vandal, *Louis XV et Elisabeth de Russie*, pp. 40–68.

55 For a striking example of Orléans' attachment to the dynastic principle see below, p. 131.

56 A.A.E., mémoires et documents, France, 445, fos 177ᵛ–178ʳ.

Chapter IV

1 J. Bodin, *Six livres de la république*, book 3, chapter 4, 418; for the origins and history of the parlement see J. H. Shennan, *The Parlement of Paris, passim*; see also the article by the same author, 'The Political Role of the Parlement of Paris, 1715–23', *The Historical Journal*, VIII, 2 (1965), 179–200.

2 H. G. Judge, 'Louis XIV and the Church', *Louis XIV and the Craft of Kingship*, p. 257.

3 B.N., ms. fr. 17044, fos 11–14.

4 Leclercq, *op. cit.*, I, 139.

5 B.N., n.a.f., collection Lamoignon, 8161, fos 95–104; ms. fr. 10543, fo. 36; Dorsanne, *op. cit.*, I, 263–67.

6 Rech, *op. cit.*, p. 126.

7 Carreyre, *op. cit.*, I, 155; A. Gazier, *Histoire générale du mouvement janséniste*, I, 258.

8 Bibliothèque des Amis de Port-Royal, Paris [hereafter Port-Royal], collection Le Paige, 416, no. 48.

9 Carreyre, *op. cit.*, I, 148; *Journal Historique de Guillaume de Lamoignon, 1713–18*, p. 37.

10 Port-Royal, collection Le Paige, 413, no. 16, 417, no. 38; B.N., n.a.f., collection Lamoignon, 8163, fos 264–66.

11 B.N., ms. fr. 10361, pp. 81–82.

12 See, e.g., A. Grellet-Dumazeau, *L'affaire du bonnet, passim*.

13 Saint-Simon (ed. Boislisle), *op. cit.*, XXIX, appendix IV, 509.

14 R. Bickart, *Les parlements et la notion de souveraineté nationale au XVIIIᵉ siècle*, pp. 143 ff.

15 Saint-Simon (ed. Boislisle), *op. cit.*, XXX, 167–80.

16 Marais, *op. cit.*, I, 208.

17 Flammermont, *op. cit.*, I, 42–49; Saint-Simon (ed. Boislisle), *op. cit.*, XXX, 166–67; Marshal de Villars, *Mémoires*, II, 462–63.

18 *Les correspondants de la marquise de Balleroy*, I, 198–99; Bibliothèque du Sénat, Paris (hereafter Sénat), ms. 422, fo. 135ʳ.

19 B.N., ms. fr. 10231, 93a; Sénat, ms. 422, fo. 159ʳ; Leclercq, *op. cit.*, II, 118.

20 Flammermont, *op. cit.*, I, 50–56. Details of the parlement's debates during these weeks are to be found in B.N. ms. fr. 10231, 93a and Sénat, ms. 422, fos 159–69.

21 Marquis de Dangeau, *Journal*, XVII, 160.

22 See below, p. 135.

23 A.N., U416, section 1, fo. 2. This journal, kept by a clerk in the parlement, Delisle, and covering most of the year 1718 provides our chief source for the debates taking place in the court up to the *lit de justice* in August of that year.

24 A.N. U420, 14 January 1718.
25 Flammermont, *op. cit.*, I, 64.
26 F.-A. Isambert (ed.), *Recueil général des anciennes lois françaises*, XXI, 40.
27 'Le roi a bien voulu écouter les remontrances de son parlement', Flammermont, *op. cit.*, I, 65.
28 P. Harsin, *Les doctrines monétaires et financières en France*, p. 158.
29 Leclercq, *op. cit.*, II, 139.
30 A. Renaudet, *Les parlements*, p. 124.
31 Wiesener, *op. cit.*, II, 171.
32 Saint-Simon (ed. Boislisle), *op. cit.*, XXXV, 22.
33 *Gazette de la régence*, p. 262, 20 June, 1718. Also note p. 263, 'lequel [Orléans] est sûr des troupes'; B.N., ms. fr. 13686, fo. 149.
34 Flammermont, *op. cit.*, I, 71.
35 *Gazette de la régence*, p. 263, 20 June, 1718; *Les correspondants de la marquise de Balleroy*, *op. cit.*, I, 329.
36 A.N., U416, section 30, fo. 3ᵛ.
37 *Gazette de la régence*, pp. 264–65; B.N., n.a.f., collection Lamoignon, 8164, fo. 48.
38 These remonstrances and the king's reply are printed in Flammermont, *op. cit.*, I, 77–87.
39 *Ibid.*, I, 88–105.
40 C. Joly, *Recueil des maximes*, chapter IX, 392–94.
41 Montesquieu, *De l'esprit des lois*, I, book 2, chapter 4, 20.
42 Flammermont, *op. cit.*, I, 106–7.
43 B.N., n.a.f., 23.933, fos 46–47.
44 Dangeau, *op. cit.*, XVII, 362.
45 *Gazette de la régence*, pp. 276–77; P. Narbonne, *Journal des règnes de Louis XIV et Louis XV*, p. 87.
46 Flammermont, *op. cit.*, I, 107–16.
47 Marquis d'Argenson, *Journal et mémoires*, I, 23; note also the remark of d'Antin, B.N., n.a.f., 23.933, fo. 61ᵛ: 'D'ailleurs le parlement était sans troupes'.
48 B.N., ms. fr. 10908, fo. 2ʳ; n.a.f., collection Lamoignon, 8165, fos 418ᵛ–426, 433ᵛ–35. For the magistrates as

rentiers see Bluche, *Les magistrats du parlement de Paris au XVIIIᵉ siècle*, pp. 212–16.
49 Flammermont, *op. cit.*, I, 126–39; A.N., U363, 10, 13 April, 1720; U421, 22 April, 1720.
50 Saint-Simon (ed. Boislisle), *op. cit.*, XXXVII, 314; Marais, *op. cit.*, I, 265; J. Buvat, *Journal de la régence*, II, 93. See p. 112. below.
51 B.N., ms. fr. 10908, fos 10ᵛ–11ʳ; n.a.f., collection Lamoignon, 8167, pp. 24–29.
52 See below, p. 112.
53 Sénat, ms. 423, fo. 118.
54 Carreyre, *op. cit.*, II, 193–202.
55 Port-Royal, collection Le Paige, 424, no. 3, pp. 73–80; Dorsanne, *op. cit.*, II, 16.
56 B.N., ms. fr. 10908, fos 15ʳ–16; A.N., U747, fos 23ʳ–26ʳ; Port-Royal, collection Le Paige, 424, no. 3, p. 90.
57 Port-Royal, collection Le Paige, 424, no. 3, pp. 110, 117; 425, no. 76.
58 Hénault, *op. cit.*, p. 291; Dorsanne, *op. cit.*, II, 37.
59 Cf. A.N., U747, fo. 41ʳ.
60 Port-Royal, collection Le Paige, 425, no. 90.
61 Hénault, *op. cit.*, pp. 316–17.
62 Mention, *op. cit.*, II, 60.
63 Port-Royal, collection Le Paige, 424, no. 3, p. 135.
64 Villars, *op. cit.*, III, 95; E.-J.-F. Barbier, *Chronique de la régence*, I, 198–99.

Chapter V

1 F. Braudel and E. Labrousse (eds), *Histoire économique et sociale de la France*, II, 271–77; Goubert, *op. cit.*, pp. 255 ff., 281; H. Luthy, *La banque protestante en France*, I, 98–104.
2 Arsenal, ms. 3857, pp. 5–6. On the uncertain provenance of this manuscript source, see the bibliographical essay above, p. 154.
3 *Ibid.*, pp. 13–15.
4 B.N., ms. fr. 7769, pp. 146–48.
5 *Ibid.*, pp. 158–70, 282; ms. fr. 6935, fos 66–67ʳ.
6 Luthy, *op. cit.*, I, 279.

7 Leclercq, *op. cit.*, I, 309–12.

8 B.N., ms. fr. 7769, pp. 552–58.

9 B.N., n.a.f. 23.929, fo. 174^v.

10 Rothkrug, *op. cit.*, pp. 147–48.

11 A.A.E., mémoires et documents, France, 1218, fos 399–407.

12 Leclercq, *op. cit.*, I, 204–5; A.N., G^{7}23.91, 15 September, 1718; A.A.E., mémoires et documents, France, 1236, fos 47–48^r.

13 B.N., ms. fr. 6942, fos 49^v–52; A.N., G^{7}23^{94}, 20 December, 1718; G^{7}23^{90}, fos 22^v–23^r.

14 A.A.E., mémoires et documents, France, 1253, fos 216–23; A.N., G^{7}28, fo. 266.

15 E. Levasseur, 'Law et son système jugés par un contemporain', p. 478; P. Harsin, *Les doctrines monétaires et financières en France*, p. 191.

16 Daire (ed.), *op. cit.*, pp. 164–65.

17 P. Harsin (ed.), *John Law, oeuvres complètes*, I, 202; M. A. Sallon, 'L'échec de Law', pp. 173–78.

18 Harsin (ed.), *John Law, oeuvres complètes*, II, 307–9, III, 77–86; Harsin, *Les doctrines monétaires et financières en France*, pp. 163–64; Daire, *op. cit.*, p. 201.

19 Harsin (ed.), *John Law, oeuvres complètes*, I, 214 (*Mémoire pour prouver qu'une nouvelle espèce de monnaie peut être meilleure que l'or et l'argent*).

20 *Ibid.*, II, 50 (Letter from Law to Desmaretz, 26 July, 1715); II, 10 (*Mémoire sur les banques*).

21 Sallon, *op. cit.*, pp. 154–55.

22 Harsin (ed.) *John Law, oeuvres complètes*, III, 86 (*Idée générale du nouveau système des finances*).

23 *Ibid.*, II, 198 (*Restablissement du commerce*, September, 1715); II, 324–5 (*Mémoire sur la politique monétaire française*, early 1716); III, 91–92 (*Idée générale du nouveau système des finances*).

24 *Ibid.*, II, 324; Luthy, *op. cit.*, I, 289.

25 Harsin (ed.), *John Law, oeuvres complètes*, II, 67–259 (*Restablissement du commerce*); Rothkrug, *op. cit.*, pp. 435–47; Harsin, *Les doctrines monétaires et financières en France*, pp. 125–26.

26 Harsin (ed.) *John Law, oeuvres complètes*, III, 39–61.

27 H. M. Hyde, *John Law*, pp. 39,

57, 64. It was suspected that Law was also in Paris towards the end of 1708, acting as a British spy, but Torcy's enquiries failed to produce any evidence to support this suspicion, A.A.E., correspondance politique, Angleterre, 226, fos 172, 174, 183–84, 205. (I am indebted to Professor J. C. Rule for drawing my attention to this correspondence.)

28 Luthy, *op. cit.*, I, 295.

29 B.N., ms. fr. 7769, p. 328; Arsenal, ms. 3857, pp. 42–44.

30 Giraud, *op. cit.*, III, 16 ff.

31 Arsenal, ms. 3857, pp. 69–70, 76.

32 Luthy, *op. cit.*, I, 314–16; Giraud, *op. cit.*, III, 61–62; P. Harsin, *Crédit public et banque d'état en France du XVIe au XVIIIe siècle*, p. 62.

33 Giraud, *op. cit.*, III, 70–72; E. J. Hamilton, 'Prices and Wages at Paris under John Law's System', p. 58.

34 Giraud, *op. cit.*, III, 73.

35 Hyde, *op. cit.*, p. 130.

36 Hamilton, *op. cit.*, p. 58.

37 Saint-Simon (ed. Norton), *op. cit.*, III, 282.

38 Arsenal, ms. 3857, p. 175.

39 Law apparently dated the destruction of the System from the promulgation of the decree of 27th May: *Ibid.*, p. 176.

40 Leclercq, *op. cit.*, II, 455–57.

41 Sénat, ms. 423, fo. 118^r.

42 Marais, *op. cit.*, I, 386.

43 *Ibid.*, I, 469.

44 Arsenal, ms. 3857, p. 200; Leclercq, *op. cit.*, II, 473.

45 Leclercq, *op. cit.*, II, 474–75.

46 Arsenal, ms. 3857, pp. 49–50; Daire, *op. cit.*, p. 442; *Correspondance complète de Madame*, *op. cit.*, II, 213.

47 *Correspondance complète de Madame*, *op. cit.*, I, 439, II, 163; cf. the duke of Perth's description of Law in 1708, 'grand et de bonne mine', A.A.E., correspondance politique, Angleterre, 226, fo. 172^r.

48 Saint-Simon (ed. Norton), *op. cit.*, III, 299.

49 C. D. Duclos, *Mémoires secrets sur les règnes de Louis XIV et de Louis XV*, II, 134.

50 Arsenal, ms. 3857, pp. 47–49.

51 *Correspondance complète de Madame,* II, 263; B.N., n.a.f., 23.933, fos 46–47.
52 Marais, *op. cit.,* I, 334.
53 Arsenal, ms. 3724, fo. 164ʳ.
54 Saint-Simon (ed. Norton), *op. cit.,* III, 299.
55 Harsin (ed.), *John Law, oeuvres complètes,* III, 140 (*Troisième lettre sur le nouveau système des finances*).
56 Harsin, *Les doctrines monétaires et financières en France,* p. 200.
57 Arsenal, ms. 3857, pp. 112–15. See p. 113–14 above.
58 Hamilton, 'Prices and Wages at Paris under John Law's System', pp. 62–63; Harsin (ed.), *John Law, oeuvres complètes,* II, 307–9 (*Mémoire sur les banques,* December, 1715).
59 Harsin (ed.), *John Law, oeuvres complètes,* II, 309.
60 *Ibid.,* III, 82; see above, p. 105.
61 Sallon, *op. cit.,* pp. 173, 179.
62 Giraud, *op. cit.,* III, 76–77; Harsin, *Les doctrines monétaires et financières en France,* pp. 173, 203.
63 E. J. Hamilton, 'Prices and Wages at Paris under John Law's System', p. 57; 'Prices and Wages in Southern France under John Law's System', p. 449.
64 Harsin, *Les doctrines monétaires et financières en France,* pp. 191, 200–01; Sallon, 'L'échec de Law', p. 148.
65 Arsenal, ms. 3857, pp. 235–37.
66 'Prices and Wages at Paris under John Law's System', *Quarterly Journal of Economics,* LI, 1936; and 'Prices and Wages in Southern France under John Law's System', *Economic Journal* (Economic History Supplement), 1937.
67 Hamilton, 'Prices and Wages at Paris under John Law's System', p. 61.
68 J. P. Poisson, 'Introduction à une étude quantitative des effets socio-économiques du système de Law', p. 266.
69 Arsenal, ms. 3857, p. 49.
70 Harsin (ed.), *John Law, oeuvres complètes,* II, 264.
71 Luthy, *op. cit.,* I, 290.
72 Sallon, *op. cit.,* pp. 190–91.
73 However, in the early months of the king's majority Orléans' attitude changed and Law was on the point of

setting out for France when the news of Philippe's death reached him: Hyde, *op. cit.,* pp. 170–73; Arsenal, ms. 3857, p. 297.
74 Arsenal, ms. 4492, p. 351.

Chapter VI

1 Saint-Simon (ed. Norton), *op. cit.,* II, 426–38.
2 Waller, *op. cit.,* p. 268 (*Epître sur la calomnie*).
3 Lescure, *op. cit., passim*; Saint-Simon (ed. Norton), *op. cit.,* III, 62–64.
4 See above, pp. 44–45.
5 Lescure, *op. cit.,* p. 226.
6 cf. Madame's remarks on Orléans' attitude to the brothers Broglie, *Correspondance complète de Madame,* II, 186. The duke de Noailles was an exception to this general rule.
7 Leclercq, *op. cit.,* III, 272. According to the duke d'Antin Orléans never totally confided in anybody: B.N., n.a.f., 23.933, fo. 62ʳ.
8 *Correspondance complète de Madame,* I, 303, II, 1; Saint-Simon (ed. Norton), *op. cit.,* II, 442–43.
9 *Correspondance complète de Madame,* II, 132; Saint-Simon (ed. Norton), *op. cit.,* III, 61, 246–52; P. Erlanger, *Le régent,* pp. 169–70.
10 Saint-Simon (ed. Norton), *op. cit.,* III, 385–86; *Correspondance complète de Madame,* I, 387–88, II, 154–57, 199 and f.n., 355. Chartres further soured relations with his father by joining an abortive court cabal against Dubois in the autumn of 1722: A.A.E., mémoires et documents, France, 1252, fos 178–79, 1253, fos 1–6; Leclercq, *op. cit.,* III, 409 ff.
11 *Correspondance complète de Madame,* II, 344; I, 327, II, 66–67.
12 *Ibid.,* II, 172, 305.
13 B.N., collection Clairambault, 529, p. 293; Waller, *op. cit.,* p. 471; Leclercq, *op. cit.,* III, 290–91; Saint-Simon (ed. Norton), *op. cit.,* III, 255, 479.
14 *Correspondance complète de Madame,* I, 204.
15 Barbier, *op. cit.,* I, 307.

16 Waller, *op. cit.*, pp. 178–80, 532–33; see also above, pp. 13–14.

17 Waller, *op. cit.*, pp. 183–84.

18 R. E. A. Waller, 'Voltaire and the regent', pp. 7–36.

19 Waller, *The relations between men of letters and the representatives of authority in France, 1715–23*, pp. 476, 541.

20 G. Atkinson and A. C. Keller, *Prelude to the Enlightenment*, p. 63.

21 J.-J. Gloton, 'L'architecture de la régence', *La régence*, pp. 44–57.

22 J. Sgard, 'Style rococo et style régence', *La régence*, pp. 10–20; J. H. Shennan, 'Louis XV: Public and Private Worlds', p. 306.

23 L. Hautecoeur, *Histoire de l'architecture classique en France*, III, 5–6; examples of Cressent's work are illustrated in A. G. Palacios, *The Age of Louis XV*, p. 79 and in the magnificent volume produced to accompany the 1974 Paris exhibition on the subject of *Louis XV: un moment de perfection de l'art français*, p. 316.

24 *Correspondance complète de Madame*, I, 259.

25 Montesquieu, *Mes pensées*, 1630, p. 1024.

26 Shennan, 'Louis XV: Public and Private Worlds', pp. 320–24.

27 cf. Saint-Pierre, *A Discourse of the danger of governing by one minister . . .*, p. 98.

28 Waller, *The relations between men of letters and the representatives of authority in France, 1715–23*, p. 474.

29 Flammermont, *op. cit.*, I, 68.

30 Leclercq, *op. cit.*, II, 131–32.

31 See above, p. 000.

32 Leclercq, *op. cit.*, II, 364.

33 Saint-Simon (ed. Norton), *op. cit.*, III, 232.

34 Waller, *The relations between men of letters and the representatives of authority in France, 1715–23*, pp. 28–39, 221, 270–71, 544, 550–51; Dr Waller has examined Orléans' relations with Voltaire in his article, 'Voltaire and the regent', cited at f.n. 18 above.

35 T. J. Schaeper, *op. cit.*, *passim*; Antoine, *Le conseil du roi sous le règne de Louis XV*, pp. 70–71, 74–75, 96; see also above, chapter I, footnotes 43 and 44.

36 Braudel and Labrousse (eds), *op. cit.*, II, 299.

37 Saint-Simon (ed. Norton), *op. cit.*, III, 144–46; Bailly, *op. cit.*, pp. 82–83.

38 Leclercq, *op. cit.*, III, 67, 74; Bourgeois, *Le secret de Dubois*, pp. 173, 190–91.

39 Barbier, *op. cit.*, I, 307.

40 Arsenal, ms. 3857, p. 67.

41 *Correspondance complète de Madame*, I, 306.

42 Waller, *The relations between men of letters and the representatives of authority in France, 1715–23*, p. 36 (citing Saint-Pierre's *Annales*); Arsenal, ms. 3724, fo. 35ʳ.

43 Saint-Simon (ed. Norton), *op. cit.*, III, 479.

44 Waller, *The relations between men of letters and the representatives of authority in France, 1715–23*, pp. 235, 280.

45 Cited in *ibid.*, p. 538.

46 Saint-Simon (ed. Norton), *op. cit.*, III, 456–57.

47 Arsenal, ms. 3724, fo. 35ʳ.

48 Louis XIV's phrase: Saint-Simon (ed. Boislisle), *op. cit.*, XXV, 156.

List of Personalities who played a significant Role during the Regency

The most outstanding ones, namely Dubois, Law, Louis XIV, the Regent himself and Saint-Simon, are treated analytically in the Index.

Aguesseau, Henri-François d' (1668–1751), procureur-général in the parlement of Paris (1700), chancellor (1717–50)

Amelot de Gournay, Michel Jean (1655–1724), president of the council of commerce.

Angervilliers, Nicolas Prosper d' (1675–1740), intendant at Strasbourg (1715–24).

Antin, Louis Antoine de Goudrin, duke d' (1675–1736), legitimate son of Madame de Montespan, president of the council for the interior (1715), later a member of the regency council.

Argenson, Marc René de Voyer, marquis d' (1652–1721), lieutenant of the Paris police (1697), keeper of the seals and president of the council for finance (1718).

Argenton, Marie Louise de Séry, countess d' (1680–1748), Orléans' favourite mistress.

Armenonville, *see* Fleuriau d'Armenonville.

Arnaud de la Briffe, Pierre (1679–1740), intendant at Dijon (1711–40).

Asfeld, Claude François Bidal, chevalier d' (1665–1743), member of the council for war.

Averne, Sophie d', succeeded Parabère as the regent's mistress in June 1721.

Baudry, Gabriel Taschereau de (1673–1755), master of requests (1711), member of the council for finance (1715).

Bernage, Louis de (1661–1737), intendant at Amiens (1708–18), and Toulouse and Montpellier (1718–24).

Berry, Marie Louise Elisabeth d'Orléans, duchess de (1695–1719), the regent's eldest daughter, married Charles, duke de Berry (1710), youngest son of the Grand Dauphin.

Berwick, James Fitz-James, duke of (1671–1734), illegitimate son of King James II of England, marshal of France (1706), member of the regency council (1720).

Bezons, Armand Bazin de (1655–1721), archbishop of Rouen (1719), member of the regency council.

Bezons, Jacques Bazin, count de (1645–1733), marshal of France (1709) and member of the regency council.

Bignon, abbé Jean-Paul (1662–1743), librarian in the *Bibliothèque du Roi*.

Bignon de Blanzy, Armand-Roland (1666–1724), intendant at Paris (1709–24).

Biron, Charles Armand de Gontaut, marquis de (1664–1756), member of the council for war, then of the regency council, and one of the *roués* in the regent's circle.

Bissy, Henri de Thiard de (1657–1737), bishop of Meaux (1704), cardinal (1713), supporter of Unigenitus.

Boisguillebert, Pierre le Pesant de (1646–1714), economic theorist.

Boulainvilliers, Henri de (1658–1722), Norman count who wrote in strong support of the French nobility.

Bourbon, Louis-Henri de (1692–1740), Monsieur le Duc. Member of the regency council (1715), succeeded Orléans as first minister.

Brancas, Louis de Brancas-Céreste, marquis de (1672–1750), member of the council for the interior.

Brancas, see below, Villars-Brancas, duke de.

Broglie, Charles Guillaume, marquis de (1668–1751), one of the regent's *roués*.

Broglie, François Marie, duke de (1671–1745), marshal of France, younger brother of Charles Guillaume.

Campredon, Jacques de, French resident diplomat in St Petersburg and later in Stockholm.

Cangé, *valet de chambre* to the regent.

Canillac, Philippe de Montboissier Beaufort, marquis de (1669–1725), one of the regent's *roués*.

Cardin le Bret, intendant at Aix-en-Provence (1704–34).

Cellamare, Antonio Joseph del Guidice, prince de (1657–1733), Spanish ambassador to France, the centre of a conspiracy against the regent (1718).

Charolais, Charles de Bourbon-Condé, count de (1700–60), younger brother of the duke de Bourbon and a member of the regency council.

Chartres, Louis, duke de (1703–52), the regent's son who succeeded his father as duke d'Orléans.

Châteauneuf, Pierre Antoine de Castagnères, marquis de (1644–1728), French ambassador at the Hague in the first years of the regency.

Chauvelin de Beauséjour, Bernard (1672–1755), intendant at Tours (1709–18).

Chavigny, Anne-Théodore Chevignard de (1687–1771), agent of Torcy, then of Dubois, later French ambassador to Portugal, Venice and Switzerland.

Chavigny, François Bouthillier de (1642–1731), bishop of Troyes (1678–97), member of the regency council from 1715.

Coëtlogon, Alain-Emmanuel, marquis de (1646–1730), member of the council for the marine.

Coigny, François de Franquetot, marquis de (1670–1759), given responsibility for the dragoons in 1718.

Conti, Louis Armand, prince de (1695–1727), member of the regency council.

Coypel, Antoine (1661–1722), court painter to Louis XIV and the regent.

Desmares, Charlotte (1682–1753), actress and mistress of Orléans.

Desmaretz, Nicolas (1648–1721), controller-general of finance (1708), dismissed at the beginning of the regency.

Destouches, Philippe Néricault (1680–1754), writer and diplomat.

Dodun, Charles Gaspard (1679–1736), member of the council for finance, appointed controller-general in 1722.

Dorsanne, abbé Antoine (1664–1728), noted Jansenist secretary to the *conseil de conscience* (1715–18).

Doujat, Jean Charles, intendant at Maubeuge (1708–20).

Effiat, Antoine Coiffier-Ruzé, marquis d' (1638–1719), member of the council for finance and later of the regency council.

Estrées, Victor Marie, duke d' (1660–1737), marshal of France, president of the council for the marine, later a member of the regency council.

Evreux, Henri Louis de la Tour d'Auvergne, count d' (1679–1753), member of the council for war.

Fagon, Louis (1680–1744), magistrate in the parlement of Paris (1702), intendant of finance (1714), member of the council for finance (1715).

Falari, Marie Thérèse, duchess de (1697–1782), Orléans' last mistress who was with him when he died.

Fénelon, François de Salignac de la Mothe (1651–1715), archbishop of Cambrai (1695), writer on social and political matters.

Ferrand de Villemilan, Antoine François, intendant at Rennes (1705–16).

Fleuriau d'Armenonville, Joseph-Jean-Baptiste (1661–1728), secretary of state for the navy (1718), keeper of the seals (1722).

Fleury, André-Hercule, abbé de (1653–1743), bishop of Fréjus (1698–1715), tutor to Louis XV (1715), cardinal and chief minister from 1726.

Fleury, abbé Claude (1640–1723), confessor to Louis XV.

Florence (Florence Pellerin, d. 1716), *danseuse* from the Opéra who was an early mistress of the regent when he was still duke de Chartres.

Flotte, Joseph de (*c.* 1657–1742), private secretary to Orléans and his agent in Spain (1709).

Fontenelle, Bernard le Bovier de (1657–1757), Cartesian philosopher and distinguished literary figure.

Fontpertuis, Angrand de, a syndic of the Compagnie des Indes.

Fortia, Joseph Charles de (1668–1742), councillor in the parlement of Paris, later first president of the grand conseil.

Foullé de Martargis, Etienne Hyacinthe, intendant at Alençon (1715–20).

Gaumont, Jean-Baptiste de (1664–1750), intendant of finance from 1722.

Gesvres, Léon Potier de (1656–1744), cardinal (1719), member of the restored *conseil de conscience* (1720).

Gilbert de Voisins, Pierre (1684–1769), distinguished lawyer and royal counsellor.
Guiche, Antoine de Gramont, duke de (1672–1725), colonel of the French Guard and brother-in-law to the duke de Noailles, vice-president of the council for war.

Harcourt, Henri, duke d' (1654–1718), marshal of France and member of the regency council.
Homberg, Wilhelm (1652–1715), Dutch scientist, friend of Orléans.
Huxelles, Nicolas de Laye du Blé, marquis d' (1652–1730), marshal of France, president of the council for foreign affairs.

Joly de Fleury, Guillaume-François (1675–1756), avocat-général in the parlement of Paris (1705), procureur-général (1717–46).
Jubert de Bouville, Louis Guillaume, intendant at Orléans (1713–31).

La Force, Henri Jacques Nompar de Caumont, duke de (1675–1726), member of the regency council.
La Grange-Chancel, François-Joseph de (1677–1758), poet, author of the *Philippiques*.
Lamoignon de Basville, Nicolas de (1648–1724), intendant at Montpellier and Toulouse (1685–1718).
Lamoignon de Courson, Urbain Guillaume de (1674–1742), intendant at Bordeaux (1709–20).
La Motte, Antoine de (1672–1731), French poet.
La Trémouïlle, Joseph Emmanuel de (1678–1720), cardinal (1706), French ambassador to the Vatican, archbishop of Cambrai (1718).
Laval, Guy André de Montmorency, count de (1682–1745), implicated in the Cellamare conspiracy.
La Vrillière, Louis Phélypeaux, marquis de (1672–1725), secretary of state, member of the regency council from 1716.
Le Blanc, Louis Claude (1669–1728), intendant at Dunkirk (1708–16), member of the council for war and then secretary of state for war (1716–23).
Le Gendre de Saint-Aubin, Gaspard François (d. 1740), intendant at Auch (1713–17).
Le Guerchois, Pierre Hector (1670–1740), intendant at Besançon (1708–17).
Le Peletier des Forts, Michel-Robert (1675–1740), member of the council for finance (1715) and of the regency council (1719), chief commissioner for finance after d'Argenson's disgrace in June 1720.
Le Peletier de Souzy, Michel (1640–1725), member of the regency council.
Le Pelletier de la Houssaye, Félix (1663–1723), appointed controller-general of finance, December 1720.
L'Escalopier, César Charles de (1671–1753), intendant at Châlons (1711–30).
Louville, Charles Auguste, marquis de (1664–1731), friend of Philip V of Spain, undertook an unsuccessful diplomatic mission to Madrid in July 1716.

Maine, Louis Auguste de Bourbon, duke du (1670–1736), elder son of Louis XIV and Madame de Montespan.

Maine, Louise Bénédicte de Bourbon-Condé, duchess du (1676–1753), wife of the duke du Maine and grand-daughter of the Great Condé. Aunt of Monsieur le Duc.

Maisons, Claude de Longueil, marquis de (1667–1715), president *à mortier* in the parlement of Paris.

Marsin, Ferdinand, count de (1656–1706), marshal of France (1703), fatally injured before Turin.

Maurepas, Jean Frédéric Phélypeaux, count de (1701–81), Pontchartrain's son, secretary of state for the *maison du roi* (1718).

Méliand, Antoine François, intendant at Lyons (1710–17).

Menguy, abbé Guillaume (d. 1728), celebrated Jansenist member of the parlement of Paris and of the council for the interior.

Mesmes, Jean Antoine de (1661–1723), first president of the parlement of Paris from 1712.

Montesquiou-d'Artagnan, Pierre de (1640–1725), marshal of France (1709) and later governor of Brittany.

Noailles, Adrien Maurice, duke de (1678–1766), nephew of the cardinal, president of the council for finance (1715–18), member of the regency council (1718).

Noailles, Louis Antoine de (1651–1729), archbishop of Paris (1695), cardinal (1706), president of the *conseil de conscience* (1715).

Nocé, Charles de (1664–1739), one of the regent's *roués*, disgraced in 1722.

Oppenord, Gilles-Marie (1672–1742), superintendent of buildings under the regency.

Orléans, Elisabeth Charlotte, duchess d' (1672–1722), second wife of Philippe I duke d'Orléans, and mother of the regent.

Orléans, Françoise-Marie de Bourbon, duchess d' (1677–1749), daughter of Louis XIV and Madame de Montespan, wife of the regent.

Orléans, Jean Philippe, chevalier d' (1702–48), illegitimate son of Philippe II d'Orléans and Madame d'Argenton.

Orléans, Philippe I, duke d' (1640–1701), brother of Louis XIV, father of the regent.

Ormesson, Henri François-de-Paule Lefèvre d' (1681–1756), magistrate in the parlement of Paris (1704), member of the council for finance (1715), intendant of finance (1722).

Orsay, Charles Boucher d', intendant at Limoges (1710–19).

Parabère, Marie-Madeleine de la Vieuville, countess de (1693–1755), Orléans' mistress for over five years between 1715 and 1721.

Pecquet, Antoine, d. 1726, secretary to the council for foreign affairs and later Dubois' chief secretary.

Polignac, Melchior de (1661–1742), cardinal (1712), implicated in the Cellamare conspiracy.

Pompadour, Léonard Hélie, marquis de (1654–1732), implicated in the Cellamare conspiracy.

Pontchartrain, Jérôme Phélypeaux, count de (1674–1747), secretary of state for the navy and the *maison du roi* under Louis XIV, ordered to leave the regency council (November 1715).

Pottier de la Hestroye, Jean, economic theorist.

Prie, Jeanne Agnès Berthelot de Pléneuf, marquise de (1698–1727), mistress of the duke de Bourbon.

Pucelle, abbé René (1655–1745), famous Jansenist member of the parlement of Paris and of the *conseil de conscience*.

Réamur, René-Antoine Ferchault de (1683–1757), entomologist and scientific polymath.

Regnault, Deslandes de, Orléans' agent in Spain.

Reynoldt, François de, lieutenant-general and deputy commander of the Swiss Guard, member of the council for war.

Rohan-Soubise, Armand Gaston Maximilien de (1674–1749), bishop of Strasbourg (1704), cardinal (1712), supporter of Unigenitus.

Rouillé du Coudray, Hilaire (1651–1729), member of the council for finance (1715).

Rousseau, Jean-Baptiste (1670–1741), Parisian-born poet of the French classical school.

Sabran, Madeleine Louise Charlotte de Foix-Rabat, countess de (1693–1768), mistress of Orléans.

Saint-Albin, Charles de (1698–1764), illegitimate son of Orléans and Florence Pellerin.

Saint-Pierre, Charles Irénée de Castel, abbé de (1657–1743), political writer.

Sauveur, Joseph (1653–1716), mathematician.

Tallard, Camille d'Hostun de la Baume, duke de (1652–1728), marshal of France, Louis XIV's representative in London for the negotiations leading to the Partition treaty (1698), member of the regency council.

Torcy, Jean-Baptiste Colbert, marquis de (1665–1746), secretary of state for foreign affairs (1696), member of the *conseil d'en haut* (1699–1715), member of the regency council from 1715.

Toulouse, Louis-Alexandre de Bourbon, count de (1678–1737), younger son of Louis XIV and Madame de Montespan, Admiral of France (1683), member of the regency council and of the council for the marine (1715).

Troyes, *see above*, Chavigny.

Turgot de Saint-Clair, Mark-Antoine, intendant at Moulins (1714–20).

Vauban, Sebastien le Prestre de (1633–1707), military engineer, who became a marshal of France (1703), author of *Projet d'une dîme royale* (1707) in favour of tax reform.

Villars, Claude Louis Hector, duke de (1654–1734), marshal of France, president of the council for war (1715), later a member of the regency council.

Villars-Brancas, Louis, duke de (1663–1739), one of the regent's *roués*.

Villeroy, François de Neufville, duke de (1644–1730), marshal of France (1693), appointed governor to Louis XV and member of the regency council (1715), disgraced in 1722.

Voysin, Daniel François (1644–1717), chancellor of France, member of the regency council.

Glossary of Terms

appel comme d'abus	A complaint to the parlement against an ecclesiastical judge accused of exceeding his powers.
arrêt	A formal judgment of the parlement.
avocat-général	Barrister-in-chief representing the king's interests in the parlement. There were three of them in the parlement of Paris.
capitation	A graduated tax introduced in 1695 which divided the taxable population into twenty-two groups determined according to social status.
chambre de justice	Extraordinary commission set up in 1716 to counter peculation amongst tax-collectors.
chambre des vacations	An assembly of magistrates from the parlement acting for the court during its summer recess. The chamber was in session from 9 September to 27 October.
cour des monnaies	Sovereign court based in Paris with authority over cases arising out of the counterfeiting or devaluation of the currency.
dixième	A tax of one-tenth levied between 1710 and 1717 on all incomes.
don gratuit	Payment accorded to the king by the provincial estates as an alternative to the *taille*. The clergy similarly voted a 'free gift' to the crown.
duc et pair	Highest rank of the nobility after the royal family.
élection	Sub-division of the *généralité* for taxation purposes.
élu	Royal official in charge of an *élection*.
généralité	Area of financial administration which developed into the chief unit of local government under the intendant.
gens du roi	Collective title applied to the procureur-général and the avocats-généraux.
grand'chambre	Location of the parlement's plenary and ceremonial sessions.
grand conseil	Sovereign court whose indeterminate yet country-wide jurisdiction allowed the king to evoke its authority in opposition to the parlement.

keeper of the seals	Temporary office-holder appointed to perform the functions of the chancellor when the latter was in disgrace, the chancellor's office being irremovable.
lettres de cachet	Sealed royal orders.
lit de justice	The parlement's most solemn assembly when the king presided over the court in person.
Madame	Court title of Monsieur's wife.
maison du roi	The civil and military establishment of the royal household. The secretary of state for the *maison du roi* had wider responsibilities than his title might imply, including the tasks of administering a number of provinces and dealing with matters relating to the clergy.
maître des requêtes	Distinguished judicial officer.
Monsieur	Court title of the king's younger brother.
Monsieur le Duc	Court title of the head of the house of Bourbon-Condé.
noblesse de robe	Nobility acquired as a result of holding high judicial office.
pays d'état	Provinces retaining their estates with the right to assess their own fiscal contribution.
petit-fils de France	Grandson of a French king: in Orléans' case, Louis XIII.
procureur-général	The king's chief representative in the parlement, responsible for the maintenance of public order.
rentes	State investments.
roués	Orléans' ironic term for his debauched cronies who, he implied, deserved to be broken on the wheel. (Now accepted in English language.)
taille	The main direct tax in *ancien régime* France. The *taille personnelle* was levied on unprivileged individuals, the *taille réelle* – confined to the Midi and the south-west – was levied on land.
traitant	Tax-farmer who was empowered to collect certain indirect taxes in return for paying a specific sum of money to the government.

France and its neighbours during the regency of Philippe d'Orléans.

List of Illustrations

Index

Names marked with an asterisk * will be found in the *List of Personalities* where detailed information is given. Places given on the map are marked with a dagger†. Figures in italic refer to illustrations.